PLATO'S REPUBLIC

**Benjamin Jowett's translation
revised by Albert A. Anderson**

unabridged

The Theater of the Mind

Agora Publications

AGORA PUBLICATIONS
PO Box 442
Lenox, MA 01240

Cover: Ideas from Plato's dialogues drawn by Donald Krueger

This is an unabridged revision of Benjamin Jowett's translation of Plato's *Republic*, as it appeared in the 1873 edition published by Scribner, Armstrong, and Company. Changes in the language have been made so that the dialogue flows more naturally in the contemporary American English idiom. Numbers in brackets are the universal Greek text pages.

Printed in the United States of America
ISBN 1-887250-25-5

TABLE OF CONTENTS

INTRODUCTION

What persists throughout the perpetual flow of events in the world? Plato's *Republic* explores that question and a host of others, perhaps answering it best by what it shows in its own endurance over a period of nearly 2,400 years.

But what actually remains of Plato's own work? How accurate is Benjamin Jowett's 1871 translation of the Stallbaum version of the Greek text? How authentic is the Greek text? What changes are introduced by the present revision of Jowett's translation? Can we ever step twice into the same river?

When we consider the wide variety of interpretations of the *Republic* that have emerged over the millennia, the challenge of finding the real Plato becomes even greater. Plotinus, in the third century of the Christian era, drew upon Plato's writings to develop his version of Neo-Platonism. A century later, Augustine formulated his version of Christian Platonism, drawing on "certain books of the Platonists."[i] At the beginning of the modern epoch, Descartes developed a form of essentialism that recollects some important features of Christian Platonism. Descartes' ontological dualism between two substances (mind and matter) was as influential on subsequent thinking about the nature of reality as Augustine's separation between the City of Man and the City of God was on politics and theology. In the twentieth century, Karl Popper considered the *Republic* to be "probably the most elaborate monograph on justice ever written,"[ii] but he interpreted it as a form of "totalitarian justice."[iii] Library shelves throughout the world are laden with interpretations and commentaries on the *Republic*, some praising it as a sacred text and others, like Popper's, linking it to the social programs of Hitler and Stalin.

Because they frequently contradict each other, these various interpretations and applications of Plato's thought cannot all be correct, and it is probable that they are all flawed in important ways. Neither this introduction nor this revised translation pretends to resolve the persistent disputes that pervade Platonic scholarship. Heraclitus was right about our inability literally to step into the same river, but I think it is possible for us to swim in the same stream of thinking, one that extends at least as far as

Parmenides' time, and probably even earlier. Rather than searching for an account of what Plato said, it is much more important to gain access to the same dialectical process in which we can participate in the twenty-first century.

The enduring aspect of Plato's work is the way of thinking manifested in his dialogues. Following Heraclitus and Parmenides, Plato used poetic language to pursue the love of wisdom. The love of wisdom is different from the possession of it. Plato's kind of thinking was fundamentally and formatively philosophical, but that means he was a seeker after wisdom, not one who pretended to have it or one who sought to propagate it. Pythagoras called himself a "lover of wisdom" rather than a wise person (*sophos*), a distinction Plato developed in *The Symposium*.[iv]

The *Republic* poses questions that endure: What is justice? What form of community fosters the best possible life for human beings? What is the nature and destiny of the soul? What form of education provides the best leaders for a good republic? What are the various forms of poetry and the other arts, and which ones should be fostered and which ones should be discouraged? How does knowing differ from believing? Several characters in the dialogue present a variety of tempting answers to those questions. Cephalus, Polemarchus, Thrasymachus, and Glaucon all offer definitions of justice. Socrates, Glaucon, and Adeimantus explore five different forms of republic and evaluate the merit of each from the standpoint of goodness. Two contrasting models of education are proposed and examined. Three different forms of poetry are identified and analyzed. The difference between knowing and believing is discussed in relation to the objects of each kind of thinking.

But it is a mistake to confuse answers presented by Plato's characters with Plato's own position on a given issue. No doubt Plato held strong beliefs about the most important subjects, but the dialogue form is not a good medium for an author who wishes to make declarations and disseminate absolute truth. The dialogue form, especially as used by Plato, is an excellent way of shifting the burden from the author to the reader or listener. If Plato created the *Republic* and his other dialogues as instruments by which to help the students in his Academy engage in the search for wisdom, then we can benefit from that same process.

Imagine that Plato arranged for a dramatic performance of Book One in order to lure his students into the dialogue.[v] Consider who might have participated in such an event. We need only think of Aristotle, who is widely believed to have spent several years in Plato's Academy, as the kind of student who attended the performance. Thrasymachus' definition and defense of justice as "the interest of the stronger" provokes a vehement refutation by Socrates. It is not difficult to imagine a vigorous exchange among Plato's students about the ideas and arguments presented in Book One, with some of them agreeing with Socrates and others taking the side of Thrasymachus. Perhaps Plato then retired to his study to write Book Two, which opens with a clear challenge to Socrates' position by Glaucon and Adeimantus, who then proceed to state a much stronger version of Thrasymachus' "realistic" ethics and politics based on a no-nonsense version of what most people think about such matters. Then Socrates begins a response to these challenges that extends through eight more books, each one adding new ideas and possibilities, and each one refuting and replacing ideas that came before. Rather than leaving the reader or listener with a clear and distinct answer to any of the questions and issues it examines, the *Republic* enables us to join the dialogue in our own context, whether it be in a classroom, among a group of friends, or in the solitude of our own mind.

If we approach Plato's text in this way, what endures is not any particular theory, concept, story, proposal, or doctrine but a way of thinking that is dialectical in the best sense of the term. Plato shows us how to think an idea through, never settling for easy answers or ready-made formulations. The serious and practical import of that process is obvious throughout the dialogue, because the questions and challenges it presents are as contemporary as this morning's news. Anyone who seeks to live a good and happy life must wrestle with the same issues that Plato faced in his own historical context. It is remarkable how current are the possibilities posed by the dialogue, but it is also obvious that our choices among the alternatives on most of the topics are just as difficult to make now as they were in Plato's Athens.

This version of Plato's *Republic* is designed for dramatic performance. Agora Publications offers an unabridged recording of this and other dialogues on compact disk and cassette. Whether read silently with the mind's eye or heard orally with the mind's ear, the goal is to provide access to philosophy for our time.

ENDNOTES

[i] Augustine, *The Confessions*, Book 8.

[ii] Karl Popper, *The Open Society and Its Enemies*, vol. 1, *The Spell of Plato* (Princeton, New Jersey: Princeton University Press, 1962), p. 93.

[iii] Ibid., chapter 6.

[iv] Cf. Plato, *Symposium*, 202–212.

[v] The inspiration for this line of thinking comes from Gilbert Ryle in *Plato's Progress* (Cambridge, England: Cambridge University Press, 1966).

THE REPUBLIC

Characters

SOCRATES, CEPHALUS, GLAUCON, THRASYMACHUS,
ADEIMANTUS, CLEITOPHON, POLEMARCHUS

Book One

[327] *Socrates:* I went down to the Piraeus yesterday with Glaucon, Ariston's son. I wanted to offer my prayers and also see how they would celebrate this new festival honoring the goddess Bendis. I was delighted with our procession, but that of the Thracians was equally beautiful. When we had finished our prayers and seen the show, we headed in the direction of the city. Polemarchus, Cephalus' son, caught sight of us from a distance and told his servant to run and ask us to wait for him. The servant grabbed my cloak from behind and said that Polemarchus wanted us to wait.

I turned around and asked him where his master was. He said that he was on his way and that we should wait for him.

In a few minutes Polemarchus arrived, along with Adeimantus, Glaucon's brother, and Niceratus, the son of Nicias, and several others who had probably been at the procession.

Polemarchus: Socrates, I see that you are already on your way back to the city.

Socrates: That's right.

Polemarchus: But do you see how many we are?

Socrates: Of course.

Polemarchus: Are you stronger than all of us? If not, you will have to stay where you are.

Socrates: Isn't there another alternative? Perhaps we could persuade you to let us go.

Polemarchus: Can you persuade us, if we refuse to listen?

Glaucon: No way.

Polemarchus: We are not going to listen; you can be sure of that.
[328]

Adeimantus: Haven't you heard about the torch-race in honor of the goddess that will take place this evening? It's on horseback!

Socrates: On horseback? That's something new. Will they carry torches and pass them to each other during the race?

Polemarchus: That's it. Not only that, but there will be an all-night festival that you definitely ought to see. After supper we'll go to the festival, other young men will meet us, and we will have a good talk. So stay; don't be stubborn.

Glaucon: Since you insist, it looks like we have to stay.

Socrates: So, we went with Polemarchus to his house where we found his brothers Lysias and Euthydemus along with Thrasymachus from Chalcedon, Charmantides from Paeania, and Cleitophon, the son of Aristonymus. Polemarchus' father, Cephalus, was also there. I had not seen him for a long time, and he now seemed to be a very old man. He was seated on a cushioned chair, and had a wreath on his head, because he had been sacrificing in the courtyard. We sat on chairs arranged around him in a semicircle.

Cephalus: Greetings, Socrates. You don't come to see me as often as you should. If I were still able to visit you, I would not ask you to come here. But at my age I can hardly get to the city, so you should come more often to the Piraeus. I want you to know that as my bodily pleasures decay, my delight in good conversation increases by the same amount. Do not deny my request. Make our house your resort and keep company with these young men. We are old friends, and you will be quite at home with us.

Socrates: There is nothing I like better, Cephalus, than talking with people your age. I regard them as travelers who have made a trip that I may make one day. I can ask them whether the road is smooth and easy, or rugged and difficult. **[329]** This is a question which I especially want to ask you now that you have arrived at what poets call the "threshold of old age." Is life more difficult toward the end? What do you have to report?

Cephalus: Socrates, I will tell you how I feel about it. Men of my age flock together. We are birds of a feather, as the old proverb says. At our meetings most of my friends are full of complaints: "I cannot eat; I cannot drink; the pleasures of youth and love are fled away. Once we had good times, but now all that is gone and life is no longer life." Some complain that their relatives have neglected them. This gets them going on a litany of evils of which old age is the cause. But to me, Socrates, these complainers seem to blame something that is not really the problem. If old age were the cause, I and every other old man would feel as they do. But this is not my own experience, nor that of others I have known. I remember well the words of the poet Sophocles. When he was an old man, someone asked: "How does love fit with age, Sophocles? Are you still the man you were?" He replied: "Be quiet! I am happy to be free of all that. I feel as if I have escaped from a deranged and raging master." His answer sounds even better to me now than it did then. Old age brings a great sense of calm and freedom from the things he mentions. When the passions diminish and relax their hold, then, as Sophocles said, we are freed not from one mad master but from many. The truth is, Socrates, that such regrets and complaints about relatives should all be attributed to the same cause—not to old age, but to character and temperament. A person who has a calm and happy nature will hardly feel the problems of aging, but to one with the opposite disposition both youth and age are hard to bear.

Socrates: I admire your words, Cephalus, but I suspect that most people are not convinced. They think that you bear old age so well, not because of your happy disposition, but because you are rich. Wealth, they say, brings many consolations.

Cephalus: You are right; they are not convinced, and there is something in what they say—but not as much as they imagine. I might answer them as Themistocles answered the man from Seriphus who was abusing him and saying that he was famous, not because of his own merits but because he was an Athenian: **[330]** "If you had been a native of my country or I of yours, neither of us would have been famous." To those who are not rich and are troubled by old age, I would make the same reply. To good people living in poverty, old age will be a burden; but evil rich people will never be at peace with themselves.

Socrates: May I ask, Cephalus, whether you inherited your fortune or earned it?

Cephalus: Socrates, that's hard to say, because both are true. Let me put it this way. In the art of making money I am midway between my grandfather and father. My grandfather, whose name I bear, doubled or tripled what he inherited, which is pretty much what I have now. But my father, Lysanias, reduced the property. I will be satisfied if I leave to my sons a little more than I received.

Socrates: That's why I asked the question. I see that you do not have excessive love for money, which is a characteristic of those who have inherited their fortune rather than earned it. In addition to the natural love of money for its use, those who make their own fortune have a second love of money, because they created it themselves, resembling the affection authors have for their own poems or parents for their children. As a result they are bad company, because they measure the value of everything in terms of wealth.

Cephalus: You are right, Socrates.

Socrates: May I ask another question? What is the greatest benefit you have gained from your wealth?

Cephalus: It's a benefit about which I could not easily convince others. Let me tell you, Socrates, that when we begin to think our last hour is near, fears and cares we never had before enter our mind. Tales of a world below and the punishment there for what we have done here once may have been a laughing-matter. Now we are tormented with the thought that those stories may be true. Whether from the weakness of age or because we are now drawing near to that other place and have a clearer view of things, suspicions and alarms crowd in on us, and we begin to reflect and consider any wrongs which we may have done to others. And if we find that we are guilty of many offenses, we begin to wake up at night like children terrified by bad dreams. But to people who have a clear conscience, sweet hope, as Pindar charmingly says, is the kind nurse of age. **[331]** He puts it this way:

> Hope which cherishes the soul of
> One who lives in
> Justice and holiness
> Is the nurse of age and the
> Companion of our journey.
> Hope is mightiest to sway the restless soul.[1]

How admirable are his words! So, the great blessing of riches—I do not say to everyone, but to a good and upright person—is that we have had no occasion to deceive or to defraud others, even without intention. When we depart to the world below, we do not worry about offerings due to the gods or debts owed to other people. Wealth contributes greatly to such peace of mind. Perhaps it has other advantages; but, all things considered, to a sensible person this is the greatest.

Socrates: Well said, Cephalus. But what, exactly, is the justice of which Pindar sings? Is it no more than telling the truth and paying your debts? Don't you think that these actions might sometimes be just and sometimes unjust? Suppose that a friend left some weapons with me while sane, but then went mad and returned to ask for them. Ought I give them back? I don't think anyone would say that I should return them or that it would be right to do so. Nor would they say that I should always tell the truth to someone in that condition.

Cephalus: You are quite right.

Socrates: Then "telling the truth and paying your debts" is not a good definition of justice.

Polemarchus: It is a good definition, Socrates, if Simonides[2] is to be believed.

Cephalus: I'm afraid that I have to go now, because I have to attend the sacred services. I'll turn over the argument to the others.

Socrates: Isn't Polemarchus your heir?

Cephalus: That he is, so I leave it to him.

Socrates: Tell me then, heir of the argument, what do you think Simonides said correctly in speaking about justice?

Polemarchus: He said that repaying a debt is just, and I think he's right.

Socrates: I'm sorry to doubt the word of such a wise and inspired man, but his meaning, though probably clear to you, is not clear to me. **[332]** Certainly he does not mean, as we were just now saying, that I ought to return weapons to someone who asks for them while insane. Yet what is loaned is considered to be a debt.

Polemarchus: True.

Socrates: Then when the person who asks me is insane, I should not pay the debt?

Polemarchus: That's true.

Socrates: When Simonides said that repaying a debt is justice, it seems he did not mean to include that case?

Polemarchus: Certainly not, because he thinks that a friend should always do good to a friend and never do evil.

Socrates: Do you mean that if returning a deposit of gold injures a friend, that is not giving the friend what we owe? Is that what you think Simonides would say?

Polemarchus: Yes.

Socrates: What about enemies? Should we give them whatever we owe them?

Polemarchus: By all means! And what an enemy owes to an enemy is evil. That's what's proper.

Socrates: Simonides, then, after the manner of poets, would seem to have spoken obscurely about the nature of justice. He really meant to say that justice is giving to each person what is proper to that person, and this he called a debt.

Polemarchus: That must have been his meaning.

Socrates: Tell me this. If we asked him what is properly given by the practice of medicine, and to whom, how do you think he would answer?

Polemarchus: He would probably say that medicine gives drugs and food and drink to human bodies.

Socrates: And what is properly given by cooking?

Polemarchus: Seasoning to food.

Socrates: And what does justice give, and to whom?

Polemarchus: Socrates, if we are to be guided by analogy, then justice is the art that gives benefit to friends and injury to enemies.

Socrates: Then by justice he means doing good to friends and harm to enemies?

Polemarchus: I think so.

Socrates: And who is best able to do good to friends and evil to enemies with respect to sickness and health?

Polemarchus: The physician.

Socrates: When they are on a voyage, facing the perils of the sea?

Polemarchus: The pilot.

Socrates: And in what sort of actions or to what result is the just person most able to do harm to an enemy and confer benefit upon a friend?

Polemarchus: In going to war against the one and in making alliances with the other.

Socrates: But when a person is well, my dear Polemarchus, there is no need of a physician?

Polemarchus: No.

Socrates: And one who is not on a voyage has no need of a pilot?

Polemarchus: No.

Socrates: Then in peacetime justice will be useless? **[333]**

Polemarchus: I don't think that's quite true.

Socrates: You think that justice may be of use in peace as well as in war?

Polemarchus: Yes.

Socrates: Like agriculture for growing corn?

Polemarchus: Yes.

Socrates: Or like shoemaking for obtaining shoes. Is that what you mean?

Polemarchus: Yes.

Socrates: So what similar service would you say that justice can provide; how can it help us in peacetime?

Polemarchus: It serves for making contracts, Socrates.

Socrates: And by contracts you mean partnerships?

Polemarchus: Exactly.

Socrates: But is the just person or a skillful player more useful and a better partner in a game of checkers?

Polemarchus: A skillful player.

Socrates: And when laying bricks and stones, is the just person more useful or a better partner than a builder?

Polemarchus: No. It's the other way around.

Socrates: Then in what sort of partnership is the just person a better partner than the builder or the harp-player? In playing the harp, the harpist is certainly a better partner than the just person.

Polemarchus: In a money partnership, I suppose.

Socrates: Yes, Polemarchus, but surely not in using money when the partners contemplate the purchase or sale of a horse. Wouldn't a person who knows about horses be a better adviser?

Polemarchus: Certainly.

Socrates: And when you want to buy a ship, wouldn't a shipbuilder or pilot be better?

Polemarchus: True.

Socrates: Then what is that joint use of money in which the just person is to be preferred to other partners?

Polemarchus: When you want a deposit to be kept safely.

Socrates: You mean when money is not being used?

Polemarchus: Precisely.

Socrates: In other words, justice is useful when money is useless?

Polemarchus: That seems to follow.

Socrates: And when you want to keep a pruning-hook safe, then justice is useful; but when you want to use it, then you hire a gardener?

Polemarchus: Yes.

Socrates: And when you want to keep a shield or a lyre, and not use them, you would say that justice is useful; but when you want to use them, then you turn to the soldier or the musician?

Polemarchus: Exactly.

Socrates: And so it is with all other things: justice is useful when they are useless, and useless when other things are being used?

Polemarchus: That is the inference.

Socrates: Then justice is not worth much, if it deals only with useless things. Let's consider another point. Isn't the one who can best strike a blow in a boxing match, or in any kind of fighting, best able to ward off a blow?

Polemarchus: Certainly.

Socrates: And a person skilled in protecting against disease is best able to spread it without being detected?

Polemarchus: True. **[334]**

Socrates: And a good camp guard is also the one who is able to discover the plans of enemies or deter their attacks?

Polemarchus: That's right.

Socrates: Then a good keeper of anything is also a good thief?

Polemarchus: I guess that follows.

Socrates: Then if the just person is good at keeping money, that same person is good at stealing it.

Polemarchus: That makes sense.

Socrates: Then after all that the just person turns out to be a kind of thief. And this is a lesson I suspect you learned from Homer when he says of Autolycus (the maternal grandfather of Odysseus, who is a favorite of his) that "He was excellent above all others in theft and perjury."[3] And so, you and Homer and Simonides all seem to agree that justice is an art of theft, which should be practiced "for the benefit of friends and for the harm of enemies." That is what you were saying, isn't it?

Polemarchus: No, certainly not that. But now I don't know what I did say. Anyway, I still think that justice is beneficial to friends and harmful to enemies.

Socrates: Well, here is another question. By friends and enemies do we mean those who are really good and bad, or only seem so?

Polemarchus: Surely we love those we think good and hate those we think are evil.

Socrates: Yes, but don't we often make mistakes about good and evil? Don't some people who seem good turn out to be evil, and others we think are evil are not?

Polemarchus: That's true.

Socrates: Then to those people the good will be enemies, and the evil will be friends?

Polemarchus: Yes.

Socrates: And in that case they will be right in doing good to evil people and harm to good people?

Polemarchus: Clearly.

Socrates: But wouldn't you say that good people are just and would not do an injustice?

Polemarchus: I would.

Socrates: But according to your reasoning it is just to harm people who do no wrong.

Polemarchus: No, Socrates, that can't be right.

Socrates: Then I suppose it is just to do good to just people and do harm to unjust people.

Polemarchus: That sounds better.

Socrates: Then let's think this through. People often misjudge others. That means they have friends who are bad, so, according to your definition of justice, they ought to harm them. They may have enemies who are good, so they ought to benefit them. But now we are saying the opposite of what Simonides said.

Polemarchus: That's true, so I think that we should correct our mistake when we used the words "friend" and "enemy."

Socrates: What mistake, Polemarchus?

Polemarchus: We assumed that a friend is one who only seems to be good.

Socrates: And how should we correct that error? **[335]**

Polemarchus: We should say that a friend *is* good. One who only seems to be and is not good, only seems to be and is not a friend. And we should say the same about an enemy.

Socrates: You would say that good people are friends and bad people are enemies?

Polemarchus: Yes.

Socrates: So instead of simply saying, as we did at first, that it is just to do good to our friends and harm to our enemies, we should say: "It is just to do good to our friends when they are good and harm to our enemies when they are evil."

Polemarchus: Yes, that change would be correct.

Socrates: But should just people harm anyone at all?

Polemarchus: Of course. They ought to harm those who are both evil and enemies.

Socrates: Polemarchus, when horses are harmed, are they better or worse?

Polemarchus: Worse.

Socrates: In other words, they are worse with respect to the unique excellence of horses, not of dogs?

Polemarchus: Yes, of horses.

Socrates: And dogs are made worse with respect to the unique excellence of dogs, and not of horses?

Polemarchus: Of course.

Socrates: And will not people who are harmed be worse with respect to the unique excellence of humans?

Polemarchus: Certainly.

Socrates: But isn't justice the unique excellence of humans?

Polemarchus: Yes.

Socrates: Then, my friend, people who are harmed become less just?

Polemarchus: That is the result.

Socrates: Can a musician make people less musical through the art of music?

Polemarchus: Certainly not.

Socrates: Or can an equestrian become a bad rider through proper training?

Polemarchus: No.

Socrates: Then can just people, through justice, make people unjust? Or, speaking generally, can good people make people bad through human virtue?

Polemarchus: That's impossible.

Socrates: That would be as wrong as to say that heat can produce cold or drought can create moisture. We should say that these are effects of the opposite causes?

Polemarchus: Exactly.

Socrates: And to cause harm is not the effect of goodness, but of its opposite?

Polemarchus: Evidently.

Socrates: And would you say that the just person is good?

Polemarchus: Certainly.

Socrates: So to injure a friend or anyone else is not the act of a just person but of the opposite, one who is unjust?

Polemarchus: I think that what you say is true, Socrates.

Socrates: Then it is wrong to say that justice consists of repaying debts and that goodness is the debt a just person owes to friends, whereas evil is the debt owed to enemies. To say this is not wise, because it is not true. We have clearly shown that intentionally harming anyone cannot be just.

Polemarchus: I agree with you.

Socrates: Then you and I are prepared to oppose anyone who attributes such a saying to Simonides or Bias or Pittacus,[4] or any other wise person? **[336]**

Polemarchus: I am quite ready to fight by your side.

Socrates: Shall I tell you who I think first said that justice is "doing good to your friends and harm to your enemies"?

Polemarchus: Who was it?

Socrates: I believe it was a rich and mighty man such as Periander or Perdiccas or Xerxes or Ismenias from Thebes, someone who had a great opinion of his own power.

Polemarchus: I think you are right.

Socrates: But if this definition of justice and just action breaks down, what other one can we find?

As we were talking, Thrasymachus tried to interrupt us and take over. He was silenced by the others who wanted to hear the conclusion. But now he came at us like a wild beast seeking to devour us. Polemarchus and I were terrified.

Thrasymachus: What kind of rubbish have you two been talking? And why this absurd politeness and deference to each other? Socrates, if you really want to know the meaning of justice, don't simply ask questions and congratulate yourself on being able to refute any answer that anyone gives, simply because you are keen enough to see that it is easier to ask questions than to answer them. You yourself have to answer and define the nature of justice. And don't tell me that it is duty, or advantage, or profit, or gain, or interest. That sort of nonsense won't work with me! I demand clarity and accuracy.

Socrates: Thrasymachus, I've heard that if you don't see a wild beast first, you will lose your voice. It's a good thing I glanced at you a moment ago, or I wouldn't be able to answer you! Please don't be so hard on us. Polemarchus and I may have made mistakes in thinking about justice, but our errors were not intentional. If we were searching for gold, we would never yield to each other and lose our chance of finding it. But we are searching for justice, something more precious than gold, so don't think we are so foolish as to submit to each other and not do our best to discover it. Believe me, my friend, we want to find it, but we are unable. So, you clever people should pity us rather than be angry with us. **[337]**

Thrasymachus: I knew it! I want you all to notice this display of Socratic irony. Didn't I tell you that whenever he was asked a question he would refuse to answer, using irony or any other dodge to avoid a direct reply?

Socrates: You have an acute mind, Thrasymachus. You know that if you ask someone what numbers make up twelve and prohibit that person from answering two times six, three times four, six times two, or four times three, then no one can answer you when you say: "That sort of nonsense won't work with me!" Suppose that person were to say: "Thrasymachus, what do you mean? If one of these numbers you forbid were the true answer to the question, should I say some other number that is not the right one? Is that your meaning?" How would you answer, Thrasymachus?

Thrasymachus: As if the two cases were at all alike!

Socrates: How do they differ? But even if they are not alike and only appear to be so, should people not say what they think is true, whether you and I forbid them or not?

Thrasymachus: I assume you are going to give one of the forbidden answers?

Socrates: I might, if on reflection I approve of one of them.

Thrasymachus: What if I give you a different answer about justice that's better than any of those? What kind of punishment would you deserve?

Socrates: The kind of punishment appropriate for the ignorant: I must learn from the wise. That's what I deserve.

Thrasymachus: What? No payment for what you learn? That's a fine idea!

Socrates: I will pay when I have the money.

Glaucon: Socrates, you do have the money. Thrasymachus, don't worry about getting paid; we will all make a contribution for Socrates.

Thrasymachus: Of course, and then Socrates will do as he always does—refuse to answer. He will take someone else's answer and pull it to pieces. **[338]**

Socrates: My good friend, how could I answer if I do not pretend to know? How could anyone answer, even with a suggestion, if that person is told by a man of authority not to utter it? The natural thing is that the speaker should be someone like you who professes to know and can tell what he knows. Will you please answer as a favor to me, to enlighten Glaucon and the rest of us?

Thrasymachus: Behold the wisdom of Socrates! He refuses to be the teacher, he goes about learning from others, and he never even says "thank you."

Socrates: It is true that I learn from others, but I emphatically deny that I am ungrateful. Money I have none, and therefore I pay in praise, which is all I have. How ready I am to praise anyone who appears to me to speak well, you will soon find out when you answer; for I expect that you will answer well.

Thrasymachus: Then listen. I say that justice is nothing else than the interest of the stronger. Now, why don't you praise me? But of course you won't.

Socrates: First I must understand you. Your answer is not yet clear. Justice, you say, is the interest of the stronger. Thrasymachus, what does that mean? Surely you don't mean that because the wrestler Polydamas is stronger than we are, and finds the eating of beef conducive to his bodily strength, that eating lots of beef is therefore equally good and just for us.

Thrasymachus: That's a dirty trick, Socrates; you take my words in the sense that is most damaging to my position.

Socrates: Then tell us your meaning more clearly.

Thrasymachus: OK. Have you never heard that forms of government differ? There are tyrannies, there are democracies, and there are aristocracies.

Socrates: Yes, I have heard that.

Thrasymachus: And the government is the ruling power in each state?

Socrates: I've heard that too. **[339]**

Thrasymachus: And different forms of government make laws in different ways. Some operate democratically; in others the aristocrats rule; and in still others a single tyrant makes the laws. It all depends on their various interests. They all claim that what is advantageous to themselves is justice for the people they rule. Anyone who violates this principle they punish as a lawbreaker, and they brand that person as unjust. That is what I mean, sir, when I say that there exists in all states the same principle of justice, and that is the interest of the established government. In all cases the government has the power, so the only reasonable conclusion is that everywhere there is but one principle of justice: the interest of the stronger.

Socrates: Now I understand you. Next we must determine whether or not you are right. But let me point out that in defining justice you used the word "interest," one of the terms you forbid me to use. It is true, however, that in your definition the words "of the stronger" are added.

Thrasymachus: A small addition.

Socrates: Whether it is large or small is not yet clear. First we must ask whether what you are saying is true. Let's agree that justice is interest of some kind, but you add "of the stronger." I'm not so sure about this addition, so we must continue.

Thrasymachus: Go ahead.

Socrates: First tell me whether it is just for subjects to obey their rulers?

Thrasymachus: Of course.

Socrates: Are the rulers of the various states you mentioned infallible, or do they sometimes make mistakes?

Thrasymachus: They sometimes make mistakes.

Socrates: So when they make laws, sometimes they make the right ones, and sometimes they don't?

Thrasymachus: I suppose so.

Socrates: When they make the right ones, they make them in accord with their interest; when they make mistakes, the laws are contrary to their interest. Is that correct?

Thrasymachus: Yes.

Socrates: And whatever laws they make must be obeyed by their subjects. Is that what you call justice?

Thrasymachus: That's right.

Socrates: Then justice, according to you, not only serves the interest of the stronger, but even works against that interest?

Thrasymachus: What's that you're saying?

Socrates: I believe I'm only repeating what you are saying. But let's think it through. Have we not agreed that the rulers, in commanding some actions, may be mistaken about their own interest? And have we not also agreed that it is just for the subjects to do whatever their rulers command? Haven't we agreed to that?

Thrasymachus: I think so.

Socrates: Then think also that you have agreed it is just to do what is contrary to the interest of the government—what you call the stronger—when the governors unintentionally command things that harm themselves. I'm assuming with you that it is just for subjects to obey all commands. In that case, wise Thrasymachus, is there any escape from the conclusion that the weaker are commanded to do, not what is for the interest of the stronger, but the opposite—what harms them? **[340]**

Polemarchus: Nothing could be clearer, Socrates.

Cleitophon: Yes, Polemarchus, if you are allowed to be his witness.

Polemarchus: Cleitophon, we don't need witnesses, because Thrasymachus himself acknowledges that rulers may sometimes command what is harmful to themselves and that for subjects to obey them is just.

Cleitophon: Yes, Polemarchus, Thrasymachus did say that it is just for subjects to do what is commanded by their rulers.

Polemarchus: And he also claimed that justice is the interest of the stronger. While admitting both of these propositions, he said that the stronger—the rulers—may command the weaker—the subjects—to do what is contrary to the interest of the rulers. Therefore, Cleitophon, it follows that justice is both for and against the interest of the stronger.

Cleitophon: But by "the interest of the stronger" Thrasymachus means what the stronger think is in their interest. That's what the weaker has to do. And that's what he means by justice.

Polemarchus: Those were not his words.

Socrates: Never mind, if Thrasymachus now says that's what he means, let's understand him that way. Tell me, Thrasymachus, did you mean to define justice as that which the stronger think is in their interest, whether it really is or not?

Thrasymachus: Certainly not. Do you suppose that I call someone who makes a mistake "the stronger" at the time the mistake is made?

Socrates: Yes, I got that impression when you admitted that the ruler is not infallible but might be sometimes mistaken.

Thrasymachus: Socrates, that's because you are only interested in refuting my position. For example, did you get the impression that someone who is mistaken about sick people is a physician when that person makes the mistake? Is a person who makes an error in arithmetic a mathematician because of the mistake? It's true we say that a physician or mathematician or grammarian has made a mistake, but that's only a way of speaking. The fact is that none of these people ever makes a mistake insofar as they are what their title implies. You are a lover of precision, Socrates. Well, it is not precise to say that artisans make mistakes to the extent that they are artisans. None of them makes a mistake unless their skill fails them, and then they cease to be skilled artisans. This is a general rule: No artisan or sage or ruler makes a mistake at the time they are what their title implies. According to the ordinary way of speaking I was using, we say that a doctor or ruler makes errors. **[341]** But to be perfectly precise, we should say that rulers, insofar as they are rulers, do not make mistakes, so they only command what is in their own interest. The subjects are required to execute those commands. Therefore, as I said at first and now repeat, justice is action in the interest of the stronger.

Socrates: Thrasymachus, do I really appear only to be interested in refuting you?

Thrasymachus: No question about it.

Socrates: And do you believe that I ask these questions only to undermine your position?

Thrasymachus: No, I don't believe it, I know it. But you won't take me by surprise, and you will never win by sheer force of argument.

Socrates: I wouldn't dream of trying. But to avoid any misunderstanding between us in the future, tell me in what sense you speak of a ruler or of the stronger. Are you using the term "ruler" in the popular or in the strict sense of the term?

Thrasymachus: In the strictest possible sense. Now go ahead: cheat and try to twist my argument all you can. I ask for no mercy from you. But you never will succeed; never.

Socrates: And do you imagine that I am so foolish as to try and cheat Thrasymachus? I might as well try to shave a lion.

Thrasymachus: You tried a minute ago, and you failed.

Socrates: Enough of these pleasantries. Now tell me: Is the physician, taken in the strict sense of the term, a healer of the sick or a maker of money? Remember, I am now speaking of the true physician.

Thrasymachus: A healer of the sick.

Socrates: And is the captain of a ship—that is, the true captain—a leader of sailors or only a sailor?

Thrasymachus: A leader of sailors.

Socrates: The fact that the captain sails in the ship is not relevant to this point; the title we give the captain indicates the captain's skill and authority over the sailors.

Thrasymachus: OK.

Socrates: Now, does each person engaged in a craft have an interest?

Thrasymachus: Certainly.

Socrates: And the craft serves that interest; that is its origin and purpose.

Thrasymachus: Yes.

Socrates: And shouldn't we say that the craft has no interest? Its only purpose is to perfect itself.

Thrasymachus: What do you mean? **[342]**

Socrates: I'll illustrate my meaning by the example of the body. If you were to ask me whether the body is self-sufficient or needs assistance, I would say that it needs assistance. That's why the science of medicine was invented. The body is fragile and often cannot survive by itself. Medicine has been developed in order to provide things that help the body thrive. Would I not be right if I gave this answer?

Thrasymachus: Quite right.

Socrates: But is the practice of medicine defective or deficient in the same way that the eye may be unable to see or the ear unable to hear? Does medicine require some other art or science to provide for the body? In other words, does the science of medicine itself have a fault or defect so that it requires a supplementary art or science to provide for its interests, and that supplementary art or science another and another without end? Or is each of them able to look after itself? Could we say that the only benefit an art or science needs to consider is that of its subject? It seems that the art or science is pure and faultless as long as it is true to itself. Consider these words in your precise sense, and tell me whether I am right.

Thrasymachus: Yes, you are right.

Socrates: Then medicine does not consider the interest of medicine, but the interest of the body?

Thrasymachus: Yes.

Socrates: Nor does the craft of horse training consider the interests of the craft of horse training. Rather, it looks after the interests of the horse. Nor do any of the other arts or crafts care for themselves, for they have no needs. They only care for the subject of their art?

Thrasymachus: So it seems.

Socrates: So, Thrasymachus, can we say that the arts are superior to their subject-matter?

Thrasymachus: Well, in a sense you could say that, but I'm not entirely happy with that formulation.

Socrates: Then no science or art considers or serves the interest of the superior but only the interest of whoever it serves—the weaker?

Thrasymachus: I would not put it exactly that way, but go on.

Socrates: Then a physician, when prescribing medicine, considers only the good of the patient. To use a metaphor, we could say that the true physician is also a ruler with the human body as a subject. Didn't we already agree that the physician, in the precise sense of the term, is not a money-maker?

Thrasymachus: Yes, we agreed on that.

Socrates: And the captain, in the strict sense of the term, is not simply a sailor but is a ruler of sailors?

Thrasymachus: We agreed about that as well.

Socrates: So, the captain will provide and prescribe for the interest of the sailors and not for the interest of the captain?

Thrasymachus: Well, I suppose you could put it that way. **[343]**

Socrates: Then, Thrasymachus, there is no ruler, to the extent that person is a ruler, who merely considers or seeks personal interest. On the contrary, rulers attend to the welfare of the citizens. Everything the ruler says and does as a ruler is concerned with what is suitable or advantageous to the citizens. Isn't that right?

When we reached this point in the discussion, it was clear to everyone that the definition of justice had been completely reversed. Instead of replying to me, Thrasymachus attacked.

Thrasymachus: Tell me, Socrates, do you have a nurse?

Socrates: Why do you ask such a question?

Thrasymachus: Because your nurse lets you snivel and never wipes your nose. You haven't even been taught how to distinguish the shepherd from the sheep.

Socrates: What makes you say that?

Thrasymachus: Because you think that a shepherd fattens and tends sheep for the good of the animal rather than for the benefit of the shepherd or the owner. You don't realize that the people who rule over states, if they are true rulers, think of their subjects as sheep to be fleeced, contemplating their own interest day and night. You are so far off in your ideas about justice and injustice, you don't even know that justice really serves the interest of the ruler, the one who is stronger, at the expense of the weaker. Justice is for those who are simpleminded. The unjust, by exercising their power, dominate the just. Those who are ruled serve the interest and happiness of those who rule rather than their own.

The just always lose to the unjust. Consider the world of business. In private contracts, whenever the unjust form a partnership with the just they come out on top. When the partnership is dissolved, the just person never walks away with more than the unjust. Or take their dealings with the state. When there is an income tax, the just will pay more and the unjust less on the same amount of income. When it's time to get paid, the one gains nothing and the other gains a lot. Or, see what happens when they hold office. The just person neglects private affairs, and, being just, gets nothing out of public service. Just people wind up being hated by friends and acquaintances, because they refuse to bend or break the law to serve themselves.

But all this is reversed in the case of the unjust person. I'm talking about someone who makes it big. That's where the unjust person's advantage is most obvious. **[344]** The truth of what I'm saying is clear when we consider the highest form of injustice in which criminals are the happiest, while those who suffer injustice or refuse to do injustice are the most miserable. Tyrants take away other people's property by fraud and force, not retail but wholesale. They make no distinction between sacred and secular or private and public. Any one of their crimes taken singly would be punished. They would suffer the greatest disgrace and would be called robbers, kidnappers, burglars, swindlers, and thieves. But when they not only take people's money but also capture them and turn them into slaves, instead of being called dishonorable names, they are considered to be happy and fortunate, not only by citizens but by all who hear of their achievements. People condemn injustice because they fear that they may be its victims, not because they shrink from committing it. I tell you, Socrates, injustice—when practiced on a large enough scale—has more strength, freedom, and mastery than justice. As I said from the beginning, justice is the interest of the stronger, while injustice is our own profit and interest.

Socrates: Thrasymachus, you have deluged our ears with your words like a bath attendant who pours water on our heads! But don't go away. We all insist that you remain and defend your position. These provocative pronouncements need to be examined. Are you going to run away before we can decide whether they are true or not? Do you consider our search for the good life so insignificant? Won't you help us determine how to conduct our lives for our greatest advantage?

Thrasymachus: Do you think that I consider this issue to be unimportant?

Socrates: Either that, or you don't care about us, Thrasymachus. It doesn't seem to matter whether we live better or worse from not knowing what you say you know. Dear friend, don't keep your knowledge to yourself. We are a large group, and any benefit you give us will be amply rewarded. **[345]** But I have to tell you that I, for one, am not convinced. I do not believe that injustice is a greater advantage than justice, even if it is uncontrolled and given free reign. Granting that there may be an unjust person who is able to commit injustice by fraud or force, this does not convince me that injustice is superior. Perhaps other people share my view, but we may be wrong. If so, you should convince us that we are mistaken when we prefer justice to injustice.

Thrasymachus: How can I convince you, if you are not already convinced by what I have just said? What more can I do? Shall I put the proof straight into your mind?

Socrates: No, certainly I don't want that! I'm only asking you to be consistent. Or, if you change, do it openly; don't try to deceive us. Let me remind you, Thrasymachus, that you began by defining the true physician in an exact sense, but you did not use the same precision in talking about the shepherd. You think that the shepherd tends the sheep, not as a shepherd who seeks their benefit, but as a banqueter seeking the pleasures of the table. You also considered the shepherd to be a merchant who only thinks about the market price. But surely the work of the shepherd seeks what is best for the sheep. What's best is achieved whenever the shepherd's work is properly performed. And that's what I said earlier about the ruler. Both in public and in private, the ruler should consider the good of the citizens. But you seem to think that rulers—true rulers—enjoy being in charge.

Thrasymachus: I don't just think so; I know it!

Socrates: Then why don't rulers volunteer to serve without pay? Isn't it because they assume that their rule is advantageous to the people they govern, rather than to themselves? **[346]** Let me ask you a question: Don't the arts differ because each has a separate power or function? My dear friend, please say what you really think, so we can make a little progress.

Thrasymachus: Yes, that's the difference.

Socrates: And doesn't each art give us a particular good rather than a general one? For example, medicine gives us health; navigation provides safety at sea; and so on.

Thrasymachus: Yes.

Socrates: And the art of earning has the special function of providing money. Would you call medicine and navigation the same art? To speak precisely, as you earlier prescribed, you wouldn't equate them—not even if the captain's health improves on a sea voyage?

Thrasymachus: Certainly not.

Socrates: Would you say that the art of earning is the same as the art of medicine, because a person is in good health on payday?

Thrasymachus: Of course not.

Socrates: Nor would you say that medicine is the ability to make money, because someone engaged in healing charges a fee.

Thrasymachus: No.

Socrates: Have we agreed that the good of each art is specially connected to it?

Thrasymachus: Yes.

Socrates: Then, if there is some good that all practitioners share, we should attribute it to something they all have in common.

Thrasymachus: True.

Socrates: Then should we say that if a practitioner benefits by receiving pay, it comes from the ability to make money, not from the unique practice in which that person is skilled?

Thrasymachus: Well, I suppose you could say that.

Socrates: Then various practitioners do not make money from the uniqueness of their practices. The truth is that the physician nurtures health and the architect designs a house, but they do have an ability in common—making money. The various professions perform their tasks to benefit their clients, but would they profit from their work unless they were paid?

Thrasymachus: I suppose not.

Socrates: Then practitioners provide no benefit when working for free?

Thrasymachus: Of course there is a benefit.

Socrates: Then, Thrasymachus, we must conclude that neither arts nor governments provide for their selfish interests. As I said a while ago, they rule and provide for the interests of their clients and for the citizens at large, for the good of the weaker and not the interest of the stronger. That's the reason, Thrasymachus, why, as I was just saying, good people are unwilling to govern. No one likes to take on other people's problems without remuneration. **[347]** A true professional, in giving orders to others, works not for self-interest but always for the benefit of others. So, in order that rulers may be willing to rule, they must be paid in one of three kinds of payment—money, honors, or a penalty for refusing to govern.

Glaucon: Excuse me, Socrates. I don't understand what you mean. Money and honors are familiar incentives, but how can a penalty be a kind of payment?

Socrates: Glaucon, I'm surprised you don't understand the only kind of payment that can induce the best people to rule. Surely you know that ambition and greed are disgraceful to good people.

Glaucon: Of course.

Socrates: That's why they will not consent to rule for the sake of money or honors. Good people do not wish to solicit payment for governing and become mercenaries, nor secretly help themselves to public funds and become thieves. They are not ambitious, so they don't care for honors. Only necessity will convince them; they must be induced to serve in order to avoid punishment. I suppose this is why seeking public office, instead of waiting to be compelled, is considered to be disgraceful. The person who refuses to rule runs the risk of being ruled by someone else who is less capable. What could be worse than that? Good people take office, not because they crave it, but because they can't avoid it. They are not lured to rule by the idea of personal benefit or enjoyment; they are impelled by necessity because they are unable to entrust the task of ruling to someone who is better, or even as good as they are. If a city were composed entirely of good people, then avoiding office would be as prevalent as seeking office is at present. In that case, we would have convincing proof that by nature a true ruler seeks not selfish interest, but the interest of all citizens.

So, I'm a long way from agreeing with Thrasymachus that justice is the interest of the stronger. But we can pursue this question on some future occasion. Thrasymachus also says that the life of unjust people is superior to that of just people. This new statement is much more urgent and a far more serious matter. Which of us is right, Glaucon? Which kind of life do you think is superior?

Glaucon: I think the life of the just is superior. **[348]**

Socrates: Did you hear all the advantages of the unjust life presented by Thrasymachus?

Glaucon: Yes, I heard him, but I'm not convinced.

Socrates: Then shall we try to convince him that what he is saying is not true?

Glaucon: Yes, I would like to do that.

Socrates: If we make a speech in opposition to his speech by recounting all the advantages of being just, and he answers and we rejoin, then we will be reduced to numbering and measuring the goods claimed for each side. In the end, we will have to call on a judge to decide the matter. But if instead we continue to follow our method of mutual agreement, we can both judge and advocate in our own person.

Glaucon: That's right.

Socrates: Which method do you prefer?

Glaucon: I prefer the method of mutual agreement.

Socrates: Well, then, Thrasymachus, suppose we begin at the beginning and you answer me. You say that perfect injustice is more profitable than perfect justice?

Thrasymachus: Yes, that is what I say, and I have already given you my reasons.

Socrates: And would you call one of them virtue and the other vice?

Thrasymachus: Certainly.

Socrates: I assume that you would call justice virtue and injustice vice.

Thrasymachus: What a charming notion! Is it likely I would say that, given that I say injustice is profitable and justice is not?

Socrates: Then what would you say?

Thrasymachus: The opposite!

Socrates: You would call justice vice?

Thrasymachus: No, I would rather call it sublime simplicity.

Socrates: Then would you call injustice malice?

Thrasymachus: No, I would rather call it practical intelligence.

Socrates: So, according to you, unjust people are intelligent and good?

Thrasymachus: Yes, at least it's true of those who can be perfectly unjust, and who have the power of subduing states and nations; but I suppose you think I'm talking about pickpockets. Even that occupation, if undetected, has advantages, though they should not be compared with the ones I have in mind.

Socrates: I understand what you are saying, Thrasymachus, but I still have a hard time believing that you class injustice with wisdom and virtue, and justice with the opposite.

Thrasymachus: Well, I do class them that way.

Socrates: That's a tough position to refute, Thrasymachus. If you said, as many do, that injustice is profitable but morally wrong, then I might have been able to answer you on the basis of commonly accepted principles. But now I see that you have not hesitated to rank injustice as wisdom and virtue, so I suspect that you will call injustice strong and honorable, and you will ascribe to the unjust all the qualities we previously attributed to the just. **[349]**

Thrasymachus: You speak like a true prophet.

Socrates: Thrasymachus, now that you are saying what you really believe and not amusing yourself at our expense, I won't hesitate to follow the logic of our discussion.

Thrasymachus: What difference does it make whether I believe it or not? Your job is to refute my argument.

Socrates: That's right. But will you please try to answer one more question? Would a just person try to take advantage of or outdo another just person?

Thrasymachus: Of course not. If just people did that, they could no longer be the amusing fools they are.

Socrates: In any action, would a just person try to get more than a fair share?

Thrasymachus: No.

Socrates: How would a just person regard the attempt to outdo an unjust person? Would that be considered just or unjust?

Thrasymachus: The just person would think it just and would try to gain the advantage, but would be unable to do so.

Socrates: I'm not asking about ability. My question is only whether the just person, while refusing to have more than another just person, would wish and claim to have more than the unjust?

Thrasymachus: Yes, that's right.

Socrates: And what of the unjust—does such a person claim more than the just person and do more than the just action?

Thrasymachus: Of course; the unjust person wants to outdo everybody.

Socrates: Then the unjust person will also strive and struggle to obtain more than the unjust person and exceed in unjust actions in order to have more than everyone else?

Thrasymachus: Precisely.

Socrates: Let's put it this way: A just man does not desire more than his like but more than his unlike, whereas the unjust desires more than both his like and his unlike?

Thrasymachus: I couldn't have said it better myself.

Socrates: And the unjust is good and wise, and the just is neither?

Thrasymachus: Good again.

Socrates: And isn't the unjust like the wise and good and the just unlike them?

Thrasymachus: Of course; they will be like them because they have those qualities, and the others won't be like them.

Socrates: So we can compare both to what they are like?

Thrasymachus: How could it be otherwise?

Socrates: Very good, Thrasymachus. Let's test these statements by analogy with the arts and crafts. Would you say that one person is a musician and another not a musician?

Thrasymachus: Yes, Socrates, I would say that.

Socrates: Which is wise and which is not wise about music?

Thrasymachus: Obviously the musician is wise, and the one who is not a musician is unwise.

Socrates: And a good musician is one who knows, whereas a bad musician is one who does not know.

Thrasymachus: Yes.

Socrates: Would you say the same thing of the physician?

Thrasymachus: I suppose.

Socrates: Now, my friend, would you say that a musician who tunes a lyre would want to go beyond another musician in tightening and loosening the strings?

Thrasymachus: I don't think so.

Socrates: But the musician would want to go beyond the non-musician?

Thrasymachus: Of course. **[350]**

Socrates: Now what would you say about a physician? In prescribing food and drink, would a physician wish to go beyond another physician or surpass the art of medicine?

Thrasymachus: No.

Socrates: But the physician would like to surpass the non-physician?

Thrasymachus: Yes.

Socrates: What should we think about knowledge and ignorance in general? Do you think that a person who has knowledge would choose to say or do more than another person who has knowledge? Wouldn't the person who knows say or do the same as another person who knows in the same case?

Thrasymachus: I can't deny that, not in such cases.

Socrates: And what about ignorant people? Wouldn't they desire to have more than both the knowing and the ignorant?

Thrasymachus: Yes, I suppose.

Socrates: And the possessor of knowledge is wise?

Thrasymachus: Yes.

Socrates: And the wise is good?

Thrasymachus: True.

Socrates: Then the wise and good will not desire to gain more than their like, but more than their unlike and opposite?

Thrasymachus: Evidently.

Socrates: Whereas the bad and ignorant will desire to gain more than both?

Thrasymachus: I guess so.

Socrates: But, Thrasymachus, didn't you say that the unjust exceeds both like and unlike? Were not these your words?

Thrasymachus: Yes, I did say that.

Socrates: And you also said that the just person will not exceed the like but only the unlike person?

Thrasymachus: I also said that.

Socrates: Then the just person is like the wise and good, and the unjust person is like the evil and ignorant?

Thrasymachus: That does seem to follow.

Socrates: Didn't we previously establish that we can liken both to what they are like?

Thrasymachus: Yes, that was established.

Socrates: So it turns out that the just is wise and good and the unjust evil and ignorant.

Thrasymachus: That's your position, not mine.

Socrates: Thrasymachus, I understand your reluctance in arriving at agreement, but I don't understand whether it is the hot weather that makes you perspire so much or the heat of the argument. Perhaps it is the latter, because I now see something I have never seen before: Thrasymachus blushing. Anyway, we have now agreed that justice is virtue and wisdom, and injustice is vice and ignorance. So, let's consider another point. Do you remember saying that injustice has strength?

Thrasymachus: Yes, I remember, but don't think that I approve of what you say or that I have no answer. The reason I don't answer is that I know you would accuse me of making a diatribe. Therefore either permit me to have my say, or, if you would rather ask questions, go ahead and I will answer "Very good" and will nod or shake my head, as if I were listening to an old woman telling stories.

Socrates: Don't do that, Thrasymachus, not if it is contrary to your real opinion.

Thrasymachus: Yes, I will, to please you, since you won't let me speak freely. What else would you have me do?

Socrates: Nothing in the world. If that's the way you want it, I will ask questions, and you answer.

Thrasymachus: Proceed. **[351]**

Socrates: Then I will repeat the question I asked before. What is the nature of injustice when compared with justice? Thrasymachus, you said earlier that injustice is stronger and more powerful than justice. But now that we have identified justice with wisdom and virtue, it is easy to show that justice is stronger than injustice, because injustice is ignorance. Anyone can see that. But now I want to view the matter in a new way. Will you agree that a state may be unjust and may unjustly attempt to take over other states, or may have already overpowered them, and may be holding them in subjection?

Thrasymachus: Not only will I agree, but I will add that the best and most perfectly unjust state will be most likely to do so.

Socrates: I know that was your position; but what I want to consider is whether this power must be exercised with justice, or without justice.

Thrasymachus: If you are right in claiming that justice is wisdom, then power can be exercised only with justice; but if I am right, then power can exist without justice.

Socrates: I am delighted, Thrasymachus, to see that you are not only nodding and shaking your head, but also giving excellent answers.

Thrasymachus: That is out of courtesy to you.

Socrates: And very good of you, too. Would you also be so good as to inform me whether you think that an army, or even a band of robbers and thieves, or any other group with a common purpose, could act at all if they mistreated one another?

Thrasymachus: No, they could not.

Socrates: But if they abstained from injuring one another, then they might act better?

Thrasymachus: Yes.

Socrates: Isn't this because injustice creates divisions and hatred and fighting, whereas justice imparts harmony and friendship?

Thrasymachus: I agree, because I don't want to quarrel with you.

Socrates: Thank you. I have another question. Since injustice has this tendency to arouse hatred, wherever it is found—whether among slaves or free people—will it not make them hate one another and set them at odds and render them incapable of common action?

Thrasymachus: Certainly.

Socrates: And even if injustice is found in only two people, won't they quarrel and fight and become enemies not only to one another but to all just people as well?

Thrasymachus: They will.

Socrates: Now let's suppose injustice exists only in a single person. Would you say that the injustice loses or retains its natural power?

Thrasymachus: Let's say it retains its power.

Socrates: But think again about the power of injustice. Its nature is such that wherever it takes up its abode, whether in a city, an army, a family, or in any other body, that body is first rendered incapable of united action by reason of sedition and distraction, and then becomes its own enemy as well as the enemy of the just and of everything else that opposes it? Is this not so, Thrasymachus? **[352]**

Thrasymachus: Yes, certainly.

Socrates: And isn't injustice equally suicidal when it exists in an individual? In the first place it makes that person incapable of action, lacking internal unity. In the second place such an individual becomes its own enemy and an enemy of the just. Is not that true, Thrasymachus?

Thrasymachus: Yes.

Socrates: My friend, surely the gods are just.

Thrasymachus: Whatever you say.

Socrates: But if that's true, the unjust will be the enemy of the gods, and the just will be their friend?

Thrasymachus: Take your fill of the argument, and have a good time. I won't oppose you, otherwise I might displease your friends here.

Socrates: Well then, proceed with your answers, and let me have the rest of my feast. We have shown that the just are clearly wiser and better and more able than the unjust, and that the unjust are incapable of common action. We have shown even more. When we speak of unjust people acting together at any time, that is not strictly true. If they had been entirely unjust, they would have turned against each other. It is clear that there must have been some remnant of justice in them, or they would have attacked each other as well as their victims; and they would have been unable to act together. If they had been entirely evil, they would have been entirely incapable of action. That, as I understand, is the truth of the matter, and not what you said at first. But whether the just have a better and happier life than the unjust is a further question we also promised to consider. I think that they have, and for the reasons I have given. But I think this needs further examination. It is not a light matter; it concerns nothing less than the true rule of human life.

Thrasymachus: Go ahead.

Socrates: I will begin with a question: Would you say that a horse has a natural function?

Thrasymachus: I suppose.

Socrates: And would you also say that the natural function of a horse, or of anything else, could not be done, or not done as well, by any other thing?

Thrasymachus: I don't understand what you're talking about.

Socrates: Then I'll explain. Can you see with anything other than your eyes?

Thrasymachus: Certainly not.

Socrates: Or hear with anything but your ears?

Thrasymachus: No.

Socrates: Then we can say that these are the natural functions of these organs?

Thrasymachus: That's right. **[353]**

Socrates: Isn't it possible to cut off a vine-branch either with a carving knife or with a chisel or with many other tools?

Thrasymachus: Of course.

Socrates: But they can't do the job as well as a pruning hook made for that purpose.

Thrasymachus: That's true, but what's your point?

Socrates: Can we say that this is the natural function of a pruning hook?

Thrasymachus: Of course.

Socrates: Then, can you understand my asking whether the natural function of anything is something that could not be done, or not done as well, by any other thing?

Thrasymachus: Now I understand what you mean, and I agree.

Socrates: So things not only have a natural function, but they perform that function with excellence? Let's go back to the same examples. We said that eyes have a natural function.

Thrasymachus: We did.

Socrates: And they also have an excellence, a virtue that only they possess?

Thrasymachus: I agree.

Socrates: Also, ears have a natural function and, therefore, a unique virtue.

Thrasymachus: True.

Socrates: Can we say the same for all other things; each one has a natural function and a special excellence?

Thrasymachus: Yes, we can say that.

Socrates: Now, can the eyes fulfill their natural function if they lack their own proper excellence, if they are defective?

Thrasymachus: How could they perform their natural function if they were blind and could not see?

Socrates: You mean to say, if they have lost their proper excellence, which is sight; but I have not yet arrived at that point. Right now I am only asking whether the things which fulfill their natural function do so by their own excellence, and fail to do so by their own defect.

Thrasymachus: That makes sense.

Socrates: And we can say the same of the ears; when deprived of their unique excellence, they cannot fulfill their natural function.

Thrasymachus: Yes.

Socrates: And the same may be said of all other things?

Thrasymachus: I agree.

Socrates: That means the soul also has a natural function which nothing else can perform. For example, it rules, reasons, and manages. These functions are peculiar to the soul, and they can't be assigned to anything else.

Thrasymachus: That's right. They could not be done by anything else.

Socrates: What about living—isn't that a function of the soul?

Thrasymachus: It is.

Socrates: Does the soul have its proper excellence, a virtue it alone possesses?

Thrasymachus: Yes.

Socrates: Thrasymachus, if the soul is deprived of its proper excellence, can it perform its natural function?

Thrasymachus: It cannot.

Socrates: Then a bad soul would be a bad ruler, and a good soul would be a good ruler.

Thrasymachus: Yes, that's right.

Socrates: Didn't we agree that justice is the excellence of the soul, and injustice the defect of the soul?

Thrasymachus: We agreed about that.

Socrates: Then the just soul and the just person will live well, and the unjust person will live badly?

Thrasymachus: That's what your argument proves.

Socrates: And the person who lives well is happy, and the one who lives badly is not? **[354]**

Thrasymachus: Yes.

Socrates: Then the just person is happy, and the unjust person is miserable?

Thrasymachus: So it seems.

Socrates: But happiness—not misery—is more profitable.

Thrasymachus: Of course.

Socrates: Then, Thrasymachus, injustice can never be more profitable than justice.

Thrasymachus: Socrates, let this be your entertainment on the feast day of Bendis.

Socrates: For this I am indebted to you, Thrasymachus, now that you have grown gentle and stopped being angry with me. And if I have not been well entertained, it was my fault, not yours. I'm like a glutton who snatches a taste of every dish brought to the table, without allowing enough time to enjoy the previous one. Before we even discovered the nature of justice, I left that question and started asking whether justice is virtue and wisdom, or evil and folly. Then, I couldn't help being diverted by the question about the comparative advantages of justice and injustice. The result is that I learned nothing. I still don't know what justice truly is, and therefore I don't really know whether it is or is not a virtue, nor whether the just person is happy.

ENDNOTES

[1] Pindar (518–c. 446 B.C.), Fragment 214.
[2] Simonides (556–468 B.C.) was a Greek lyrical and elegiac poet.
[3] Homer, *The Odyssey*, xix. 395.
[4] Both Bias of Priene and Pittacus of Mytilene (mid-seventh century– 570 B.C.) were numbered among the Seven Sages.

Book Two

[357] *Socrates:* I thought these words had ended the discussion, but it turned out to be only the beginning. Glaucon was not satisfied with Thrasymachus' retreat, so he attacked me with his usual audacity.

Glaucon: Socrates, do you really want to convince us that it is always better to be just than unjust, or do you merely want to pretend that you have convinced us?

Socrates: I really want to convince you.

Glaucon: So far you've failed. Tell me how you would analyze goodness. Isn't there a kind of good that is desirable for its own sake, independent of its consequences, such as joy and delight in harmless pleasures?

Socrates: I agree.

Glaucon: And what would you say about another kind of good that is desirable not only in itself but also because of its consequences, such as thinking, seeing, and being healthy?

Socrates: I would say yes to that kind of good.

Glaucon: And isn't there a third form of good, one that is annoying in itself but valuable for what it produces? Consider body-building, medical treatment, and earning a living. We don't choose such activities for their own sake but for their results.

Socrates: Yes, there is also that kind. But why are you asking these questions?

Glaucon: Because I want to know how you would classify justice.

Socrates: I would say it is the best kind of good, desirable both for its own sake and for its consequences. [358]

Glaucon: That's not what most people think. They consider justice to be of the third kind, the annoying kind pursued for the sake of rewards and reputation but otherwise to be avoided.

Socrates: I know that's their opinion, and it was also what Thrasymachus had in mind when he scorned justice and praised injustice. I seem to be a slow learner.

Glaucon: Then listen to me, as you did to him, so we can see whether you and I agree. Thrasymachus gave up too soon, like a snake charmed by your voice. I'm far from satisfied with what has been said about the nature of justice and injustice. I want to know both what they are in themselves, apart from rewards and consequences, and what power they have in our soul. If it's all right with you, I will revive the argument presented by Thrasymachus. First, I'll talk about the popular view of the nature and origin of justice. Next, I'll show that all people who practice justice do so against their will, not as something good but as a necessity. Finally, I will argue that their approach makes sense, because they believe that the life of the unjust is far better than the life of the just. Don't think that I agree with what they say, Socrates, but I am confused and nearly deaf from the voices of Thrasymachus and so many others. I have never heard a satisfactory proof for the claim that justice is better than injustice, and I think you are the person most likely to make that case. Therefore, I will praise the unjust life to the best of my ability, and that will set the stage for you to praise justice and censure injustice. Do you approve of my plan?

Socrates: I certainly do. I can't imagine a topic a reasonable person would rather discuss.

Glaucon: Wonderful! Then I will begin with their account of the nature and origin of justice. Most people would say that doing injustice is naturally good and suffering injustice is naturally bad. However, the bad outweighs the good. Once people have experienced both doing and suffering injustice, they conclude that it is impossible to escape the bad and obtain the good. So they agree to avoid doing injustice in order to avoid suffering it. [359] This is the origin of laws and contracts. What people make into law, they then consider lawful and just. This means that justice is, by nature, a compromise between what they think is best—to do and not suffer injustice—and what is worst—to suffer injustice without the ability to retaliate. Because justice is a mean between these two alternatives, it is tolerated not as something good but as the lesser evil. It is respected because it restricts people's ability to do injustice. They say that a real man would never submit to such an agreement if he could avoid it; he would be crazy to do so. Socrates, this is the popular view of the nature and origin of justice.

To show that justice is merely the inability to do injustice, imagine a situation in which a just person and an unjust person have complete freedom to do what they want. Let's watch and see where desire leads them. In that way we will catch the just person in the act of taking the same road as the unjust—following self-interest, which everyone understands to be good. They are only diverted onto the path of justice by the force of law, which is equal for all. The kind of freedom I have in mind once also belonged to Gyges, the ancestor of Croesus the Lydian. According to tradition, Gyges was a shepherd serving the king of Lydia. One day when he was in the field, there was a storm and an earthquake which opened the earth where he was feeding his flock. Amazed by what he saw, he descended into the chasm that held many wonders, including a hollow bronze horse with doors in its side. When he opened one of the doors, he saw a corpse of more than human size. It was wearing nothing except a gold ring, which he took from its finger and climbed out of the hole. The custom among the shepherds was to meet to deliver a monthly report to the king about the flocks. Gyges joined them, wearing his new ring. As he was sitting among them, he chanced to turn the setting of the ring toward the palm of his hand. He instantly became invisible, and the other shepherds began to talk about him as if he was not there. **[360]** This amazed him, so he turned the ring again, and he reappeared. He tested the ring several times, always with the same result. When he turned the setting inwards, he became invisible; he reappeared when he turned it outwards. When he had figured this out, he managed to be chosen as the messenger to the court. As soon as he arrived, he seduced the queen and, with her help, murdered the king and took over the kingdom.

Let's suppose there were two such magic rings, one worn by a just person and the other by an unjust person. Nobody is strong enough to remain just in such a situation. No one would remain honest who could safely take anything from the marketplace, or go into any house and copulate with anyone, or kill or release from prison anyone they choose, generally acting with godlike power among human beings. Then the actions of the just would be no different from the actions of the unjust; they would seek the same goal. This clearly proves that people are just not freely or because they think that justice is in their interest—they are just out of necessity. Whenever people can be safely unjust, they will be unjust. In their hearts, they believe that injustice is far more profitable to the individual than justice, and those who follow this line of thought would say that they are right. Imagine someone with that kind of impunity who never does any wrong or never touches what belongs to someone else. Most people would consider such a person to be a complete fool, although they would praise that person in public out of fear that they too might suffer injustice. Well, I think I've said enough about that point.

In order truly to judge the lives of the just and the unjust, we must totally separate them. How is that to be done? Let the unjust person be completely unjust, and the just person completely just. Nothing should be removed from either of them, and both should be perfect examples of their type. First, think of the unjust person as accomplished in a craft, like skillful pilots or physicians who know their powers and attempt only what is within their limits. [361] If they fail at any point, they are able to recover and make corrections. In the same way, the unjust should practice injustice skillfully, remaining undetected to achieve greatness. If you are detected, you fail—the high point of injustice is to be considered just when you are not. To a perfectly unjust person, we must attribute the most perfect injustice, subtracting nothing. While doing the most unjust deeds, they must acquire the greatest reputation for justice. When they take a false step, they must be able to recover. If any of their unjust actions come to light, they must be able to speak effectively to cover up their crimes. They must employ force when force is required, using courage, strength, money, and friends as needed.

Now let's compare the unjust person with the simple and noble just person—as Aeschylus says, one who not merely seems but is good. Let's remove the appearance of justice, because if people seem to be just, they might be honored and rewarded, and then we won't know whether they are just for the sake of justice or for the sake of honors and rewards. Let's clothe the just person only in justice. Let's imagine the opposite condition to that of the unjust person: our just person is the best possible human being but is considered to be the worst. Let's see whether virtue serves as protection against infamy and its consequences. Until the hour of death, the just person is just, but seems to be unjust. When both have reached their extreme condition, the one of justice and the other of injustice, let's judge which of the two is happier.

Socrates: Glaucon, my dear friend, you have vigorously polished these two, as if they were statues to be put on exhibit.

Glaucon: I'm doing my best. Now that we know what they are like, we should be able to figure out the kind of life that awaits them. Socrates, you may think that my description is a bit too rough, so please don't take these words as mine. Imagine them as coming from the mouths of those who praise injustice.

They will tell you that in the case I described, just people will be scourged, racked, and bound; will have their eyes burned out; and, after suffering every other kind of evil, they will be impaled. This will teach them that they ought to seem, not to be, just.

They will say that the words of Aeschylus are more truly spoken of the unjust than the just, **[362]** because the unjust are pursuing reality—they do not live for appearances; they really want to be unjust, not merely to seem so:

> His mind is like a deep and fertile soil
> Out of which his prudent counsels spring.[1]

The unjust person is considered to be just, and can therefore rule; can freely choose whom to marry and arrange the marriages of others; can trade and deal freely, always pursuing self-interest, never worrying about being unjust. In every public or private struggle, the unjust person wins at other people's expense. Out of the riches gained, friends benefit and enemies suffer. Furthermore, the unjust person can offer abundant sacrifices and present magnificent gifts to the gods, honoring both gods and humans in far better style than the just person. For this reason, the unjust are dearer to the gods than the just. Socrates, both in the eyes of the gods and of human beings, the life of the unjust appears to be preferable to the life of the just.

Socrates: I would like to answer you, Glaucon, but I think your brother has something to say.

Adeimantus: Socrates, I hope you don't think our case is complete.

Socrates: Why, Adeimantus, what else needs to be said?

Adeimantus: The most important point hasn't even been mentioned.

Socrates: Well, as the proverb says, "Let brother help brother." You can fill in what he omitted, though I think Glaucon has already said enough to throw me and leave me powerless to help justice.

Adeimantus: Nonsense! I want you to hear the other side of Glaucon's argument. It is necessary to explain his meaning. We should also consider the argument of those who praise justice and condemn injustice only by looking at their consequences. Parents and teachers are always telling young people that they should be just. But why? Not for the sake of justice, but out of concern for reputation. **[363]** They promise powerful positions, good marriages, and all the other advantages which Glaucon said go to the unjust because of their high standing in public opinion. But this group makes more of appearances than the other one. They throw in the good opinion of the gods, and they tell you that the heavens will shower benefits on you because of your holiness. This agrees with the testimony of noble Hesiod and Homer. Hesiod says that for those who are just the gods make:

> The oaks to bear acorns at their summit, and the bees in the middle;
> And the sheep are bowed down with the weight of their own fleeces.[2]

Many other lessons of that kind are provided for them. Homer sings a similar song, telling of one whose fame is:

> As the fame of some blameless king who, like a god,
> Maintains justice; to whom the black earth brings forth
> Wheat and barley, whose trees are bowed with fruit,
> And his sheep never fail to bear, and the sea gives him fish.[3]

Musaeus and his son offer even grander heavenly gifts to the just. They take them to another world, where they attend a symposium of the holy ones. Lying on couches with crowns on their heads, they spend their time drinking. Perhaps their idea is that being eternally drunk is the greatest reward for virtue. Some poets extend the rewards for justice to future generations, promising earthly immortality through posterity.

This is how they praise justice. But for the unjust and the unholy they imagine a different set of consequences. They bury them in the muck of Hades, or make them carry water in a sieve. Even while they are still living, they live in infamy, suffering the punishment that Glaucon described for the just people who have the reputation of being unjust. Although they offer nothing new, that's how they praise the just and condemn the unjust.

Socrates, there's yet another way of talking about justice and injustice, not by the poets but by the people themselves. **[364]** Everyone agrees that justice and virtue are honorable but painful and boring, whereas injustice and vice are pleasurable and easy to obtain—to be avoided only because of law and public opinion. They also say that honesty is usually less profitable than dishonesty, and they don't hesitate to call evil people happy and to honor them both in public and in private if they are rich and powerful. They despise and ignore good people who are weak and poor, even though they admit that they are better than the others. Most amazing is what they tell us about virtue and the gods. They say that the gods send disaster and misery to many good people and fortune and happiness to evil people. Priests and prophets beg at rich people's doors, claiming that they have the power through charms and sacrifices to forgive their sins and those of their parents. This is done with festivals and games. They also promise to harm enemies, regardless of whether they are just or unjust, all for a small fee. Through magic and incantations they persuade the gods and appeal to the authority of the poets like Hesiod, who sing of vice and its attraction:

> Vice may be easily found and
> Many are they who follow after her;
> The way is smooth and not long.
> But before virtue the gods have set toil.[4]

He says the path to virtue is tedious and steep. Others appeal to Homer, who testifies that we can influence the gods to indulge us:

> The gods, too, may be moved by prayers;
> And men pray to them and turn away their wrath
> By sacrifices and entreaties,
> And by libations and the odor of fat,
> When they have sinned and transgressed.[5]

They produce a host of texts by Musaeus and Orpheus, whom they call children of the Moon and the Muse. They perform their rituals according to those books, persuading individuals and whole cities that they can atone and be purified for their deeds, not only for the living but also for the dead, through sacrifices and childish games. They call them mysteries, which they say will deliver us from the pains of Hades; but if we ignore them, no one knows what dreadful things await us. **[365]**

Socrates, when young people hear such talk about how virtue and vice are regarded by gods and humans, what are they going to think? I mean the clever ones who, like bees gathering nectar, land on everything they hear in order to gather ideas about the best way to live. They will probably ask Pindar's question:

> Can I by justice or by crooked ways of deceit ascend a loftier tower,
> which shall be a house of defense to me in all my days?

Based on what they have heard, they will conclude that there is no sense in my being just unless people think I am just. Otherwise it only leads to pain and loss. On the other hand, if I am unjust but have the reputation of being just, then I can have a wonderful life. Wise people say that appearance is the master of truth and the lord of happiness, so I will devote myself to appearance. I will clothe myself in virtue, but I will follow the sly and crafty fox, as the sage Archilochus advises. I hear someone object that it is not easy to hide evil; I answer that nothing great is easy. Yet this is the road to happiness, the logical way to go. As for covering our tracks, we can do that through political parties and secret agencies. And there are teachers of rhetoric who will show us how to persuade courts and legislatures. So partly by force and partly through persuasion, I will break the law and not be punished. Still another voice says that we can never fool or force the gods. But if there are no gods or if the gods don't care about human beings, we don't need to hide from them. And even if there are gods and they do care about us, we only know about them from the poets who proclaim their laws and trace their genealogies. According to them, we can influence the gods by prayers and gifts. So, either we believe the poets or we don't. If we believe them, then it is better to be unjust and offer them a share of the profits. **[366]** If we are just, we escape being punished by the gods, but we will lose the benefits of injustice. If we are unjust, we can reap the benefits and appease the gods by praying for forgiveness. "But there is a world below where we or our children will suffer for our crimes." I will reply: "Yes, my friend, but there are rituals and mysteries that can invoke the powerful gods who forgive. That's what the mighty cities tell us; and the children of the gods, their poets and prophets, say the same."

Then on the basis of what principle should we choose justice over injustice? If we combine injustice with deception, we will do well both with gods and human beings, here and hereafter. This is what we learn from popular opinion and from the highest authorities. Knowing all this, Socrates, how can anyone who has intelligence, money, power, or rank praise justice rather than laugh at it? Even if there is someone who can refute me, someone who thinks that justice is best, that person will not be angry with those who are unjust. Such people will forgive them, knowing that people do not willingly choose justice. Only those who have a divine nature or who have attained true wisdom will hate injustice. Of course there are also those who condemn injustice because they are too old, cowardly, or weak to be unjust. This is supported by the fact that those same people are the first to be unjust when they have the power.

Socrates, this entire line of argument can be traced to a single source. My brother and I both told you at the beginning of this discussion that we were amazed to find that of all the so-called experts on justice, no one has praised justice or blamed injustice except for the glory, honor, and benefit that flows from them. This is true of the ancient heroes whose words have been preserved as well as the people of our own time. No one has adequately described either in verse or in prose the essential nature and power of justice or injustice as they are found inside a person, invisible to any human or divine eye. No one has shown that justice is the greatest good and injustice the greatest evil. **[367]** If this had been the common theme, if you had tried to persuade us of this since our childhood, we would not have to watch each other to make sure that nobody does something wrong. We would all watch ourselves to avoid having the greatest evil inside our own person. I'm sure that Thrasymachus and many others would use the language I have merely been repeating, expanding it, grossly perverting the true nature of justice and injustice. I am using all the words at my command only because I want to hear you take the opposite side. I ask you not only to show the superiority of justice over injustice, but also explain what they do to those who possess them, what makes one good and the other bad for that person. As Glaucon also asked, please don't appeal to reputation. Unless you dress the just in the garb of injustice and the unjust in the guise of justice, we will conclude that you do not praise justice but only its appearance. We will think that you are only encouraging us to keep injustice in the dark and that you really agree with Thrasymachus in thinking that justice is really someone else's good—the interest of the stronger—whereas injustice is actually self-interest, but harmful to the weaker. You have already classified justice among the best kind of good things, the type that is desired for its results but even more for its own sake. You placed it with sight, knowledge, and health, real and natural goods that are intrinsically valuable, not the kind that is merely conventional. Leave it to others to praise the rewards and the appearances of justice. I can tolerate that way of arguing because it comes from them, but you have spent your whole life thinking about this, so I expect something better from you unless you tell me yourself that you cannot provide it. Therefore, I ask you not only to prove that justice is better than injustice but to show what each does to the person who possesses them, what makes one good and the other bad, whether seen or unseen by gods and human beings.

Socrates: Glaucon and Adeimantus, I have always admired the quality of your minds, but this display is especially impressive. **[368]** Glaucon's lover did well when he began his poem of praise for your performance at the battle of Megara by saying:

"Sons of Ariston, divine offspring of a glorious hero."

That's well put, because there is something truly divine in being able to argue as you have for the superiority of injustice and to resist being seduced by your own rhetoric. Based on your character, I am convinced that you are not swayed by these speeches, but if I considered only what you said, I wouldn't trust you. Yet the more I trust you, the less I trust myself. You leave me in a dilemma: on one hand, I feel my own inability to defend the cause of justice, because you are not convinced by the answer I gave to Thrasymachus about the superiority of justice to injustice, leading me to believe that I am not up to the job; on the other hand, it would be irreverent to remain silent when justice is attacked in this way. So, I must do my best to help defend justice.

Glaucon: Socrates, on behalf of everyone here, I beg you not to give up but to continue the discussion. We really would like to know the truth about the nature of justice and injustice and about their relative benefits.

Socrates: This will not be an easy search. It requires keen eyesight, but we seem to be a bit nearsighted. So, I suggest that we use a method designed to help people who have to read small letters at a great distance. If we are lucky, we can read the same letters up close and in larger form, and then proceed to identify the smaller ones.

Adeimantus: That's true, but how does it apply to justice and injustice?

Socrates: Don't we sometimes think of justice as a quality of an individual and sometimes as a quality of a republic?

Adeimantus: Yes.

Socrates: And isn't the republic larger than the individual?

Adeimantus: That's right.

Socrates: Then there will be more justice in the larger, so it will be easier to see. **[369]** Therefore, I suggest that we first consider the nature of justice and injustice as they appear in the republic, and then examine the individual, going from the larger to the smaller and comparing them.

Adeimantus: That's an excellent plan.

Socrates: Let's imagine through our words how the republic comes into existence so that we can see how justice and injustice come into existence as well.

Adeimantus: That makes sense.

Socrates: Once we have done that, we can hope to get a better look at what we are seeking.

Adeimantus: Much better.

Socrates: Are you sure you want to do this? It's not going to be easy, so you might want to think about it.

Adeimantus: I have thought about it; there is nothing else I'd rather do.

Socrates: As I understand it, a republic comes into existence out of human needs. We all want many things, but none of us is self-sufficient. Can you think of any other origin of a republic?

Adeimantus: None at all.

Socrates: Because we have many wants, many people are needed to provide for them; we need one kind of helper for one purpose and another kind for another purpose. When these helpers and partners come together in one place, we call that collection of people a republic.

Adeimantus: True.

Socrates: So they trade goods and services, one giving and the other receiving, each thinking that the exchange is good for them.

Adeimantus: That's right.

Socrates: Then let's create a republic in our imagination, beginning with our needs.

Adeimantus: That's where we should begin.

Socrates: The first thing we need is food, simply to stay alive.

Adeimantus: True.

Socrates: Then we need a place to dwell, clothing, and that sort of thing.

Adeimantus: Yes.

Socrates: To provide these things in our republic, one person must be a farmer, another a builder, and someone else a weaver.

Perhaps we should add a shoemaker and somebody to take care of our body.

Adeimantus: A good idea.

Socrates: So the most basic republic must include four or five people.

Adeimantus: That's clear.

Socrates: How should they proceed? Should each person work for all the others, the farmer, for example, producing food for everyone? Or should the farmer ignore the others, spending a quarter of the time raising enough food for personal needs and three-quarters of the time building, weaving, or making shoes? **[370]** That way we wouldn't have to bother with other people and could simply mind our own business.

Adeimantus: I think the first alternative is better.

Socrates: I think you are right, because it occurs to me that we are not all alike. We each have our own nature, and as a result we are each inclined to different occupations.

Adeimantus: Very true.

Socrates: Will the work be done better when a worker has several jobs or only one?

Adeimantus: Only one.

Socrates: And there's no doubt that the job will be spoiled when it's not done at the right time.

Adeimantus: No doubt.

Socrates: The reason is that business won't wait for the worker to do the work at leisure, but it must have first priority.

Adeimantus: It must.

Socrates: Then more things are produced more easily and with better quality when a person leaves other occupations and does one thing which comes naturally and does it at the right time.

Adeimantus: That's correct.

Socrates: Then we will need more than four citizens in our republic. The farmer won't make plows, hoes, or other such equipment, at least not good ones. The same is true of the builder, the weaver, and the shoemaker; they all need many tools, which they are not likely to make themselves.

Adeimantus: True.

Socrates: So we will need carpenters, metalworkers, and many other craftspeople in our little republic, which is now beginning to grow.

Adeimantus: It's definitely getting bigger.

Socrates: But it won't be very large even if we add cowherds, shepherds, and other herders so that the farmers can have oxen to pull the plow and the builders and weavers can have animals to pull and carry their loads of raw materials.

Adeimantus: No, but the republic won't be small either if it contains all these people.

Socrates: Furthermore, it's nearly impossible to place the republic where no imports are needed.

Adeimantus: You're right; it's impossible.

Socrates: So we will need another group to bring what we need from other places.

Adeimantus: We will.

Socrates: But if our traders take nothing with them, they will return empty-handed. **[371]**

Adeimantus: Of course.

Socrates: That means we must not only produce enough at home for our own needs, but we need ample goods of high quality to supply our customers.

Adeimantus: That makes sense.

Socrates: Won't that require even more farmers and craftspeople?

Adeimantus: It will.

Socrates: Then, of course, we will need merchants to import and export our goods.

Adeimantus: Yes.

Socrates: We will probably trade by sea, so a large number of skillful sailors will be required.

Adeimantus: Yes, a large number.

Socrates: But how will they exchange goods within the republic? That was our original objective.

Adeimantus: They will have to buy and sell.

Socrates: For that we will need a marketplace and a common currency.

Adeimantus: That's right.

Socrates: Now suppose that a craftsperson—a farmer, for example—brings some goods to the market, arriving at a time when there is nobody who wants to trade. Does this mean the farmer must sit and wait for a customer in the marketplace, even though there is farm work to be done?

Adeimantus: Not at all. There will be people who identify this need and take care of the selling—in well-managed republics they are commonly the people who are physically weakest and unable to do anything else. All they have to do is stay in the marketplace, take money from those who want to buy goods, and, in exchange, give money to those who want to sell.

Socrates: Then this need will introduce retailers into our republic. Retailer is the name we give to the people who buy and sell in the agora, whereas those who go from one republic to another we call traders.

Adeimantus: Those are appropriate terms.

Socrates: There is one more group of workers that we would not include in our republic because of their intellect but who are able to do hard physical labor, a service they sell for money. We call them laborers, another part of our population.

Adeimantus: That sounds good.

Socrates: And now, Adeimantus, with the addition of laborers, is our republic complete?

Adeimantus: Perhaps it is.

Socrates: Then where are justice and injustice? In what part of our republic can we find them?

Adeimantus: I can't imagine where they are to be found, unless it is in the relations of the citizens with each other. **[372]**

Socrates: You may be right, but we should not leave it at that; we need to examine your suggestion carefully. Let's first consider their lifestyle as we have provided for it. Won't they produce grain, wine, clothes, and shoes as well as build houses? They will work in the summer stripped and barefoot, but in the winter they will wear both clothes and shoes. They will feed on barley-meal and wheat flour, kneaded and baked, making excellent cakes and breads, serving them on a mat of reeds or clean leaves. While they feast, they and their children will recline on beds of yew or myrtle boughs, drinking wine, wearing garlands on their heads, and singing hymns to the gods. They will enjoy making love, but avoid producing too many children so that they can live within their means, avoiding poverty and war.

Glaucon: But Socrates, you haven't provided any delicacies for their banquet.

Socrates: True, I forgot about that. Of course they should have delicacies—some salt, olives, cheese, onions, and greens, boiled with herbs as they do in the country. For dessert we will serve them figs, chick-peas, and beans; they will drink in moderation while roasting myrtle-berries and nuts over the fire. Living on such a diet, they can expect to live in peace and reach a ripe old age, passing on a similar life to their children.

Glaucon: Right, Socrates, and if you were establishing a republic of pigs, isn't this exactly how you would feed them?

Socrates: Then how would you do it, Glaucon?

Glaucon: They should have the amenities of the good life. To be comfortable, people are used to lying on couches and dining from tables; they should have delicacies and dessert in the modern fashion.

Socrates: Now I understand. You don't merely want to consider how a republic comes into existence, you are interested in establishing a luxurious one. That's not a bad idea, because in such a republic we are likely to see how justice and injustice develop. I think that we have already described a true republic, a healthy one, but if you would like to consider a luxurious one, let's do that. I suppose that few people will be satisfied with the simple life. [373] They will want to add couches, tables, and other furniture; delicacies, perfumes, incense; and prostitutes and pastries of all kinds. We should not limit our imagination to the needs I spoke about before, such as houses, clothes, and shoes. We must call upon painters and embroiderers, so gold, ivory, and similar materials will be needed.

Glaucon: I agree.

Socrates: Then our original healthy republic is too small, so we must create a larger one. We must fill it with a multitude of occupations which go far beyond basic needs, such as hunters; and imitators (both visual artists who work with shape and color and musicians), poets and the rhapsodists who cling to them, actors, dancers, contractors; and people who make all kinds of ornaments, especially the ones used by women. And we will need more servants. Won't we need tutors, wet nurses, baby sitters, hairdressers, beauticians, pastry makers, and chefs? And what about swineherds? We didn't need them in the healthy republic, but now we need them and herds of other kinds of animals if people wish to eat meat.

Glaucon: No doubt.

Socrates: With such a lifestyle, won't they have a greater need for doctors?

Glaucon: Much greater.

Socrates: In our first republic we had enough land to support our population, but won't there be too little now?

Glaucon: You are right about that.

Socrates: Then we'll need a piece of our neighbor's land for pasture and farming. But they will want a piece of ours, if, like us, they go beyond basic needs and devote themselves to the unlimited acquisition of wealth.

Glaucon: That seems inevitable.

Socrates: And then we will go to war, Glaucon. That will be the next step.

Glaucon: I don't see how we can avoid it.

Socrates: It's premature to say whether waging war produces good or bad, but we have already discovered the causes of war which are also the causes of nearly all public and private evils in a republic.

Glaucon: That's for sure.

Socrates: Then once again we must enlarge our republic, this time adding nothing less than a whole army, one capable of fighting invaders to defend both our property and our citizens. **[374]**

Glaucon: Why? Aren't they able to defend themselves?

Socrates: Not if we were right about the principle we presented when we began to shape our first republic. You remember, don't you, that we said a single person cannot excel in many jobs.

Glaucon: I do remember.

Socrates: And don't you think waging war is a profession?

Glaucon: Certainly.

Socrates: Doesn't it deserve as much attention as the job of making shoes?

Glaucon: Of course.

Socrates: We did not allow the shoemaker to do the work of the farmer, the weaver, or the builder, because we wanted well-made shoes. We assigned to the shoemaker and every other worker one job for which that person was naturally suited. That person was to stay with that job for a whole lifetime, never missing the right moment to excel. And what work is more important than that of the soldier? Or is waging war so easy that a person may be both a soldier and a farmer or a shoemaker, or simultaneously practice some other occupation? Could anyone even be a good dice or checkers player who simply played for fun, without doing that and nothing else since childhood? Just picking up a tool won't make you a skilled worker or teach you the martial arts; such equipment is useless to the person who has never paid any attention to it or lacks knowledge of its nature and its use. So how could anyone take up a shield or any other weapon and on that same day become a good soldier, whether with heavy-armed or any other kind of troops?

Glaucon: Yes, a tool that taught its own use would be worth a lot.

Socrates: So, the greater the work of those who guard our republic, the more time, devotion, and training they will need.

Glaucon: I suppose that's right.

Socrates: And won't they need a nature suitable for this work?

Glaucon: Certainly.

Socrates: Then our job is to select people with natures suited to the task of guarding the republic?

Glaucon: Yes, we must do that.

Socrates: That won't be easy, but we must do our best.

Glaucon: We must. **[375]**

Socrates: Come to think of it, a watch-dog and a guard have a common talent. Do you think there is much difference between well-born youth and a well-bred dog?

Glaucon: What do you mean?

Socrates: I mean that they both should be perceptive, fast enough to catch an enemy, and strong enough to fight and defeat whatever they catch.

Glaucon: Well, yes, I guess they both need all those qualities.

Socrates: And to fight well, they must be courageous?

Glaucon: Certainly.

Socrates: Is any creature likely to be courageous if it is not high-spirited, whether horse, dog, or any other? Haven't you noticed how such spirit makes the soul of any animal fearless and invincible?

Glaucon: Yes, I have noticed that.

Socrates: Now we have a clear idea of the physical qualities required to guard our republic.

Glaucon: We have.

Socrates: And the soul of such a guardian must be high-spirited.

Glaucon: Yes.

Socrates: But, Glaucon, people with such a high-spirited nature are likely to be aggressive toward each other, and hostile to everyone else.

Glaucon: That is a problem.

Socrates: Our goal is to have them gentle to their friends and dangerous to their enemies, otherwise they will wind up destroying themselves before they encounter an opponent.

Glaucon: We must avoid that.

Socrates: But how are we to do that? Where can we find a gentle nature that is also high-spirited? These two qualities apparently contradict each other.

Glaucon: True.

Socrates: On the other hand, a good guardian must have both of those qualities, so if it is impossible to combine them, it seems that a good guardian is impossible.

Glaucon: I'm afraid you are right.

Socrates: Glaucon, when we find ourselves at such an impasse, we need to think again. My friend, I think we deserve to be in this difficulty. If we had stayed with our original image, this problem wouldn't have appeared.

Glaucon: I don't follow you.

Socrates: I mean that natures which combine these opposite qualities do exist.

Glaucon: Where can we find them?

Socrates: Many animals are examples, but think again of the well-bred dogs we discussed before. They are quite gentle with their friends, but they are just the opposite with strangers.

Glaucon: That's right.

Socrates: Then it's not impossible or unnatural to find guards who have a similar combination of qualities?

Glaucon: I guess not.

Socrates: So could we say that the guardian should combine a high-spirited nature with the qualities of a philosopher?

Glaucon: What? I don't understand what you are trying to say. **[376]**

Socrates: The quality I have in mind is found in dogs, something remarkable in such an animal.

Glaucon: What quality?

Socrates: Whenever a dog sees a stranger, it becomes angry, but it welcomes an acquaintance, even if the stranger has never harmed it and the acquaintance has never done it any good. Didn't this ever strike you as peculiar?

Glaucon: I never noticed that, but I agree now that you have pointed it out.

Socrates: This magnificent quality of a dog makes it a true philosopher.

Glaucon: How so?

Socrates: Because dogs distinguish the face of a friend and that of an enemy by the criteria of knowing and not knowing. Surely a being is fond of learning who distinguishes between what is friendly and what is unfriendly by the test of knowledge and ignorance.

Glaucon: No doubt.

Socrates: Isn't the love of learning the same as philosophy—the love of wisdom?

Glaucon: They are the same.

Socrates: So can we also say of human beings that the person likely to be gentle to friends and acquaintances will also be a lover of wisdom and knowledge?

Glaucon: We can say that.

Socrates: Then a really good and noble guard of the republic will combine high spirit, speed, strength, and a love of wisdom.

Glaucon: Yes.

Socrates: Now that we have identified their desirable qualities, how are we to rear and educate them? If we answer that question, will it shed light on our main question—how do justice and injustice come to exist in the republic? We don't want to leave out anything that is relevant, but we also want to avoid saying too much.

Adeimantus: Socrates, I think this is an important topic to explore.

Socrates: Well, Adeimantus, my friend, that means we must not give up the job even if it gets rather long.

Adeimantus: Certainly not.

Socrates: Then let's take our time and tell a story about their education.

Adeimantus: Let's do that.

Socrates: How should we educate them? Can we do better than the traditional education which has two divisions, gymnastics for the body and the arts[6] for the soul?

Adeimantus: I don't see how we can do better.

Socrates: Shall we begin by teaching the arts and then go on to gymnastics?

Adeimantus: Yes.

Socrates: When you speak about the arts, do you include literature or not?

Adeimantus: I do.

Socrates: But literature may be either true or false, isn't that right? **[377]**

Adeimantus: It is right.

Socrates: And young people should be educated by both kinds, beginning with the false.

Adeimantus: I don't understand what you mean.

Socrates: You know, we begin by telling stories to children that are mostly false but contain a grain of truth. We tell them these stories before they are old enough to learn gymnastics.

Adeimantus: True.

Socrates: That's what I meant when I said we should teach the arts before gymnastics.

Adeimantus: Now I understand.

Socrates: You also know that the beginning of any kind of work is its most important part, especially when it deals with young and tender things during the period when they are most easily formed.

Adeimantus: I do know that.

Socrates: Then should we be so careless as to allow children to hear just any story made up by anyone who comes along, taking ideas into their minds that are the exact opposite of the ones they should have when they grow up?

Adeimantus: We can't allow that.

Socrates: Then we must first supervise the storytellers, accepting what is good and rejecting what is bad. We will convince mothers and nurses to tell children only stories that have been approved, in this way forming their minds rather than simply tending their bodies. But that means we will have to throw out most of the stories now being told.

Adeimantus: Which ones are you talking about?

Socrates: The great ones which serve as a model for the minor ones; because they are of the same type, they have the same kind of power. Don't you think so?

Adeimantus: Perhaps, but I don't know what you mean by the great ones.

Socrates: The ones told by Homer, Hesiod, and the other poets who have always been the great storytellers for humankind.

Adeimantus: Which stories do you have in mind, and what's wrong with them?

Socrates: Something quite serious. They lie. What's more, the lies are bad ones.

Adeimantus: Can you be more specific? When do they lie?

Socrates: Whenever they speak falsely about the nature of gods and heroes, as when a painter paints a portrait that has no likeness to the original.

Adeimantus: Yes, you are right to condemn that sort of thing. But what stories do you mean?

Socrates: First of all, consider the story the poet tells about Uranus, a horrible lie about the highest of beings—I mean what Hesiod says Uranus did, how Cronus retaliated, and then the injuries his son inflicted on him.[7] **[378]** Even if such stories were true, they shouldn't be told to young and thoughtless people; it would be best to bury them in silence. But if they must be told, then it should be done as part of a secret ritual in which they sacrifice not a common pig, but a huge victim that is hard to get so that the number of listeners will be as small as possible.

Adeimantus: Socrates, I agree that those stories are extremely objectionable.

Socrates: Yes, Adeimantus, such stories should not be told in our republic. We should not teach young people that if they commit the worst crimes they are far from doing something outrageous and that they may punish their father anyway they like when he does something wrong, because they are simply following the example of the highest and greatest of the gods.

Adeimantus: I agree with you; in my opinion these stories are not fit to be repeated.

Socrates: And if we want the people who guard our republic to consider fighting among themselves to be repulsive, nothing should be said of wars and plots and battles among the gods, all of which is false. Nor should we tell them about the battles of the giants or allow such scenes to be embroidered on clothing. We should also keep quiet about the various other fights among gods, heroes, and their friends and relatives. We should tell them that quarreling is unholy and that so far there has never been a fight among our citizens. Elderly men and women should say this to children when they are young, and the poets should tell them similar stories when they grow up. By no means should they hear about Hephaestus tying up Hera, his own mother, or how, on another occasion Zeus threw him out because he took his mother's side when she was being beaten. And all those battles among the gods in Homer should never be repeated in our republic, even if they are supposed to have an allegorical meaning. Young people can't distinguish what is allegorical from what is literal. Anything they take into their minds at that age is likely to become indelible and unalterable, so it is especially important that the stories young people first hear should be models for virtuous thoughts.

Adeimantus: You are right about that; this is essential to our republic. But what if someone asks where such models are to be found? How should we answer?

Socrates: Adeimantus, right now you and I are not poets but founders of a republic. **[379]** In that role we ought to know the general forms in which poets should compose their stories, but it is not our job to create them.

Adeimantus: That's true, but what kind of things should we allow them to say about the gods in these stories?

Socrates: Well, something like this: Divinity should always be presented as it truly is, whether in epic, lyric, or tragic poetry.

Adeimantus: Right.

Socrates: Isn't the divine always good and, therefore, rightly said to be good?

Adeimantus: Of course.

Socrates: Nothing good is harmful, is it?

Adeimantus: No.

Socrates: And what isn't harmful can do no harm?

Adeimantus: Certainly not.

Socrates: If it does no harm, it doesn't do anything bad.

Adeimantus: That's right.

Socrates: So if it doesn't do anything bad, it can't cause anything bad.

Adeimantus: That would be impossible.

Socrates: Isn't what is good also beneficial?

Adeimantus: Yes.

Socrates: Therefore, the cause of well-being?

Adeimantus: Yes.

Socrates: Then the good is not the cause of all things, but only of good things, never of bad things?

Adeimantus: Yes.

Socrates: So the divine, if it is good, is not responsible for all things, as many people say, but the cause of only a few things, not of everything that happens—few are the good things in human life, and many are the bad. And if only what is good can be attributed to the divine, some other cause has to be found for the bad.

Adeimantus: I think what you say is true.

Socrates: Then we should not listen to Homer or any other poet who foolishly says:

> At the threshold of Zeus
> Lie two casks full of lots,
> One of good, the other of bad;[8]

or who says that the person to whom Zeus gives a mixture of the two—

> Sometimes meets with good
> At other times with bad fortune;

or that the person who is given the cup of unmixed bad—

> Wild hunger drives over the divine earth;

or again—

> Zeus, who is the dispenser of good and bad to us.

And if anyone says that Athena and Zeus brought about the breaking of oaths and treaties that was really caused by Pandarus,[9] or that the strife and conflict of the gods was instigated by Themis and Zeus, we will not approve such stories.[10] **[380]** Nor will we allow young people to hear the words of Aeschylus when he says that

A god who desires utterly to destroy a house
Plants guilt among mortals.

If a poet writes about the sufferings of Niobe, which is the subject of the tragedy in which these lines of poetry occur, or of the house of Pelops, or of the Trojan War, or any similar topic, either we must forbid saying that these are the works of a god, or, if they are attributed to a god, there must be a good explanation. The poet must say that the god did what was right and just and that the people were better for being punished. But to say that those who are punished are miserable, and that a god is responsible for their misery, that we must forbid. We might allow the poet to say that bad people are miserable because it is necessary to punish them and that they are made better by receiving divine punishment. But that a god, being good, is the source of evil for anyone, that must be vehemently denied, not allowed to be sung or said by old or young people in prose or verse in any well-ordered republic. That kind of fiction is suicidal, destructive, and blasphemous.

Adeimantus: I agree with you about this law, and I'm ready to vote for it.

Socrates: Then let this be one of the laws and prescriptions governing the making of poems and speeches—divinity is not the cause of all things but only of the good.

Adeimantus: That is quite satisfactory.

Socrates: What do you think about making a second principle? Do you consider the divine to be a magician, slyly appearing first in one form and then in another, sometimes actually changing and becoming different, and sometimes deceiving us with the appearance of such transformations? Or is divinity one and the same, fixed and immutable in a single form?

Adeimantus: I'll have to think about that.

Socrates: Think about it this way. If anything changes, that change must be brought about either by itself or by something else.

Adeimantus: That's necessarily true.

Socrates: And things that are at their best are least liable to be changed or made worse. For example, when the human body is most healthy and strong, it is least liable to be affected by food, drink, or hard work; and the most vigorous plant suffers least from wind, the heat of the sun, or other such forces.

Adeimantus: Naturally.

Socrates: Isn't this true of the soul as well? **[381]** The bravest and wisest soul is least affected by external influences.

Adeimantus: True.

Socrates: I suppose the same principle applies to the things we make such as furniture, buildings, and clothing; when they are well made and in good condition, they are least liable to be changed by time and circumstances.

Adeimantus: That's right.

Socrates: Then can we say that every good thing—whether made by art, by nature, or by both—is least liable to be changed from the outside?

Adeimantus: Yes, we can say that.

Socrates: Can we also say that divinity, and everything that belongs to it, is in the best possible state or condition?

Adeimantus: Yes, we can say that as well.

Socrates: Therefore, the divine is the least likely to take many forms.

Adeimantus: That's so.

Socrates: Could the divine change itself?

Adeimantus: If it is going to change at all, it would have to change itself.

Socrates: For better or for worse?

Adeimantus: If there is a change, it must be for the worse. We can't think that the divine is in any way lacking in beauty or goodness.

Socrates: That's right, Adeimantus. But would anyone, whether divine or human, desire to become worse?

Adeimantus: Impossible.

Socrates: Then it is impossible that divinity should ever be willing to change. Being the most beautiful and the best, it remains forever in the same form.

Adeimantus: In my judgment, that necessarily follows.

Socrates: Then, my friend, let none of the poets tell us that

> The gods in the disguise of strangers
> Prowl about cities, having diverse forms;[11]

and let no one slander Proteus and Thetis; nor in tragedy or any other kind of poetry introduce Hera, disguised as a priestess,

> Asking an alms for the life-giving daughters of the river Inachus.

Let's have no more lies of that kind. Nor must we have mothers under the influence of the poets frightening their children with horrifying stories

> Of certain gods who go about
> At night in the likeness, as is said,
> Of strangers from every land.

Let them take care not to blaspheme the gods and at the same time make their children into cowards.

Adeimantus: We should definitely prohibit that.

Socrates: Although the gods are themselves unchangeable, is it possible for them to cause us to imagine various forms in order to bewitch and deceive us?

Adeimantus: Let's explore that possibility.

Socrates: Can you imagine that a god would lie or deceive, either through words or actions, by making false images?

Adeimantus: I can't say.

Socrates: Don't you know that a true lie, if I may use that expression, is hated by gods and human beings alike? **[382]**

Adeimantus: What do you mean?

Socrates: I mean that no one wants to be deceived in their most important aspect, which concerns the most important matters. That's where we most fear being possessed by a lie.

Adeimantus: I still don't understand what you are saying.

Socrates: That is because you think I am trying to be profound. All I'm saying is that when our most important aspect, our mind or soul, is deceived or misinformed about realities, that is what we humans hate most. That's where we least want to be deceived by a lie.

Adeimantus: There is nothing we hate more than that.

Socrates: As I was saying, this ignorance of a lie within the soul is what I called a true lie. On the other hand, a mere verbal lie is only an image, a shadowy imitation of a previous state of the soul, not a pure, unadulterated falsehood. Isn't that right?

Adeimantus: Perfectly right.

Socrates: And the true lie is hated not only by the gods but also by humans?

Adeimantus: Yes.

Socrates: But a verbal lie is sometimes useful, not something hateful—for example, when we deal with enemies, or when it is used as a kind of medicine or preventative against people we call our friends who are deceived or insane and are about to do some harm. Or, consider the mythical stories we were just talking about. We don't know the truth about ancient times, so we put falsehood to use by making it as much like the truth as possible.

Adeimantus: We certainly do that.

Socrates: However, can any of these reasons apply to the gods? Can we suppose that a god is ignorant of antiquity and therefore needs to make false images of it?

Adeimantus: That would be ridiculous.

Socrates: Then there is no lying poet in the divine.

Adeimantus: Certainly not.

Socrates: Would a god tell a lie through fear of an enemy?

Adeimantus: That's inconceivable.

Socrates: May a god have friends who are foolish or mad?

Adeimantus: A god has no friends who are mad or foolish.

Socrates: Then we can imagine no motivation for a god to lie?

Adeimantus: None at all.

Socrates: So we can conclude that any divine being is absolutely incapable of falsehood?

Adeimantus: Yes.

Socrates: Then the gods are absolutely simple and true both in what they say and do, never changing, never deceiving through dreams, visions, signs, or words. **[383]**

Adeimantus: Your words reflect my own thoughts.

Socrates: I assume you also agree that this is the second model according to which we should form our ideas about divine things; the gods are not magicians who transform themselves, nor do they deceive human beings in any way.

Adeimantus: I do agree.

Socrates: Then even though we admire Homer, we do not admire the lying dream Zeus sends to Agamemnon.[12] Nor will we praise the lines of Aeschylus in which Thetis says that Apollo, at her wedding—

> Was celebrating in song her fair progeny
> Whose days were to be long, and know no sickness.
> And gathering all in one he raised a note
> Of triumph over the blessedness of my lot
> And cheered my soul.
> And I thought that the word of Phoebus
> Being prophetic and divine would not fail.
> And now he himself who uttered the strain,
> He who was present at the banquet, and who said this—
> He was the very one who slew my son.

These are the kind of stories about the gods that will make us angry. We will not support their public performance, nor will we allow them to become part of the education of the young. The guards of our republic should be true worshippers of the divine and resemble it as much as is possible for a human being.

Adeimantus: I fully agree with you about these principles, and I think they should become laws.

ENDNOTES

[1] Aeschylus, *Seven against Thebes*, 592–594.

[2] Hesiod, *Works and Days*, 232f.

[3] Homer, *The Odyssey*, xix. 109ff.

[4] Hesiod, *Works and Days*, 287–289.

[5] Homer, *The Iliad*, ix. 497ff.

[6] The Greek word "*mousikē*" includes music, the various forms of poetry, dance, and all of the other arts inspired by the Muses.

[7] Hesiod, *Theogony*, 154, 159.

[8] Homer, *The Iliad*, xxiv. 527–532.

[9] Homer, *The Iliad*, ii. 69.

[10] Homer, *The Iliad*, xx. 1–74.

[11] Homer, *The Odyssey*, xvii. 485–486.

[12] Homer, *The Iliad*, ii. 1–34.

Book Three

[386] *Socrates:* So, Adeimantus, we have identified the kinds of stories about the gods that should be told to our guards beginning in their childhood. In that way we will encourage them to honor the gods and their parents, and to be friends with each other.

Adeimantus: Yes, Socrates, and we were clearly right in doing that.

Socrates: And if they are to be courageous, should we not also teach them lessons that will take away their fear of death? Can any person be courageous who is afraid of death?

Adeimantus: Certainly not.

Socrates: Would someone who believes in the reality and terror of the world below avoid fearing death, choosing death in battle rather than defeat and slavery?

Adeimantus: Impossible.

Socrates: Then we must take control of these stories and others, asking the people who tell them not to condemn but rather to commend the world below. We must make it clear to them that their descriptions are untrue and do not benefit our future warriors.

Adeimantus: That is our responsibility.

Socrates: Then let's eliminate obnoxious passages, beginning with this verse:

> I would rather be a serf on the land of a poor portionless man who is not well to do, than rule over all the dead who have come to nought.[1]

We must also delete this verse:

He feared that the mansions—grim and squalid—which even the gods abhor, should be seen both by mortals and immortals.[2]

Or again:

O heavens! Is there in the House of Hades soul and ghostly form but no mind at all?[3]

Again:

To Teiresius alone had the gods given wisdom; the other souls do but flit as shadows.[4]

And again:

The soul flying from the limbs had gone to Hades, lamenting her fate, severed from strength and youth.[5]

Again:

And the soul, with shrilling cry, passed like smoke beneath the earth.[6] **[387]**

And:

Like bats in the hollow of a mystic cavern fly shrilling and hold to one another whenever any of them, dropping out of the string, falls from the rock, so did they with shrilling sound hold together as they moved.[7]

We must ask Homer and the other poets not to be angry when we strike out these and similar passages. It is not that they lack poetry, or because they fail to please the ear, but because the more they charm us, the less they are fit for the ears of boys and men who should be the champions of freedom and fear slavery more than death.

Adeimantus: No doubt.

Socrates: We should also reject all of the terrible and frightening names that describe the underworld, such as Cocytus, Styx, ghosts under the earth, sapless shades, and any others of the same sort. The mere mention of such words makes a shudder penetrate the deepest part of the soul of those who hear them. I am not saying that these stories are worthless, but there is a danger that they will weaken the efficiency of our guards.

Adeimantus: We do have reason to fear that.

Socrates: Then we must eradicate such stories.

Adeimantus: True.

Socrates: We must compose and tell a different kind.

Adeimantus: Clearly.

Socrates: Then we will not show famous people weeping and wailing?

Adeimantus: We will eliminate such descriptions along with the others.

Socrates: But would it be right to get rid of them? Remember that we said a good person would not consider another good person's death to be terrible.

Adeimantus: Yes, I do remember that.

Socrates: Therefore such a person would not grieve for a departed friend, thinking something terrible has happened.

Adeimantus: That's right.

Socrates: That kind of person is self-sufficient and does not need other people in order to be happy.

Adeimantus: True.

Socrates: Losing a son or brother or wealth would be less terrible to these than to other kinds of people.

Adeimantus: That's for sure.

Socrates: Therefore, they will be unlikely to grieve and will calmly bear bad luck of this kind.

Adeimantus: Yes, such people will feel misfortune less than others will.

Socrates: Then we would be right in getting rid of weeping and wailing that can make worthy people into useless women and inferior men. The people we educate to defend the republic would be ashamed to act like that. **[388]**

Adeimantus: That's right.

Socrates: Then once again we will beg Homer and the other poets not to present Achilles,[8] who is the son of a goddess,

> Lying on his side, then on his back, and then on his face; then starting up again in a frenzy full sail upon the shores of the barren sea, taking dusky ashes in both hands and pouring them over his head,[9]

crying and mourning in the various modes that Homer has described. Nor should he describe Priam, kinsman of the gods, as

> Rolling in the dirt, calling each man loudly by name.[10]

Even more seriously will we plead with him not to depict the gods lamenting and saying

> Alas! my misery! Alas! that I bore the bravest to my sorrow.[11]

But if we must hear the gods, the greatest of them should not speak in false words like these:

> Oh heavens! with my eyes I behold a dear friend of mine driven round and round the city, and my heart is sorrowful![12]

Or, again,

Woe is me that I am fated to have Sarpedon, dearest of men to me, subdued at the hands of Patroclus, the son of Menoetius.[13]

My dear Adeimantus, if our young people truly believe in such improper representations of the gods, instead of laughing at them as they should, they will never believe that they, being mere mortals, will be dishonored if they say and do the same. Instead of having shame and self-control, they will be whining and sobbing when they face the smallest difficulty.

Adeimantus: What you say is true, Socrates.

Socrates: So, following our previous reasoning, we will condemn such actions until we find a better alternative.

Adeimantus: That's a sound plan.

Socrates: We should also not allow our guards to indulge in excessive laughter, because such fits are likely to cause violent opposite emotions.

Adeimantus: I agree.

Socrates: So worthy people, and especially not gods, should never be represented as overcome by laughter.

Adeimantus: As you say—especially not the gods. **[389]**

Socrates: Then we should not allow the kind of expressions used by Homer when he describes how

Inextinguishable laughter arose among the blessed gods, when they saw Hephaestus bustling about the mansion.[14]

You would say that we should not admit such descriptions?

Adeimantus: If you want me to take responsibility, then it is certain that we should not allow such language to be used in our republic.

Socrates: But we should also venerate the truth. If, as we said, a lie is useless to the gods but useful to people—as a form of medicine—only physicians should prescribe that kind of remedy. Common people should not be allowed to meddle with it.

Adeimantus: Clearly not.

Socrates: Of all people, only the rulers of our republic have the right to lie, either to citizens or to foreigners. They will do this for the good of the republic. Nobody else should have anything to do with it. Lying to the rulers would be a far worse offense than when a patient hides the truth about an illness from a physician; or when an athlete conceals a physical condition from the coach or trainer; or when a sailor fails to inform the captain what is happening on a ship.

Adeimantus: How true!

Socrates: Then if the rulers catch anyone else in the republic telling lies,

> Any of the craftsmen, whether priest, physician, or carpenter,[15]

they will punish them for introducing a practice that destroys republics no less than ships.

Adeimantus: They must, if actions are to follow words.

Socrates: Now, Adeimantus, let's consider moderation. Will our young people need that quality?

Adeimantus: Certainly.

Socrates: And for most people, that means being obedient to their rulers but in control of their own pleasures of eating, drinking, and sexual activity.

Adeimantus: True.

Socrates: Then would you praise or blame Diomedes' command in Homer?

Friends, sit still and obey my word![16]

And what about the verses that follow?

The Greeks marched breathing prowess,[17]
In silent awe of their leaders.[18]

And the others of the same kind?

Adeimantus: I think they are good. **[390]**

Socrates: Then what about this line:

O heavy with wine, who has the eyes of a dog and the heart
of a deer.[19]

And what do you think of the ones after it? Would you say that
these or any other impertinent remarks common people make to
their superiors, whether in verse or in prose, are well chosen or
not?

Adeimantus: They are not well chosen.

Socrates: Such words may be amusing, but they do not promote
moderation and are likely to harm our young people. Do you
agree?

Adeimantus: Definitely.

Socrates: What do you think of having the wisest person say that
nothing is more glorious than—

When the tables are full of bread and meat, and the cup
bearer carries round wine drawn from the bowl and pours it
into cups.[20]

Would a young person's self-control be improved by hearing
such a thing? Or consider the other verse that claims

Hunger is the worst way of encountering destiny and death.[21]

What would you say about the story of Zeus who, while all the
other gods and people were asleep, lay awake devising plans,

which he instantly forgot when Hera appeared? Overcome by lust, he would not even go into the house but desired to lie with her on the ground, declaring that he had never been so aroused, not even when they deceived their dear parents and made love for the first time.[22] Or consider the tale of how Hephaestus caught Ares and Aphrodite in a net while they were in the act of adultery.[23]

Adeimantus: Socrates, I strongly object to having them hear anything of that sort.

Socrates: But they should hear about feats of endurance by famous people, whether acted out or told, as recounted in these verses:

> He smote his breast, and thus reproached his soul,
> Endure, my soul, thou has endured worse.[24]

Adeimantus: That's more like it.

Socrates: In addition, we should make sure that they are neither tempted by bribes nor by love of money.

Adeimantus: That's important.

Socrates: So, we should not sing to them of—

> Gifts persuading gods, and persuading reverend kings.[25]

Nor should we approve of Achilles' tutor Phoenix when he advises him to accept gifts to assist the Greeks but not to reconcile with them without receiving bribes.[26] And we will not agree that Achilles took Agamemnon's gifts because he was a moneygrubber and even demanded a ransom for a dead body.[27]

Adeimantus: We should never allow such things. **[391]**

Socrates: As much as I love Homer, I must say that it is downright impious to speak that way about Achilles or to believe it when other people talk that way. I cannot approve what Achilles said to Apollo:

> Thou hast wronged me, O far-darter, most abominable of
> deities. Verily I would get even with thee, if I only had the
> power.[28]

We must also reject stories such as his disobedience to the river-
god,[29] whom he was ready to attack, or the dedication of his own
hair to the dead Patroclus—hair that had already been dedicated
to the other river-god Spercheius. Equally offensive are stories of
his dragging Hector around the tomb of Patroclus[30] and his
slaughter of the captives at the funeral pyre.[31] We can no more
believe this than we can accept that Achilles, who was Chiron's
pupil, and the son of a goddess and of Peleus (himself the most
moderate of men, who was descended from Zeus) was so
disturbed as to be simultaneously the slave of two warring
passions—of meanness tainted by greed and overwhelming contempt
for gods and human beings.

Adeimantus: Socrates, you are absolutely right to object to all of
it.

Socrates: Then let's also suppress and refuse to believe the
stories about Poseidon's son Theseus, and of Peirithous, the son
of Zeus, who are accused of committing abominable rapes. We
will also condemn stories about other heroes and sons of gods
who are falsely accused now of doing unholy and horrible things.
Let's require the poets to explain that either such acts were not
committed, or that they were not committed by the sons of
gods—but not both. They cannot be allowed to convince young
people that gods are the perpetrators of evil, and heroes are no
better than ordinary people. As we said, such claims are neither
appropriate nor true. We have already proved that evil can never
come from a god.[32]

Adeimantus: Definitely not.

Socrates: Stories of this kind will have a bad effect on those who
hear them. People will begin to excuse their own evil acts when
they believe that such things are being done by—

> The relatives of Zeus, whose paternal altar
> Is in the heavens and on the mount of Ida

and who have

> The blood of deity yet flowing in their veins.[33]

Let's put an end to them before they undermine the morals of our young people.

Adeimantus: By all means, let's do that! **[392]**

Socrates: Now, Adeimantus, are there any other kinds of stories that we should consider? I think we have finished making all the necessary rules about gods, demigods, heroes, and the world below.

Adeimantus: I agree.

Socrates: Then what should we say concerning stories about human beings? Clearly that remains to be discussed.

Adeimantus: True.

Socrates: But I don't think we can settle that question at this point.

Adeimantus: Why not?

Socrates: Because to do that we would have to say that poets and story-tellers make grave mistakes about human beings when they say that the unjust are happy and just people miserable, and that injustice is profitable when it is undetected, and that justice is good for other people but harmful to yourself. We would have to forbid them to say such things and command them to sing and say the opposite.

Adeimantus: Of course. Is anything wrong with that?

Socrates: That is precisely what we have been trying to discover from the beginning of this discussion.

Adeimantus: Ah, now I understand.

Socrates: So, we must wait until we have discovered the nature of justice and why it is naturally beneficial to the person who possesses it, whether or not that person is considered by other people to be just.

Adeimantus: That's true.

Socrates: Then let's turn our attention from subject matter to style, so that when we have finished we will have considered both form and content.

Adeimantus: I don't know what you mean.

Socrates: Well, it's important that you understand, so I will explain. I assume you are aware that the stories told in mythology and poetry are about what has happened in the past, what is happening in the present, or what will happen in the future.

Adeimantus: Certainly.

Socrates: And it can take the form of simple narration, imitation, or both narration and imitation.

Adeimantus: Socrates, I'm afraid you have lost me again.

Socrates: I guess I'm not much of a teacher, because I have so much difficulty being understood. So, like a bad speaker, I will not take on the whole subject but will break off a piece and use it to illustrate my meaning. Remember the opening lines of *The Iliad* where Chryses begs Agamemnon to release his daughter? **[393]** When Agamemnon becomes irate, Chryses invokes the anger of the god against the Greeks. Homer is speaking in the first person up to the point where he wrote these lines: "And he beseeched all the Greeks, especially these two sons of Atreus, the chiefs of all the people." The poet is speaking in his own voice, never leading us to suppose that he is anyone else. But then he assumes the voice of Chryses, and he does everything he can to make us believe that the speaker is not Homer, but the elderly priest himself. This is the general form of the narrative both in *The Iliad* and in *The Odyssey*.

Adeimantus: Now I see what you mean.

Socrates: And we would call it narrative when the poet presents both the speeches and the passages between them.

Adeimantus: That's right.

Socrates: But when Homer speaks in the voice of someone else, he assimilates his style to that of the person who he tells you is going to speak.

Adeimantus: Exactly.

Socrates: And this assimilation of himself to someone else is an imitation—either by voice or by gesture—of the person whose character he assumes.

Adeimantus: Yes.

Socrates: So, in this case can we say that the poet's narrative proceeds by way of imitation?

Adeimantus: Of course.

Socrates: Now if the poet appears throughout the work and is never concealed, then his narration would proceed without imitation. To make my meaning clear, I will return to my example. Suppose Homer had said: "The priest came with his daughter's ransom in his hands, beseeching the Greeks, and above all the kings." Then, instead of speaking in Chryses' voice, Homer would continue in his own and the imitation would change into narration. He would have said—since I'm no poet, I will have to drop the meter—: "Cryses came and prayed to the gods on behalf of the Greeks, so that they might take Troy and return home in peace—if only Agamemnon would give back his daughter, take the ransom, and worship the gods. Thus he spoke, and the other Greeks respected him and agreed. But Agamemnon was wrathful, ordering him to depart and not come back, warning that the scepter and wreath of the god would not protect him. He said that Chryses' daughter would not be released until she had grown old with him in Argos. Then he told him to go away and not annoy him if he intended to get home safely. **[394]** And the old man departed in fear and silence. When he left the camp he called upon Apollo by his many names, saying that if he had ever pleased the god by building his temple and offering sacrifices, he prayed that this might be rewarded by having the arrows of the god make the Greeks pay for his tears," and so on. This is how the entire work becomes a narrative.

Adeimantus: I understand.

Socrates: Or you might imagine the opposite where intermediate pieces of narration are omitted and only the dialogue remains.

Adeimantus: I understand. That's how it's done in writing tragedy.

Socrates: That's exactly what I mean. Now I think you see clearly what you did not see before. In some cases poetry and mythology are completely imitative, for example in tragedy and comedy, as you said. But in the opposite style the poet is the only speaker—the dithyramb is a good example. And epic poetry as well as other types frequently combine both styles. Do you follow me?

Adeimantus: Yes, Socrates, I follow you completely.

Socrates: Do you remember the topic we began when I said that we had finished talking about subject matter and that we should consider style?

Adeimantus: I do remember.

Socrates: I meant that we should consider whether the poets, in telling their stories, should be allowed to imitate, and, if so, whether the entire work should be imitative or only part of it, and if so, which part it should be? Or should we prohibit imitation entirely?

Adeimantus: I think you are asking whether tragedy and comedy should be admitted into our republic.

Socrates: Yes. But there may be even more to that question. I don't yet know, but wherever the wind carries the argument, we should be prepared to go.

Adeimantus: I'm ready for the journey.

Socrates: Then, Adeimantus, I want to know your opinion concerning whether our guards ought to be imitators. But perhaps you answered the question earlier when you agreed that a person can only do one thing well.[34] Perhaps if people tried to do many things, they would be excellent in none of them.

Adeimantus: No doubt.

Socrates: Should we say the same principle applies to imitation? A person can imitate one thing better than many things?

Adeimantus: The same principle applies. **[395]**

Socrates: Then if you are right about that, the same person will be unable to pursue any occupation worth mentioning and at the same time be an imitator who is spending the whole time copying others. Even when two kinds of imitation are closely allied, as are comedy and tragedy, you seem to believe that the same person cannot excel in both. Is that your opinion?

Adeimantus: That's right. The same person cannot be excellent in both.

Socrates: Any more than they can be rhapsodists and actors at the same time.

Adeimantus: True.

Socrates: And actors in comedy differ from actors in tragedy, though both are imitations.

Adeimantus: Yes, both comedy and tragedy are imitations.

Socrates: Adeimantus, it seems to me that human nature is divided into even smaller parts than these. People are not only unable to imitate many actions well, but they are also incapable of performing well the many actions that the imitations copy.

Adeimantus: Quite true.

Socrates: Then if we follow the principle on which we first established our republic, our guards should be relieved of every other occupation and devote themselves entirely to generating freedom in the republic, focusing their full attention on this and no other goal. They should not practice or imitate anything else. But if they do imitate anything, already as children they should emulate the character of people appropriate to their profession—those who are moderate and self-controlled, reverent, courageous, free, and so on. But by no means should they be allowed to imitate what is disgraceful, for fear that they might become what they imitate. Have you noticed how imitations, already in young people, are absorbed into a person's character and become second nature in body, voice, and mind?

Adeimantus: Yes, Socrates, I have observed that tendency.

Socrates: Then if we want them to be good, we will not allow the men under our care to play the part of either a young or an old woman, quarreling with her husband, and competing with the gods by boasting and bragging about her good fortune. Much less should they imitate a woman who is suffering, grieving, or weeping, and certainly not one who is sick, or is in love or in labor.

Adeimantus: I could not agree more!

Socrates: They should also not act the part of either male or female slaves.

Adeimantus: Definitely not.

Socrates: They should also not imitate bad men—cowards or anyone else who does the opposite of what we just prescribed: slandering, satirizing, or abusing each other or themselves, whether drunk or sober. Nor should they act like insane people, either in word or deed. Madness, like evil, in men or women, must be recognized but not displayed. **[396]**

Adeimantus: I agree fully.

Socrates: Should they imitate metalworkers or any other craftspeople, or oarsmen, or the people who keep time for them, or anyone else of that sort?

Adeimantus: How could they imitate them if they are not permitted to have anything to do with such activities?

Socrates: Should they be allowed to imitate the neighing of horses, the bellowing of bulls, the sound of rivers, the roll of the ocean, thunder, and that kind of thing?

Adeimantus: Of course not. If they are forbidden to be mad, then they should not copy madness.

Socrates: Then, if I understand what you are saying, you think there is one kind of narration to be used by a really good and admirable person, and another sort appropriate for a person with another type of character and who is educated in a different way.

Adeimantus: What two kinds do you mean?

Socrates: Imagine that a decent person encounters what another good person says or does in a narration. In that case, I assume one would not be ashamed to imitate and would be ready to play the part of the good person who is behaving solidly and wisely. But when that person is made weak by illness, lust, intoxication, or some kind of accident, one would be less inclined to copy that kind of activity. But when a character is worthless, no person will want to waste any time on that role. They will refuse to wear the costume of inferior people, unless they might briefly do it for some good. They would be ashamed to play a role they never practiced, nor will they want to model themselves after anything evil and ugly. All of this is beneath them—unless it is for fun.

Adeimantus: That's how I would expect them to perform.

Socrates: They will adopt a narrative style of the sort we illustrated from Homer, the mixed form that is both imitative and narrative; but it will contain a lot of narration and little imitation. Is that what you have in mind?

Adeimantus: Exactly. That is the style we should foster.

Socrates: But the other kind of character is willing to narrate anything, and the worse such people are, the less will they try to avoid. **[397]** They will be ready to imitate anything, not as a joke but seriously and before a large audience. As I was just saying, they will make the sound of thunder, the howl of the wind, the rattle of hail, as well as the sounds of pulleys, pipes, flutes, and all sorts of instruments. They will bark like dogs, bleat like sheep, and crow like roosters. Their entire craft will consist of imitating voice and gesture, and they will not use much narration.

Adeimantus: That is how they will act.

Socrates: So these are the two kinds of style you would identify.

Adeimantus: That's right.

Socrates: And would you agree that one of them is simple and has only little variation? And when the harmonics and rhythm are also chosen for their simplicity, a person who performs correctly retains the same style and stays within the limits of a single harmonic mode and also keeps close to the same rhythm?

Adeimantus: That sounds right to me.

Socrates: By contrast, the other style involves all sorts of harmonic variations and many different kinds of rhythm so that the music can reflect the variety and the complexity of the words?

Adeimantus: True.

Socrates: Is it also true that these two styles, or some combination of them, encompass all of poetry and every other form of speaking and writing? That means nobody can say anything except in one or another of those styles.

Adeimantus: Yes, they encompass all.

Socrates: Would you favor admitting all of these styles into our republic, including the mixed ones, or only one or two of the pure forms?

Adeimantus: I would prefer admitting only the pure imitation of the best people.

Socrates: Adeimantus, don't forget that the mixed style is quite charming, and that the mimetic style, which is the opposite of the one you have chosen, is the most popular, especially with young people and their teachers, as well as the general public.

Adeimantus: I admit it is the most pleasant.

Socrates: I take it you are saying that this complex style is not appropriate for our republic, because our citizens are not complex. One person plays only one part.

Adeimantus: The complex style is definitely not suitable for our republic.

Socrates: I suppose that is why in this republic, and only in this republic, a shoemaker will be nothing but a shoemaker (not also a pilot); a farmer will only be a farmer (not also a judge); and a soldier will be a soldier and not also go into business.

Adeimantus: That is precisely the kind of republic we want. [398]

Socrates: Therefore, if one of these multiform men who has the power to imitate everything comes to our republic and offers to present himself and his poetry, we will worship him as a pleasant and holy and wonderful being. But we will also tell him that there is no place for someone like him in our republic, because the law will not allow such people. Once we have anointed him with myrrh and placed a garland of wool on his head, we will send him away to some other republic. In our own we will employ the simpler and more austere kind of storyteller who will utilize the style of good people and follow the models we prescribed when we first established the education of our soldiers.

Adeimantus: That's how we will do it, if we have the power.

Socrates: My friend, now that we have treated both its form and content, I think we have finished our reflections on that aspect of musical education that deals with stories and myths.

Adeimantus: I think so too.

Socrates: Next we should consider melody and song.

Adeimantus: It is plain that they come next.

Socrates: Since we have agreed on the basic principle, couldn't everyone say what has to be said about those elements?

Glaucon: Socrates, I'm afraid that the word "everyone" does not include me, because right now I could not say what needs to be said. I could only guess.

Socrates: Glaucon, could you at least tell us with certainty that a song or an ode has three parts—the words, the melody, and the rhythm?

Glaucon: Yes, that much I do know.

Socrates: Concerning the words, surely there is no difference between the ones that are set to music and those that are not? Both will follow the same principles we have already determined.

Glaucon: I agree.

Socrates: And will the melody and rhythm go with the subject matter?

Glaucon: Certainly.

Socrates: Do you agree that we do not need funeral-songs and lamentations?

Glaucon: Yes, Socrates, I agree that such lamentations would add little of value to our republic.

Socrates: Glaucon, you are a musician, so you can tell us what kind of melodies express sorrow.

Glaucon: I think you are referring to the mixed or tenor Lydian and the full-toned or bass Lydian modes, but there are others that are similar.

Socrates: Then I suppose these are the ones we should banish from our republic. They are not beneficial either to women of good character or to men.

Glaucon: That's right.

Socrates: And do you agree that drunkenness, softness, and laziness are destructive to the character of our guards?

Glaucon: Of course.

Socrates: So, what kind of music promotes intoxication and indolence? **[399]**

Glaucon: The Ionian and the Lydian modes are called "loose" or "slack." I think they are the ones you have in mind.

Socrates: Do those forms of music have any military use?

Glaucon: Just the opposite. So, it seems that only the Dorian and the Phrygian remain.

Socrates: I don't know much about music, but for our republic we need warlike melodies and songs that a brave person can sing in times of danger when courage is needed. We need music that is appropriate when the battle is not going well or when a person suffers wounds, faces death, or confronts some other crisis. We need music that helps them face fate with calmness and endurance. And then we also need music that is suitable for times of peace and liberty, the kind that can be used for supplication or persuasion, whether to the gods or to other people. We need music that makes people willing to listen to others when they request or advise, the kind that promotes moderation and wise submission. If this is the kind of republic we wish to construct, I request that you preserve these two kinds, the music of compulsion and the music of liberty, of the unfortunate and the fortunate, of courage and moderation.

Glaucon: The two kinds I mentioned would well serve our purposes.

Socrates: Then if we use only the Dorian and Phrygian modes in our songs and melodies, we will not need complex scales and structures.

Glaucon: That's correct.

Socrates: That means we will also not need people who make instruments with many strings or those capable of multiple harmonies.

Glaucon: They would be useless in our republic.

Socrates: But what about flute-makers and flute-players? We would not want to include them because the flute is the most versatile of instruments in the composite use of harmony. Is panharmonic music itself not an imitation of the flute?

Glaucon: Clearly.

Socrates: Then only the lyre and the harp remain to be used in town, and the shepherd's pipe is suitable for the country.

Glaucon: That arrangement follows from our basic principles.

Socrates: Is it surprising that we chose Apollo and his musical instruments rather than Marsyas[35] and his instruments for our republic?

Glaucon: Not at all surprising.

Socrates: By the dog of Egypt, I now realize we have unconsciously been purging this republic we recently called luxurious!

Glaucon: And I think we are wise in doing so.

Socrates: Well, then let's finish the job. Since we have taken care of the harmonies, we naturally come to rhythms. They should be subject to the same principles, which means we should not have complex or diverse systems of meter. We need to figure out what rhythms express a courageous and harmonious life. **[400]** First come the words, then the rhythms should be adapted to them, not the other way around. Glaucon, you are in charge of choosing the proper rhythms—just as you did the harmonic modes.

Glaucon: Socrates, I can't say which rhythms are best. I only know that there are three basic principles out of which metric systems are composed, just as in sounds there are four elements into which the harmonics can be classified. But I can't tell you about the kinds of life to which these rhythms correspond.

Socrates: Then we will have to consult the musical expert Damon. He can tell us what rhythms express subservience, insolence, fury, or any other kind of vice as well as which ones express the opposite of those qualities. I have a vague recollection of his mentioning a complex rhythm from Crete. I also remember a dactylic and a heroic form that he arranged to compensate for the rise and fall—I'm not sure how—passing into short and long times. Unless I am mistaken, he spoke of an iambic as well as a trochaic rhythm, and he assigned them to short and long quantities. Also, in some cases he seemed to praise or disapprove of the movement of the foot quite as much as the rhythm. In any case, his words were applicable to both, and I'm not sure which he meant. But, as I said, we should refer this matter to Damon, because of the difficulty of the subject. Do you agree?

Glaucon: I do agree that we should leave this matter up to him.

Socrates: But you are able to determine that grace or clumsiness is the effect of good or bad rhythm, good or bad style, and good or bad harmony. And we have accepted the principle that rhythm and harmony are regulated by the words, not the other way around.

Glaucon: Yes, rhythm and harmony should follow the words.

Socrates: Is it right to say that words and style depend on the character of a person's soul?

Glaucon: Yes.

Socrates: And everything else depends on the words?

Glaucon: That's right.

Socrates: Then good language and harmony and grace depend on simplicity. I mean the simple elegance of a true and noble mind, not the simplicity that is a euphemism for the simple-minded.

Glaucon: I agree about that kind of simplicity.

Socrates: So, our young people should make this their constant guide if they are to achieve what is most important for them.

Glaucon: They should.

Socrates: And these same qualities seem to prevail everywhere—in the arts and crafts such as painting, weaving, embroidery, architecture, interior design, as well as in natural things such as the bodies of animals and plants. **[401]** In all things there is either appropriateness or inappropriateness. Discord, disharmony, and gracelessness are closely connected to clumsy speech and bad character, whereas grace and harmony are the sisters of moderation and good character.

Glaucon: Well said.

Socrates: Tell me, Glaucon, should we supervise only the poets to make sure that they imitate only the character of good people if they are allowed to write poetry in our republic? Or should we exercise the same control over the other artists to prevent them from exhibiting malignant, lustful, indecent, or graceless forms in sculpture, building, or any of the other arts? Should we prohibit them from practicing their arts in our republic, so that they do not corrupt our citizens? I don't think you want our guards growing up among perverted images, as if they were grazing in a pasture of poisonous plants, feeding on noxious herbs and flowers day after day, bit by bit, until they quietly gather a destructive mass of corruption in their souls. It would be better if our artists were able to grasp the true nature of grace and beauty. Then our young people would dwell in a healthy land among fair sights and sounds. Exquisite works will exude qualities that fill their senses like a fresh breeze and invisibly draw even the soul of a child into harmony with the beauty of reason.

Glaucon: There could be no better education for our young people.

Socrates: Glaucon, don't you think this is why education in the arts is so powerful? Rhythm and harmony find their way to the inner part of the soul and establish themselves there, bringing grace to the well educated. The opposite is true for those who are badly educated. And a person properly educated in the arts will be able to recognize flaws both in art and in nature, to praise and enjoy what is good and beautiful, and in that way become good and beautiful. **[402]** That same person, while still young, will condemn and dislike what is bad even before knowing the reason why it is bad, but once reason is developed will greet the good and beautiful as an old friend.

Glaucon: Yes, I agree that these are the reasons why proper education in the arts is so important.

Socrates: It is like learning to read. First we have to recognize the various letters of the alphabet in their many combinations, ignoring their size. Until we are able to identify them in their various forms, we cannot be considered truly literate.

Glaucon: I agree.

Socrates: Or suppose that we see letters reflected in water or in a mirror. It is only when we know the letters themselves that we are able to recognize them in their various manifestations, and such knowledge exists through a single art.

Glaucon: Exactly.

Socrates: Then am I correct in saying that neither we nor the guards whose education we are planning can ever become true musicians until we know the forms of moderation, courage, freedom, generosity, and others like them as well as their opposites? We will recognize that they are all part of the same art and practice, and not slight them or their images wherever they occur, whether large or small.

Glaucon: Yes, Socrates, you are right.

Socrates: Then when a beautiful soul participates in the form of beauty and is in harmony with itself, that is the best possible sight for anyone who is able to view it.

Glaucon: The best by far.

Socrates: And is the best the most desirable?

Glaucon: Definitely.

Socrates: And do you think the true musician would love the most beautiful person, but not one who is inharmonious?

Glaucon: I think that is true if the disharmony is in the soul, but a mere bodily defect would not get in the way of such a lover.

Socrates: It sounds as though you are speaking from personal experience, and I agree with you. But tell me, is intense pleasure in harmony with moderation?

Glaucon: How could it be? That kind of pleasure can drive you out of your mind just as extreme pain does.

Socrates: Does excessive pleasure promote goodness?

Glaucon: Not at all. **[403]**

Socrates: Does it encourage lewdness and overindulgence?

Glaucon: Yes, in their most extreme forms.

Socrates: Do you know of any pleasure that is stronger or more intense than sexual pleasure?

Glaucon: No, and none that is more likely to drive you crazy.

Socrates: But the right kind of love is orderly, good, moderate, and harmonious.

Glaucon: That's true.

Socrates: Then we should separate violence and irrationality from true love.

Glaucon: Definitely.

Socrates: So genuine lovers should not indulge in violent pleasure if they really want to practice the right kind of love.

Glaucon: Yes, Socrates, they should stay away from violence and irrationality.

Socrates: Then I suppose you would favor making a law for the republic we are founding that a man who loves a boy should kiss him graciously and only with permission—as a father would his son. And I assume you would apply the same rule to their entire relationship; if he goes beyond that limit, he would be considered to be crude and unrefined.

Glaucon: I would vote for such a law.

Socrates: Would you agree that we have come to the end of what we should say about the arts? What is the purpose of the arts if not the love of beauty?

Glaucon: I do agree.

Socrates: After education in the arts, our young people should receive physical education.

Glaucon: Certainly.

Socrates: This form of education should also begin when they are young and continue throughout their lives. I would appreciate hearing your opinion on this subject, Glaucon, but I believe that it is not the excellent condition of the body that improves the soul, but an excellent soul that improves the body. What do you say to that?

Glaucon: I have the same opinion.

Socrates: That means that a well-educated mind will take care of the details of caring for the body, so we can be brief and simply point the way by forming general principles.

Glaucon: Good.

Socrates: Then our young people should stay sober, as we already said, because of all people it is unfitting for guards to be drunk and not know where in the world they are.

Glaucon: It would be absurd for a guard to have to be guarded by someone else.

Socrates: Now what should we say about their food? These people are athletes in the greatest of all contests, are they not?

Glaucon: They are.

Socrates: Consider the customary training for athletes—would that be suitable for our guards? **[404]**

Glaucon: I'm not sure.

Socrates: I'm sorry to say that the conventional training athletes get makes them drowsy and is hazardous to their health. Haven't you noticed that they sleep away their lives and that they are susceptible to dangerous illnesses if they depart even slightly from their routine?

Glaucon: Yes, I have observed that.

Socrates: Then we need a more appropriate kind of training for our military athletes, who should be like dogs who never sleep, with acute sight and hearing. They must adjust to many changes of water and food, endure summer heat and winter cold, while maintaining their health.

Glaucon: That is also how I think about their training.

Socrates: The best form of physical education would be the twin of that simple art of education we were just describing.

Glaucon: What do you mean?

Socrates: I think there is a kind of physical training that is simple and suitable especially for military action.

Glaucon: I'm still not sure what you have in mind.

Socrates: You can learn what I mean from Homer. As you know, when his soldiers are on a campaign, he feeds them on military rations. They do not eat fish, even though they are on the shores of the Hellespont,[36] nor boiled meat, but only roasted meat, which is the most convenient food for soldiers. It requires only a fire and avoids the trouble of carrying pots and pans.

Glaucon: Now I understand.

Socrates: And Homer never mentions sweets and spices. Even our professional athletes know that a person who seeks to be in good condition should abstain from things like that.

Glaucon: Yes, they know that they are right in avoiding them.

Socrates: Then you would not approve of eating the kind of dinners served in Syracuse or introducing fancy recipes from Sicily.

Glaucon: I would advise them to avoid such things like poison.

Socrates: I suppose you would also disapprove of Corinthian prostitutes as their dinner companions if they are to stay in shape.

Glaucon: Of course I would.

Socrates: No doubt you would also rule out the famous pastries made in Athens.

Glaucon: Absolutely forbidden!

Socrates: This kind of dining and living is like the complex musical compositions we discussed—melodies and songs with many different harmonies and rhythms.

Glaucon: Exactly.

Socrates: In that case complexity fostered excess, and here it promotes disease. But just as simplicity in music engenders moderation in the soul, simplicity in physical training nurtures health in the body.

Glaucon: That's quite true, Socrates.

Socrates: When license and disease multiply in a republic, many law courts and hospitals will open. Lawyers and doctors will develop a high opinion of themselves when the free people of the republic flock to their offices. **[405]**

Glaucon: That seems unavoidable.

Socrates: Glaucon, would it not be a sorry situation in a republic when not only common people and manual workers but even those who pretend to have a liberal education rely on professional doctors and judges for health and justice? If they were properly educated, would they need to look elsewhere to find order and harmony, relying on others to prescribe and judge? Is it not shameful if they cannot do it for themselves?

Glaucon: Nothing is more shameful.

Socrates: But is it not even more shameful if people then spend their whole lives in litigation, hanging around courthouses either as plaintiff or defendant? They have so little sense of what is right and good that they think they are smarter than others because they are so clever and cunning. They use every dirty trick and every loophole, every dodge and evasion, in order to escape. But what do they gain? Not much. They do not realize that being able to put your life in order without the approval of a drowsy judge is far better and more satisfying.

Glaucon: You are right; that way of life is far more shameful.

Socrates: And to return to medicine, isn't it also disgraceful to run to doctors not for an accident, a wound, or a seasonal illness but because of the maladies that come from indolence and luxury? Such people fill their bodies with fluids and gasses like a swamp, requiring the clever sons of Asclepius[37] to invent names for diseases such as flatulence and catarrh.

Glaucon: Yes, those really are strange and bizarre new names for diseases.

Socrates: I don't think such disorders existed in the time of Asclepius. I base this view on Homer's story about the hero Eurypylus. After he was wounded, he drank a mixture of Pramnian wine, sprinkled with flour and cheese, which actually causes inflammation. **[406]** Yet the sons of Asclepius who were at the Trojan War do not blame the woman who gave him the drink, nor did they criticize Patroclus, who ordered the medication.

Glaucon: But that was a strange drink to give to a person in his condition.

Socrates: It is not so strange if you remember that formerly, before the time of Herodicus, the guild of Asclepius did not practice the present system of medicine, which is concerned with tending disease. Herodicus was an athletic trainer who became quite sick. By blending physical training and doctoring, he found a way first to torture himself and eventually the rest of the world.

Glaucon: How did he do that?

Socrates: He invented a form of lingering death. He had an incurable illness which he spent all his time tending. Unable to cure himself or occupy himself with something else, he spent the rest of his life treating his disease. He was in constant agony if he deviated even slightly from his medical routine. And so, thanks to his skill and cunning, he spent many years dying while reaching old age.

Glaucon: What a noble prize for his cleverness!

Socrates: Yes, it is exactly the reward for a person lacking the wisdom of Asclepius who failed to instruct his descendants in these arts—not because he lacked knowledge or experience but because he knew that in a well-ordered republic people have work to do. Nobody has the leisure to spend every day being doctored for illness. We criticize this in the case of common workers but fail to apply it to people who are rich and who we suppose are fortunate.

Glaucon: How so?

Socrates: When carpenters get sick, they ask the doctor for a quick remedy—a laxative, something to make them vomit, or even surgery. But if they are told that they must undergo a tedious program or lengthy bed rest, they quickly reply that they have no time to be ill. They say that there is no point in a life spent nursing a disease and neglecting their proper work. So, they say goodbye to that kind of medicine and return to their usual ways. Either they get well as they go about their normal business, or they die and put an end to it.

Glaucon: I think that attitude toward medicine suits such people.

Socrates: Without meaningful work, what good would their life be? **[407]**

Glaucon: It would not be worth much.

Socrates: But a rich person has no work, so being kept from working would not make life intolerable.

Glaucon: That's what they say.

Socrates: I guess you never heard what Phocylides said: Once you have made your fortune, then you should practice goodness.

Glaucon: I don't think you should wait that long.

Socrates: True, but let's not quarrel with him about that. The primary question is whether rich people should practice goodness and if living without it is unbearable. We have agreed that a life spent tending an illness is intolerable for a carpenter or other worker, but are things different for a wealthy person who is trying to follow Phocylides' advice?

Glaucon: Socrates, I have no doubt that excessive care of the body, when it goes beyond basic physical exercise, is a barrier to practicing goodness. It hinders the ability to manage a house, an army, or even a routine public office.

Socrates: The worst part is that people will attribute their headaches or dizziness to learning, thinking, and serious reflection, fearing that these cause their problems. People who are always worrying about their body and nursing some kind of illness have neither the time nor the inclination to cultivate and achieve goodness.

Glaucon: I agree with you.

Socrates: Perhaps Asclepius also agreed and that is why he directed the art of medicine to people who have a healthy constitution and who adopt healthful habits but suffer from a certain ailment. Those people he cured by purgation and surgery and sent them away to live a normal life that would benefit the republic. But he would not have tried to treat bodies already destroyed by disease, pretending that emptying and filling them could restore them. He did not intend to lengthen useless lives so that they could produce children as frail as they are. He saw no point in curing people who could not live a full life. Such people have little value either to themselves or to the republic.

Glaucon: You seem to regard Asclepius as a statesman.

Socrates: I think that is obvious. We see it reflected in the example of his sons who were not only physicians but also distinguished themselves in battle at Troy. **[408]** I'm sure you remember how, when the arrow shot by Pandarus wounded Menelaus, they—

> "Sucked the blood out of the wound, and sprinkled soothing remedies."

But (as in the case of Eurypylus) they did not prescribe what Menelaus should eat or drink. They considered their treatment to be sufficient for a man who is healthy and sound, even if he happened to drink that Pramnian wine concoction. But they ignored unhealthy and immoderate people whose lives were of no use either to themselves or to others. The art of medicine was not designed for them, even if they were as rich as Midas.

Glaucon: Those sons of Asclepius were men with good sense.

Socrates: Yes, and you should expect that they would be. But Pindar and the writers of tragedy present a different picture. Even though they claim that Asclepius was the son of Apollo, they say that he was bribed to heal a rich man who was on the verge of death and that he was struck by lightning as punishment. But we should follow the rule we have established and refuse to believe both that he was the son of a god and greedy. If he was greedy, he was not the son of a god; if he was the son of a god, he was not greedy.

Glaucon: I think you are right about that, Socrates, but now I have a question for you. Don't we need good physicians in our republic? And if we do, would not the best be those who have the widest possible experience treating people with both good and bad constitutions, just as good judges need to be familiar with all kinds of people, not only good ones?

Socrates: Yes, I agree that we need both good judges and good physicians. But do you know who I think are the good ones?

Glaucon: I will if you tell me.

Socrates: I will try. First let me point out that you are comparing two things that are not alike.

Glaucon: What do you mean?

Socrates: You compare judges and physicians, but they are quite different. Skillful physicians not only need to know their art, but even when they are young should become acquainted with various kinds of disease. It would actually help if they were not always healthy but had experienced various kinds of illness in their own body. Glaucon, as I understand it, the body is not the instrument by which they treat the body. If that were the case, we would not want them ever to be sick. But they cure the body with the mind, and an unhealthy mind cannot cure anything.

Glaucon: That makes sense.

Socrates: But things are different with a judge who governs mind with mind. **[409]** For that reason they should not be reared among evil minds. It would be wrong to have them associate with criminals while young so that they would be exposed to all sorts of crime and experience it first-hand, as in the case of bodily disease. A good and sound mind, in order to form a sound judgment, ought to avoid being contaminated by bad habits. This is why good people are often considered to be simple-minded and naïve, easy targets for those who are evil and criminal. They lack examples of evil in their own souls.

Glaucon: That often happens to such people.

Socrates: For that reason, judges should not be too young. They must learn about evil not from their own souls but from observing it in others over a long period, guided not by experience but by knowledge.

Glaucon: Yes, I think that would be the best kind of judge.

Socrates: Well, I think that answers your question. And I think we can say that such a judge is also good, because a person is good whose soul is good. Now consider people who are cunning, are always expecting evil, and who have committed many crimes. When they are among their own kind, they are extremely clever in taking precautions and outsmarting others whom they judge against their own measure of evil. But when they get into the company of good people, those who have the experience that comes with age, they appear to be quite foolish, especially because of their inappropriate mistrust. They cannot recognize honest people because they have nothing in themselves with which to compare the other person's character. However, because the bad outnumber the good, they encounter evil people more often than good ones, giving them the illusion that they are wise rather than foolish.

Glaucon: That's quite true.

Socrates: So it is safe to say that the wise and good judge we are seeking is not this kind of person. The other sort will suit us better. Glaucon, in my opinion those who are bad cannot really know those who are good, but a person with a good nature, educated by time, will acquire knowledge of both goodness and evil. The good person, not the evil one, is wise.

Glaucon: That is also my opinion.

Socrates: Then I assume this is the kind of law and the kind of medicine you will prescribe for our republic. **[410]** These arts will serve people who are naturally good both in body and in soul. But individuals whose bodies have incurable disease will be allowed to die, and the ones whose souls are incorrigible they will execute.

Glaucon: That is clearly best for them and for the republic.

Socrates: This means that young people who have been educated by the simple arts that foster moderation will do everything they can to stay away from law courts.

Glaucon: No doubt about it.

Socrates: And in the same way sound physical education will influence them to have as little as possible to do with medicine.

Glaucon: I think that's true.

Socrates: So they engage in the hard work of physical exercise in order to develop the courageous aspect of their nature, not merely as a means of increasing their bodily strength, like the kind of athletes who train only to develop their muscles.

Glaucon: That's right.

Socrates: Then it would be a mistake to believe that the arts are designed to educate the soul and physical education is intended to train the body.

Glaucon: Then what is their purpose?

Socrates: I think that those who teach both kinds of art intend to improve the soul.

Glaucon: I'm not clear about what you mean.

Socrates: Have you noticed what happens to the mind when a person is exclusively devoted to physical training, or have you observed the opposite effect when someone is devoted only to the arts inspired by the Muses?

Glaucon: What effects are you talking about?

Socrates: I mean the tendency of athletes to become too hard and brutal and the others to become soft and effeminate.

Glaucon: Now I understand. People who engage only in athletic training often become too savage, and those who confine themselves to the musical arts become softer than is good for them.

Socrates: That fierce and savage quality, when properly educated, becomes courage and bravery, but when it is out of control it turns harsh and brutal.

Glaucon: That often happens.

Socrates: Lovers of wisdom tend toward the more gentle side, but if this tendency goes too far, they become too soft. When rightly educated, they will be civilized and moderate.

Glaucon: True.

Socrates: And should we require our guards to have both of these qualities?

Glaucon: We should.

Socrates: We also expect that these qualities should be harmonized.

Glaucon: Definitely.

Socrates: A harmonious soul is both moderate and courageous. **[411]**

Glaucon: Yes.

Socrates: But an inharmonious soul is cowardly and crude.

Glaucon: It is.

Socrates: Now consider what happens when you listen to music and let it pour into your soul through your ears, which are like a funnel. You spend your time singing and enjoying songs; at first the sweet and soft strains of the sort we were just describing will temper the passion and spirit within you, just as iron when heated becomes malleable and useful rather than brittle and useless. But if this softening continues, then the passion of your soul melts and disappears. The sinews of your soul are cut and you become a feeble warrior.

Glaucon: That's what happens.

Socrates: If your spirit is naturally weak, this happens quickly, but if it is vigorous, the force of the music weakens the spirit and excites you. Soon you are ignited, but then extinguished. Instead of being vigorous, you become irritable, ill-tempered, and discontent.

Glaucon: Exactly.

Socrates: And in physical training, if you work hard and eat well, ignoring music and philosophy, at first the great condition of your body fills you with pride and your spirit is doubled.

Glaucon: That's a good description.

Socrates: But if you do nothing else, never cultivating the Muses or developing a love of learning and a taste for the arts, then your mind becomes weak, dull, and blind, never being awakened or nourished by questioning, and the senses are never purified and refined.

Glaucon: A sorry state.

Socrates: Eventually you begin to hate reasoning and logic, become uncultured and resemble a wild beast—violent and fierce. Knowing no other way of dealing with others, you live in an ignorant and evil condition, with no sense of harmony and grace.

Glaucon: That's absolutely true.

Socrates: Thus there are two arts that the gods gave to human beings, one designed to cultivate a courageous spirit and the other to nurture the love of wisdom. They apply only indirectly to the body and the soul, the ultimate goal being to harmonize them and attune them to each other. **[412]**

Glaucon: That seems to be how it is.

Socrates: If you mingle the arts with physical training in the right proportion, fitting them properly to your soul, then you can be called a true musician, one who creates a harmony far greater than the harmony achieved by someone tuning the strings of an instrument.

Glaucon: A beautiful image.

Socrates: Glaucon, it seems we will always need that kind of conductor in our republic if it is to endure.

Glaucon: Yes, we must have a true musician to preserve order.

Socrates: Then these are the basic principles of nurture and education. I don't think we need to go into further detail describing their kind of dances, how they hunt or chase game with dogs, the specific form of physical training, or their horse races. These will all follow the general principles we have identified, and they will not be difficult to discover.

Glaucon: I agree.

Socrates: Now—what is our next question? Don't you think we should inquire about who should be the rulers and whom they should rule?

Glaucon: Certainly.

Socrates: It seems obvious that older people should rule the younger ones.

Glaucon: That's clear.

Socrates: And from that group it should only be the best who rule.

Glaucon: That's also clear.

Socrates: Can we say that the best farmers are the ones who are most skilled in farming?

Glaucon: Yes.

Socrates: Then the best guards in our republic would be the ones who are best at guarding the republic.

Glaucon: Yes again.

Socrates: To do that, they must not only be powerful but also politically wise and be devoted to the welfare of the republic.
Glaucon: True.

Socrates: Don't you think that people are most devoted to what they love?

Glaucon: That makes sense.

Socrates: And are they most likely to be devoted to what is of shared benefit and what promotes mutual well-being in good or evil fortune, but have the opposite attitude when they have nothing in common?

Glaucon: That's how it is.

Socrates: Then we should select from our guards the ones who, throughout their lives, show the greatest desire to do what is good for the republic and never do what will harm it.

Glaucon: They would be the best leaders.

Socrates: But we would have to watch them carefully at every stage of their lives, making sure that they maintain their devotion to the republic, never abandoning it either through force or seduction.

Glaucon: I don't understand what you mean by abandoning it.

Socrates: Then I'll explain. When you abandon a belief, your act is either voluntary or involuntary. It is voluntary when you learn that the belief is false, but it is involuntary if you think the belief is true. **[413]**

Glaucon: I understand what you said about the voluntary, but not about the involuntary.

Socrates: Don't you think that people are unwillingly deprived of what is good, and willingly deprived of what is evil? And would you agree that not having the truth is bad, and having the truth is good? And I'm sure you would agree that understanding things as they are is to have the truth.

Glaucon: Yes, I agree, and I believe that people are deprived of the truth against their will.

Socrates: And don't you think that this happens because it is stolen, taken by force, or because they were bewitched?

Glaucon: Socrates, I still don't fully understand.

Socrates: I must be talking as obscurely as the people who write tragedies. I mean that there are two kinds of theft. In the first, people are enchanted by persuasion and change their minds, and in the other one, time is the silent culprit who causes them to forget. Now do you understand?

Glaucon: Yes.

Socrates: Those who are forced to change their opinion usually do so because of some kind of pain or suffering.

Glaucon: That I understand, and I agree.

Socrates: Do you also agree that people who are bewitched change their mind because they are under the spell of either pleasure or fear?

Glaucon: Yes, it seems that all forms of deception are a kind of spell.

Socrates: Well then, as I was saying, we need to find out which guards will best protect their own conviction that what is best for the republic should rule all of their actions. We must begin watching them when they are young and challenge them with tasks in which they are most likely to forget or be deceived. We will select those who remember and are not deceived and reject the others. Isn't that how we should do it?

Glaucon: Yes.

Socrates: And as they mature we should prescribe additional labors and struggles and contests and watch for the same qualities.

Glaucon: We should also do that.

Socrates: Then we should perform a third kind of test in which we try to enchant them. Just as horse trainers expose young colts to loud noises and shouts to see if they are shy or timid, we should put our young people in the midst of various kinds of terror. We should also attempt to lure them with pleasures, testing them more thoroughly than gold is tried in the fire. That will allow us to determine whether they are armed against all enchantments. We will find out which are good guards of themselves and of the arts they have learned, retaining their inner harmony and rhythm so that they can best serve both themselves and the republic. The ones who emerge from the trial at each stage—as a child, as a young person, and as an adult—victorious and pure, will be appointed as rulers and guards of the republic. [414] They will be honored in life and in death by receiving a magnificent funeral and being remembered with great monuments. The other kind we will reject. Glaucon, this seems to be the way we should choose our rulers and guards, but I am only speaking in general, without pretending to give exact details.

Glaucon: In general, I agree with you.

Socrates: We will call them "guards" in the fullest sense of the term, those who fight for us abroad and those who keep the peace at home, saving us from anyone who has the power or the will to harm us. But the young people we have been calling guards might better be designated as assistants who carry out the orders of the rulers.

Glaucon: A good proposal.

Socrates: Let's see how you like the next proposal. I think we need to invent one of those lies we talked about before,[38] a supreme lie that might deceive even the rulers but at least the rest of the republic.

Glaucon: What sort of lie do you mean?

Socrates: It's nothing new, Glaucon, only an old Phoenician tale about what has often happened before in other places, but not in our time—at least that's what the poets say, and they have convinced many people. I don't think it is likely to happen again, and I fear it will be difficult to get people to believe it.

Glaucon: Socrates, you seem quite reluctant to tell this story.

Socrates: You will understand why when you have heard it.

Glaucon: Go ahead, don't be afraid.

Socrates: Well, I will speak, but it's difficult to look you in the eye when I do. And I'm having trouble finding the words, so I will proceed gradually. First we will tell it to the rulers, then to the military, and finally to the rest of the people. They will be told that their childhood was a dream and that the education and training they received from us was only an illusion. In reality, during that period they were being shaped and nourished in the womb of the earth, where they, along with their weapons and other equipment, were manufactured. When they were fully formed, the earth—their mother—sent them into the world. We will tell them that they should think of their republic as a mother and a nurse, defending her from all attacks and treating all of the other citizens as siblings, children of the same soil.

Glaucon: No wonder you were ashamed to tell that lie.

Socrates: Wait, there is more to come. **[415]** Citizens, we will say to them, you are all children of the same mother, yet the god formed you in different ways. Some of you have the power to command—you were composed of gold. You hold the place of greatest honor. Others are made of silver and designed to be assistants to the leaders. Still others are to be farmers and craftspeople, made of brass and iron. Normally you will breed your own kind, but because you come from the same original family, sometimes a golden parent will have a silver child, or a silver parent a golden child. And the god proclaims to the rulers a fundamental principle that above all they should watch over their offspring and see which elements are mixed into their nature. And if the child of a golden or a silver parent has a mixture of brass and iron, then the ruler should not take pity on that child but send it away to become a farmer or craftsperson. At the same time, children may spring from the ranks of farmers and craftspeople with a gold or silver nature and rise to become leaders or assistant leaders. There is a prophecy that says if a person with a brass or iron nature takes the lead in a republic, it will be destroyed. Glaucon, my friend, is there any chance we can get our citizens to believe this story?

Glaucon: I don't think it will work for the present generation, but perhaps we can persuade their children or their grandchildren and their descendants.

Socrates: I understand the difficulty, but even that approach would encourage them to care more for the republic and for each other. So let our story spread by word of mouth. In the meantime, wewill arm our earth-born children and send them out under the command of their rulers. We will let them select the best place to camp in order to prevent any rebellion that might arise within the republic and defend themselves against any enemies who might come down like wolves and attack the flock from the outside. Once they have made their camp, they should sacrifice to the gods and prepare their dwellings.

Glaucon: What kind of dwellings will they have?

Socrates: The kind that will protect them against the cold of winter and shield them from the heat of summer.

Glaucon: Then they will live in houses?

Socrates: Yes, but houses fit for soldiers, not for moneymakers.

Glaucon: What is the difference?

Socrates: Let me explain it this way. **[416]** Don't you think it would be terrible for a shepherd to keep watchdogs that were poorly disciplined or hungry or had bad habits and for those reasons turned on the sheep, behaving not like dogs but wolves?

Glaucon: That would be horrible.

Socrates: Similarly, we should make sure that our guards and their assistants, who are much stronger than ordinary citizens, do not attack them like savage tyrants rather than protecting them as gentle friends.

Glaucon: We should avoid that at all cost.

Socrates: Don't you think that education is the best preparation and precaution?

Glaucon: But they are well educated. We have already taken that precaution.

Socrates: I'm not so sure about that, Glaucon. But I'm quite certain that they ought to be and that true education, whatever it is, should civilize and humanize them in their relationship with each other and with the people under their protection.

Glaucon: That's right.

Socrates: Not only their education but also their houses and their property should be regulated so as not to interfere with their service as guards or tempt them to prey upon other citizens. All sensible people will agree with that.

Glaucon: They will.

Socrates: Then let's consider what way of life is appropriate for them. First of all, they should have only the amount of property that is absolutely necessary. Their houses should be open to anyone who wishes to enter, not locked and bolted. Their food should be appropriate for trained warriors who are moderate and brave. They should receive enough pay from the other citizens so they can meet expenses at the end of the year without either a surplus or debts. They will have common meals and live together, as in a military camp. We will tell them that they have ample gold and silver from the god placed inside their soul. Therefore they have no need of the earthly dross that mortals call gold. They should avoid polluting what is divine with the common metal that has been the source of so many unholy deeds, keeping their own metal pure. **[417]** Unlike the citizens, they will not be allowed to touch or handle silver or gold, not even be under the same roof with it, and certainly not wear it or drink from it. This will be their salvation and will preserve the republic. If they acquire land and money of their own, they will become farmers and caretakers instead of guards—enemies and tyrants instead of helpers and allies. Hating and being hated, plotting and being plotted against, they will live in greater fear of domestic than foreign enemies. This will lead to disaster both for them and for the republic. For all these reasons, we should make these rules concerning houses and other property. This will be our law!

Glaucon: Yes!

ENDNOTES

[1] Homer, *The Odyssey*, xi. 489.
[2] Ibid., xx. 64.
[3] Homer, *The Iliad*, xxii. 103.
[4] Homer, *The Odyssey*, x. 495.
[5] Homer, *The Iliad*, xvi. 856.
[6] Ibid., xxiii. 100.
[7] Homer, *The Odyssey*, xxiv. 6.
[8] Homer, *The Iliad*, xxiv. 10.
[9] Ibid., xviii. 23.
[10] Ibid., xxii. 414.
[11] Ibid., xviii. 54.
[12] Ibid., xxii. 168.
[13] Ibid., xvi. 433.
[14] Ibid., i. 599.
[15] Homer, *The Odyssey*, xvii. 383.
[16] Homer, *The Iliad*, iv. 412.
[17] Ibid., iii. 8.
[18] Ibid., iv. 431.
[19] Ibid., i. 225.
[20] Homer, *The Odyssey*, ix. 8.
[21] Ibid., xi. 342.
[22] Homer, *The Iliad*, xiv. 291.
[23] Homer, *The Odyssey*, viii. 266.
[24] Ibid., xx.17.
[25] Quoted by Suidas as attributed to Hesiod.
[26] Homer, *The Iliad*, ix. 515.
[27] Ibid., xxiv. 175.
[28] Ibid., xxiii. 151.
[29] Ibid., xxi. 222.
[30] Ibid., xxii. 394.
[31] Ibid., xxiii. 175.
[32] See p. 380.
[33] Cf. Aeschylus, *Niobe*.
[34] See pp. 369–370.
[35] Marsyas was a satyr who played the flute, best known for his sexual appetites and behavior.

[36] The Hellespont is now called the Dardanelles, a strait that connects the Aegean Sea with the Sea of Marmara.

[37] In Greek mythology, Asclepius, the son of Apollo, was the god of medicine.

[38] See p. 389.

Book Four

Adeimantus: Socrates, now I have a question for you. How would you answer the objection that these people do not live a good life and which is their own doing? Although the republic really belongs to them, they get little good from it. Other people are permitted to acquire land, build elegant houses and furnish them lavishly, provide the best hospitality, sacrifice to the gods for their personal benefit, use and wear gold and silver, and enjoy all the other advantages of good fortune. But our poor leaders seem to be no more than hired bodyguards who do nothing in the republic but protect lives and property enjoyed by others.

Socrates: Yes, Adeimantus, and you can add to those charges that they are merely given room and board and never paid the high salaries given to others. **[420]** Consequently, they cannot take trips for pleasure, give expensive gifts to their lovers, or enjoy any of the other luxuries of those who are generally considered to be prosperous. There are many similar charges you could add to your indictment.

Adeimantus: Then let's include all those complaints as well.

Socrates: So your question concerns how we should defend ourselves against those charges.

Adeimantus: Exactly.

Socrates: I believe we will find a way to reply if we continue on the same path we have been following. It may well be that the guards are living the most prosperous kind of life in the way we described, but that is not the issue right now. The central goal in constructing a republic is to foster the welfare of the whole, not merely to promote the interest of a special group. We said that we are most likely to find justice in a republic that is designed to promote the common good,[1] but injustice will prevail in a poorly ordered republic. Once we determine which republic is just and which is unjust, then we can decide which is happier. Right now we are forming the good republic, not bit by bit or for the sake of a few of its members, but as a whole. Later on we can consider the opposite kind of republic. If we were painting a statue and someone were to object that we are not painting the most beautiful part of the body with the most beautiful colors, telling us that the eyes should be purple instead of black, we would be right to resist such advice. We might say to our critic something like this:

> My friend, we do not wish to beautify the eyes to the point where they are no longer eyes. What really matters is whether, by treating each part properly, we make the entire face beautiful. So please do not force us to make the guards so prosperous that they will become something other than guards. Of course we could dress the farmers in stately robes and gold jewelry, inviting them to plow the soil whenever they like. And we might allow potters to lie on couches, feast by the fireside, and pass round the wine cup. They could keep their wheel nearby so they could work as potters whenever they are in the mood. Come to think of it, we could let everyone prosper in the same way, producing a truly happy republic. But please do not suggest such things, because then farmers will no longer be farmers, potters will cease to be potters, and nobody will show any of the distinctions that form the republic. [421] This might not be a serious problem if only shoemakers became corrupt and stopped working. But if those who guard the republic and enforce its laws only pretend to do their job, that would destroy the republic, because they are essential to its order and well being.

Adeimantus, we have been thinking that the guards should preserve rather than destroy the republic, but those who paint that other picture are imagining people at a party enjoying the food and drink, not citizens building a republic. Therefore, we should determine whether the goal in selecting guards is to make them happy and prosperous or whether we are seeking the welfare of the republic as a whole. If we are concerned about the republic itself, then the guards, their assistants, and everyone else should do their work as well as possible. That way each group can follow its nature and participate in the well being of all.

Adeimantus: Socrates, I think you have responded well to the indictment.

Socrates: Then I'm curious about how you will respond to what I have to say on a related issue.

Adeimantus: What issue?

Socrates: There seem to be two major factors that corrupt and destroy skilled workers and their work.

Adeimantus: What are they?

Socrates: Wealth and poverty.

Adeimantus: How do they do that?

Socrates: It happens this way: When potters get rich, they no longer pay much attention to their craft.

Adeimantus: That makes sense.

Socrates: They become lazy and careless.

Adeimantus: True.

Socrates: Then they become worse as potters.

Adeimantus: Much worse.

Socrates: At the opposite extreme, if they have no money, they are unable to buy tools and the other things they need, nor will they have the means to teach others how to practice the craft.

Adeimantus: That's right.

Socrates: That means both wealth and poverty will cause the workers and their work to degenerate.

Adeimantus: I agree.

Socrates: Adeimantus, we have discovered more dangers for the guards to remember so they can keep them from sneaking into the republic.

Adeimantus: What dangers? **[422]**

Socrates: I'm still talking about wealth and poverty. One of them is the parent of extravagance and laziness, and the other spawns selfishness and brutality. They both undermine republics.

Adeimantus: I cannot disagree with what you say, Socrates, but now I have another question. If we have no wealth, how could our republic wage war—especially against a rich and powerful enemy?

Socrates: That might be a problem if there were one such enemy, but not if there were two.

Adeimantus: What?

Socrates: Remember that you will have trained warriors on your side, and they would be fighting against rich people.

Adeimantus: Yes.

Socrates: Adeimantus, don't you think that one well-trained boxer would be a match for two fat and rich opponents who are not boxers?

Adeimantus: What if they attacked at the same time?

Socrates: Imagine that the boxer first retreated and then attacked the first one who follows, perhaps doing this several times in the heat of a scorching sun. Don't you think more than one enemy of that kind could be defeated under those circumstances?

Adeimantus: Yes. That's not hard to imagine.

Socrates: And can we say that rich people have even less experience in military service than in boxing?

Adeimantus: I think that is generally true.

Socrates: Your warriors would be able to win even if outnumbered several times.

Adeimantus: I believe that's right.

Socrates: Now suppose that instead of fighting a war with one of those rich republics, your citizens sent an ambassador instructed simply to tell the truth: "Unlike you, we are not permitted to possess gold and silver. Therefore, if you join with us in waging war, you can keep the loot." Tell me Adeimantus, who would choose to fight against lean and rugged dogs rather than fight with those dogs on their side against fat and tender sheep?

Adeimantus: True, but don't you think that the poor republic would be in danger if the wealth of several other republics were to be combined into a single one?

Socrates: Republics? I think you are naïve in calling any but ours by the name "republic."

Adeimantus: Then what should we call them?

Socrates: We should call them by greater names, each one being many rather than one, as in a game that people play. Each one of them is already divided by two warring factions—one rich and one poor. **[423]** And they are similarly composed of smaller ones; so it would be a mistake to treat them as a single one. But if you deal with them as many, giving the money, the resources, or even the population of the one to the others, you will have many friends and few enemies. Your republic, as long as it maintains the basic order you have established in it, will be the greatest republic, not just in appearance and reputation but in reality, even if it had only a thousand warriors. You will never find one equal to it either among Greeks or barbarians, although there are many that seem to be much greater because of their size.

Adeimantus: I think that's right.

Socrates: And is this not the best way to limit the size of a republic both in population and territory?

Adeimantus: What way?

Socrates: The republic may expand to any size that is consistent with its unity. That is the limit.

Adeimantus: That is an excellent rule.

Socrates: Then this is another mandate to convey to the guards—that the republic should be neither too large nor too small but a size that maintains it as one.

Adeimantus: They will have no trouble at all with that assignment!

Socrates: Yes, it will be about as easy to follow as the command that when the guards produce inferior children they should send them away, and that superior children from humble families should be promoted to become leaders. But remember the general principle: each individual person should follow the kind of life determined by nature. That way they will tend to their own business and become a single person rather than several people, just as the republic itself should be one rather than many.

Adeimantus: Right. That order will be even easier to follow than the other one.

Socrates: Adeimantus, we should not suppose that these commands are in themselves all that crucial or important, nor should we try to prescribe rules for everything. In fact, they are all quite trivial if we observe the one great thing, as they say, although I would rather not call it great but sufficient.

Adeimantus: What is that?

Socrates: Education. If they are well educated and become reasonable people, they will find their way through these matters as well as many others I need not elaborate—sex, marriage, children, and the like. [424] As far as possible they should follow the maxim that says friends have all things in common.

Adeimantus: Excellent.

Socrates: If the republic begins well, it gains force like a spinning wheel. Good nurture and education produce good character, and people with good character who are nourished by a good education continually improve. As with other animals, this is how the breed itself is improved.

Adeimantus: That makes sense.

Socrates: In brief, the rulers should take special care to preserve the arts and physical training in their original form and resist innovation. They should be on guard when a poet says that people are most attracted to—

The song which is the newest that the singers have.[2]

They will fear that the poet is praising, not new songs, but a new kind of song. But they should not praise such things, nor should that be presented as the poet's meaning. Innovation in the arts is dangerous to a republic because when artistic style changes, the fundamental laws of the republic change with it. That is what Damon says, and he has persuaded me.

Adeimantus: Socrates, you can count me among those who are persuaded and hold Damon's view.

Socrates: Then do you believe that the guards should build their main watchtower among the arts?

Adeimantus: Yes, Socrates, because that is where it is easiest for disorder to be overlooked and sneak into the republic.

Socrates: People think it is simply a form of harmless play.

Adeimantus: It is harmless in itself, but the real danger lies in the spirit of disorder that penetrates into habits and customs and finds a home. It gains force and invades agreements and contracts. From there it proceeds to laws and constitutions and finally overthrows all private and public order!

Socrates: Is that how it happens?

Adeimantus: That's what I believe.

Socrates: Then, as we said before, young people should be educated according to strict guidelines from the beginning, because if education is unregulated and young people are lawless, they will be unable to become serious and law-abiding adults. **[425]**

Adeimantus: Of course.

Socrates: So education must begin with their earliest play in which the spirit of law and order is conveyed to children through the arts. This way of life will accompany them in all their activities as they grow and serve to restore any part of the republic that has failed.

Adeimantus: Very true.

Socrates: Once they are properly educated, they will be able to discover and deal with minor matters that have been neglected by their predecessors.

Adeimantus: What do you mean?

Socrates: I mean etiquette and manners in general, such as when young people are to be silent in the presence of adults; how they should show respect by sitting and standing at the proper time; what forms of honor should be shown to parents; what kind of clothing should be worn, appropriate hairstyles, and good posture. Do you agree?

Adeimantus: Yes.

Socrates: Then it would be silly to legislate about such things. Whatever rules we put in writing would soon become outdated.

Adeimantus: No doubt about that.

Socrates: Therefore, Adeimantus, we will assume that the initial direction of a person's education will shape the future. Doesn't like follow like?

Adeimantus: It does.

Socrates: The final outcome will be unique to that person, a grand finale, which may be good or the opposite of good.

Adeimantus: That's how it happens.

Socrates: So, I would definitely not attempt to make laws about such matters.

Adeimantus: A wise decision.

Socrates: Now what about business conduct and the various bargains and contracts people make in the agora? What should we say concerning relations between managers and workers, about lawsuits dealing with insult and injury, or the order in which legal cases should be tried? How should judges and juries be appointed? Questions may arise about imposing dues and fees and similar issues pertaining to administering harbors, towns, and markets. Is it necessary for us to legislate about all of these particulars?

Adeimantus: Socrates, there is no need to impose such laws on good people. They can figure out the appropriate arrangements for themselves.

Socrates: Yes, my friend, if some god will preserve the very principles of law we established earlier.

Adeimantus: Otherwise they will spend their lives making and amending petty regulations in the vain attempt to reach perfection.

Socrates: Perhaps we could compare them to sick people who lack the self-control to give up their bad habits.

Adeimantus: That's a good analogy.

Socrates: What a beautiful existence such people have, constantly treating and complicating their disorders, hoping that they will be cured by the latest panacea someone recommends to them. But no matter what remedy they try, they always get worse rather than better.

Adeimantus: You describe them well. **[426]**

Socrates: And the most amusing thing about them is that they consider anyone who tells them the truth to be their worst enemy. They do not want to hear that unless they stop overeating and getting drunk, and give up sloth and indiscriminate sex, nothing will cure them—not drugs or surgery or even magic spells and protective charms.

Adeimantus: Socrates, I don't see anything amusing about people who get angry when someone gives them good advice!

Socrates: You don't seem to think much of such people.

Adeimantus: That's putting it mildly.

Socrates: Then I suppose you would not applaud a republic that acts the way they do. Don't you think that badly governed republics resemble them when they announce that anyone who seeks to change their constitution risks the death penalty, but that those who adopt their politics and sweetly serve them, indulging and fawning on them, doing their bidding and skillfully gratifying them, are considered to be the best kind of people and are honored as wise and mighty?

Adeimantus: Yes, those republics are as bad as the people are, and I have no respect for them.

Socrates: But don't you admire the virility and dexterity of people who are so adept in serving such republics?

Adeimantus: I do, but not the ones who are deluded by the applause of the crowd into believing that they are true statesmen and that they really deserve to be admired.

Socrates: Adeimantus, don't you think you are a bit too hard on them? If a man does not know how to measure and many others who cannot measure tell him that he is six feet tall, how can he help believing them?

Adeimantus: I don't suppose he can.

Socrates: Then don't be angry with these amusing creatures who are constantly passing laws in the hope that they will finally bring an end to fraud and dishonesty in business and the other activities we were just discussing. They don't know that they are really cutting off Hydra's head and that two more will immediately grow in its place.

Adeimantus: I guess they are more comical than contemptible. **[427]**

Socrates: Then a true lawmaker will not bother with that kind of legislation either in a poorly governed or in a well-governed republic. In the former they are hopeless and in the latter they are unnecessary. Good laws will flow naturally from good people and good institutions.

Adeimantus: Then what legislative work do we have left?

Socrates: I don't think we have any, but Apollo, the god at Delphi, must enact the first and greatest—the most noble laws of all.

Adeimantus: Which ones do you have in mind?

Socrates: Those that regulate establishing temples and religious rituals and the general rules concerning how to serve gods, demigods, and heroes. Also, how to bury the dead and the rites that need to be observed to remain in the good graces of those who inhabit the other world. We humans are ignorant of such matters, and as founders of a republic we know it is unwise to trust any other interpreter. We must turn to our ancestral deity, the one who sits at the very center, on the navel of the world, and transmits them to all human beings.

Adeimantus: You're right, Socrates. That's how it should be done.

Socrates: Now tell me, Son of Ariston, where in all this can we find justice? Now that you have founded your republic, bring a light and begin the search. Ask your brother and Polemarchus and the rest of our friends here to help discover the home of justice and injustice and determine the difference between them. Which one should a person choose in seeking true happiness, whether visible or invisible to gods and human beings?

Glaucon: Adeimantus don't let Socrates get away with that! He promised to search for justice himself, saying that it would be unholy to abandon justice and fail to do everything in his power to come to her rescue.

Socrates: Thanks for reminding me, Glaucon. I will keep my word, but all of you must help out.

Glaucon: We will.

Socrates: Then I think I know how we can make the discovery. Let's say that if the republic has been properly ordered, then it is completely good.

Glaucon: That necessarily follows.

Socrates: Then do you believe that your republic is wise, courageous, moderate, and just?

Glaucon: I do.

Socrates: Once we find some of these qualities, we can assume that the ones we have not yet discovered remain to be found.

Glaucon: That makes sense. **[428]**

Socrates: Let's suppose that we are looking for one thing out of four. If we find it first, that is the end of the search. But if we first find the other three and can eliminate them, then the one that remains is the one we are seeking.

Glaucon: True.

Socrates: Then that is how we should proceed in the present case.

Glaucon: I agree.

Socrates: Wisdom is the first one we saw in your republic, but there seems to be something strange about it.

Glaucon: What is that?

Socrates: When we say that a republic is wise, don't we mean that it practices good judgment?

Glaucon: Yes—we mean good judgment.

Socrates: People make good judgments by knowledge, not by ignorance, so can we say that good judgment is a kind of knowledge?

Glaucon: Clearly.

Socrates: But don't we find many different kinds of knowledge in a republic?

Glaucon: Of course.

Socrates: For example, consider the knowledge of the carpenter. Is that the kind of knowledge that leads us to say that a republic is wise and has good judgment?

Glaucon: No! That only means it is skilled in making things out of wood.

Socrates: Then you don't think we should call a republic wise because it has the kind of knowledge that judges best about making things out of wood.

Glaucon: Certainly not.

Socrates: Then what about knowing how to make things out of brass, or some other knowledge of that kind?

Glaucon: Not by any knowledge of that sort.

Socrates: And if it knows how to grow crops, that would give it a name in the field of agriculture?

Glaucon: I suppose that's right.

Socrates: Then do any of the citizens of your recently founded republic possess a kind of knowledge that advises about the entire republic rather than some particular thing? Does anyone know how to make the best policy concerning both citizens and foreigners?

Glaucon: Certainly.

Socrates: Then what is this knowledge, and who has it?

Glaucon: It is the knowledge of leading possessed by and those we called guards, in the fullest sense of the term.[3]

Socrates: Then what should we call a republic that has this kind of knowledge?

Glaucon: We should call it wise in the sense of having good judgment in leading people.

Socrates: Do you think there will be more good leaders or more metalworkers in a republic?

Glaucon: There will be far more metalworkers.

Socrates: Of all the groups that are named because they possess a certain kind of knowledge, don't you think good leaders will be the smallest?

Glaucon: The smallest by far. **[429]**

Socrates: Then do we agree that the nature of the smallest group in a republic—those who govern or rule—justifies calling the whole republic "wise"? And can we say that this is the only knowledge properly called wisdom?

Glaucon: Yes, Socrates, we do agree about that.

Socrates: Glaucon, somehow we have discovered the nature and the place in the republic of one of the four things we are seeking.

Glaucon: I'm quite satisfied with our method.

Socrates: Then it should not be difficult to see the nature of courage and where that quality resides when a republic is called courageous.

Glaucon: I'm not quite sure what you mean.

Socrates: Anyone who calls a republic cowardly or courageous will refer to those who go into battle and fight for the republic.

Glaucon: Nobody would think of any other group.

Socrates: Other citizens may be courageous or cowardly, but would that make us think of the republic itself as one or the other?

Glaucon: Certainly not.

Socrates: So, the republic will be courageous because of a group in which resides a never-failing quality that maintains an opinion about the right kind of fear, which the legislators instilled in their education. Is this what you call courage?

Glaucon: I'm sorry, Socrates, I don't understand what you are saying. Could you say it again?

Socrates: I mean that courage is a kind of preserving.

Glaucon: What kind of preserving?

Socrates: Preserving the opinion about the nature of danger implanted by the law through education. When I say "never-failing," I mean that a person holds and does not lose this opinion even under the influence of pleasure and pain or desire and fear. Would you like me to illustrate my meaning?

Glaucon: I would like that a lot.

Socrates: I suppose you know that when people want to dye wool cloth a true purple, they begin by selecting a white cloth and prepare it carefully so that the white ground will readily take the purple hue. Then, when they proceed with the dyeing, the color remains fast, so that even if it is washed with lye, the color will remain in full bloom. And you also know how this or any other color looks when the ground has not been properly prepared.

Glaucon: Yes, it is washed-out and looks ridiculous.

Socrates: Perhaps now you can understand our goal in selecting the guards, educating them in the arts, and providing them with physical training. **[430]** We were designing ways to prepare them to accept the dye of the law so that the color of their beliefs about danger and other important matters would be indelibly fixed by their nurture and training. We wanted to make sure that they would not be washed away by the potent lye of pleasure—the mighty agent that fades the soul far more effectively than any other—or grief, fear, and desire, the most powerful of solvents. Courage is the name I give to this power of preserving true opinion based on law, about true and false dangers—unless you wish to suggest another name.

Glaucon: I do not have any better one to suggest. I assume you are excluding untutored courage, such as that of an animal or a slave. Don't you think this is something other than courage formed by law and that it ought to have another name?

Socrates: Your assumption is correct.

Glaucon: Then I agree in calling this quality courage.

Socrates: Perhaps it would be more accurate if we called it the courage of a citizen, but we can pursue the idea of courage more fully some other time. Right now we are looking for justice, so we have said enough about courage.

Glaucon: Yes, we have said all we need to say.

Socrates: Then we still need to find two qualities for the republic—moderation and the main goal of our search, justice.

Glaucon: True.

Socrates: Do you think we can find justice without bothering with moderation?

Glaucon: I don't know how we can do that. And I would hate to bring justice to light and lose sight of moderation. So please do me a favor and consider moderation first.

Socrates: How can I refuse such a request?

Glaucon: Then let's continue.

Socrates: At first glance, moderation is more like harmony and proper arrangement than the first two qualities that we have considered.

Glaucon: How so?

Socrates: As I think of it, moderation is a kind of order and control of various pleasures and desires. It seems to be implied when we say that someone has self-control, is master over oneself, and similar phrases.

Glaucon: That's right.

Socrates: But there is something funny about the expression "self-control." The one doing the controlling is also the one who is controlled. The master is also mastered. **[431]**

Glaucon: That does sound strange.

Socrates: But I think these expressions refer to two different aspects of the human soul, one better and the other worse. When the better one controls the worse, then we say the person has self-control. This is intended as a form of praise. If the worse aspect, which is far larger than the good one, dominates a person— because of poor nurture or bad company—then we censure that person for being immoderate and lacking self-control.

Glaucon: I think that is a good explanation.

Socrates: Now let's look at the republic we have created, and you will find an example of such conditions. If the republic is properly called master of itself, then moderation and self-control are terms that express the rule of the better aspect over the worse.

Glaucon: As I look at it, I find that what you say is true.

Socrates: Pleasures, desires, and pains are plentiful and diverse in a republic, especially in children, women, slaves, and in the majority of so-called free citizens.

Glaucon: That is easy to see.

Socrates: But the simple and moderate desires that obey reason and are guided by mind and sound opinion are confined to only a few people, the ones who are best by nature and through education.

Glaucon: That's true, Socrates.

Socrates: Glaucon, do you find both of these aspects in your republic, with the common desires of the majority controlled by the wisdom of the few?

Glaucon: I do.

Socrates: Then if any republic can be called a master of pleasures and desires and self-controlled, this one deserves that designation.

Glaucon: Agreed.

Socrates: And can we call it moderate for the same reason?

Glaucon: Yes.

Socrates: Also, if there is any republic in which the rulers and the people who are ruled agree about who should rule, it will be this one.

Glaucon: There is no doubt about that.

Socrates: With the citizens in such agreement, where will we find moderation—in the rulers or in those who are ruled?

Glaucon: I suppose we will find it in both.

Socrates: Then do you see how close we were to the mark when we guessed that moderation is a kind of harmony?

Glaucon: Why do you say that?

Socrates: Because moderation is unlike courage and wisdom, which are to be found only in one part of the republic, making it either brave or wise. **[432]** Moderation extends to the whole, running through all the notes of the scale, producing a harmony of all elements—the weaker, the stronger, and the intermediate. And that is true whether you are talking about strength in wisdom, power, numbers, wealth, or any other domain. Therefore, we rightly describe moderation as harmony and agreement about the rule of what is naturally superior over what is inferior both in republics and in individuals.

Glaucon: I fully agree with you.

Socrates: Well, we have so far discovered three of the four forms we are seeking, and we have seen how the republic participates in them. Now we must look for the fourth one. How do you think we can find it? Clearly, it is justice we want.

Glaucon: Yes, at least that is clear.

Socrates: Then, Glaucon, the time has come for us, like hunters surrounding a thicket, to look sharp so that justice does not slip out of sight and disappear. I'm sure it is around here somewhere, so if you see it first, let me know.

Glaucon: I wish I could spot it first, but I don't think there is much chance of that. However, you will find that I am a companion who can just see well enough to observe what you point out.

Socrates: Then say a prayer and follow me.

Glaucon: I will follow, but you must lead the way.

Socrates: There is no path, and the woods are dark and confusing. But we must push on.

Glaucon: I'm right behind you.

Socrates: Look over there, Glaucon! I see some tracks. I don't think it will be able to get away now.

Glaucon: That's good news.

Socrates: Ah, how stupid we are!

Glaucon: Why?

Socrates: For a long time now, justice has been rolling around at our feet, and we were so foolish that we failed to see it, like people who go looking for something they are holding in their hand. That's what we have been doing, looking off into the distance and missing the obvious.

Glaucon: What do you mean?

Socrates: I mean it has been on our lips and in our ears, and we have failed to recognize it.

Glaucon: Socrates, that's a long introduction for someone who is eager to hear the outcome!

Socrates: Then tell me whether or not I am right. **[433]** Remember the original principle on which we founded the republic. We insisted from the beginning that all people should serve the republic in the one way for which they are best suited by nature. I think that is the essence of justice.

Glaucon: Well, we have been saying that all along.

Socrates: Not only have we said it, but we have also heard it often from others: Justice is doing your own work and not meddling in the affairs of other people.

Glaucon: That does sound familiar.

Socrates: So, my friend, in an important sense, doing your own work is what it means to be just. Do you know why I say that?

Glaucon: No, but I'm eager to find out.

Socrates: Because it is the form that would remain in the republic even if moderation, courage, and wisdom were removed. It is the productive power that brings all of them into existence, exists in them, and preserves them. But once the other three are discovered, justice is the fourth form that remains to be found.

Glaucon: And so it is necessary.

Socrates: If someone were to ask which of these four provides most by its presence to the goodness of the republic, we would have a hard time answering. Is it the agreement among the ruler and those who are ruled, the preservation of the opinion held by the guards and ordained by law concerning the true nature of danger, or the good judgment and vigilance of the rulers? Or is it the one found in children, women, ordinary workers, slaves and free people, rulers, and those who are ruled that contributes most to the well-being of the republic? I mean the principle of doing our own work.

Glaucon: That is a difficult question to answer.

Socrates: Can we at least agree that the power that comes from all people doing their own work competes with wisdom, moderation, and courage in achieving excellence in the republic?

Glaucon: Yes, we can agree on that.

Socrates: And we call this competing excellence by the name "justice"?

Glaucon: Exactly.

Socrates: Let's look at it another way. Would we not assign to the rulers of the republic the responsibility of judging lawsuits?

Glaucon: Certainly.

Socrates: Don't you think that they will follow the principle that individuals are neither to take what belongs to someone else nor to have someone else take what is theirs?

Glaucon: I think they will take that as their basic principle.

Socrates: And would you say that principle is just?

Glaucon: It is.

Socrates: Would you say that from this point of view justice is having what belongs to you and doing what is proper to you?

Glaucon: That sounds right. **[434]**

Socrates: Now consider another point. Suppose that a carpenter starts doing the work of a cobbler, or that a cobbler practices carpentry, and they exchange tools and even the privileges enjoyed by the other. Or suppose that one person does the work of both. Do you think that causes any harm to the republic?

Glaucon: I don't think so.

Socrates: But what if a craftsperson or someone best suited by nature to engage in business—either by wealth, force, or popular vote—became a warrior? Or what if a warrior tried to become a legislator or a leader, even if entirely unfit for that kind of work? Do you think that this exchange of roles is the sort of meddling in other people's affairs that would ruin the republic?

Glaucon: Definitely.

Socrates: Then you seem to believe that any transformation or meddling among these three kinds of life would be harmful to the republic and could properly be called malicious.

Glaucon: Precisely.

Socrates: And would you call that kind of malice injustice?

Glaucon: By all means.

Socrates: Then we have identified injustice. On the other hand, when businesspeople, warriors, and leaders do their own work, this is justice, and it will make the republic just.

Glaucon: Socrates, I find this account to be completely convincing.

Socrates: Don't be too quick to endorse it without qualification. We must test this way of thinking about justice both in the individual and in the republic, and only then can we embrace it without reservation. If it does not hold up under examination, then we must think again. Our present task is to finish the inquiry we started when we assumed that we should first examine a larger example of justice and then proceed to find it in the individual. We said that a larger version exists in the republic, so we designed the best one we could, believing that we would find justice in a good one. What we found in the republic, we should then apply to the individual. If the two correspond, then our account of justice passes the test. But if we find a significant difference in the individual, then we must go back to the republic and look again. Perhaps when we rub them together like two sticks, the friction will light a fire and justice will shine forth. Only then can we be content with this account of justice. **[435]**

Glaucon: I think that's the right way to proceed. Let's continue with that method.

Socrates: Now consider two things, one larger than the other. If we call them by the same name, is that because they are alike or unlike?

Glaucon: Because they are alike.

Socrates: Then a just person will not differ from a just republic but, because of the form of justice, will be like it.

Glaucon: Yes.

Socrates: Did you not say that a republic is just when the three different kinds of citizen—who are moderate, courageous, or wise by nature—do their own work?

Glaucon: Yes.

Socrates: When you consider individual people, do you think it is right to claim that they have these same three forms in their soul and, because they possess the same nature, that they should be called by the same name?

Glaucon: Certainly.

Socrates: My friend, we seem to have come upon another of those easy questions: Does the soul have those three forms or not?

Glaucon: Easy? Socrates, I think this shows the truth of the saying that nothing good is ever easy.

Socrates: So it seems. Glaucon, I must confess that the kind of inquiry we are currently using will not yield a precise answer to this question. To make the complete journey would be longer and harder than if we settle for a solution similar to the previous one.

Glaucon: The shorter road would satisfy me. Don't you think it is adequate for our present purpose?

Socrates: I think it is sufficient.

Glaucon: Then let's not hesitate but continue with the inquiry in the same way.

Socrates: Don't you think it is necessary to agree that these same forms exist both in individuals and in the republic? From what other source could they come? For example, consider the quality of courage. Would it not be ridiculous to think that this characteristic of the Thracians, the Sythians, and, generally speaking, of the northern republics, comes from anywhere but the individuals who constitute those republics? Must we not say the same of the love of learning, which distinguishes our part of the world, or the love of money that characterizes both the Phoenicians and the Egyptians? **[436]**

Glaucon: I agree fully.

Socrates: Is it difficult to understand this?

Glaucon: Not at all.

Socrates: But the difficulty begins when we pose the question of whether these forms are three or one. Do we learn with one part of ourselves, become angry with another, and desire to satisfy our natural appetites with a third? Or is the entire soul involved in each of those activities?

Glaucon: You are right. That is more difficult.

Socrates: Then let's see if we can figure out whether they are the same or different.

Glaucon: How should we go about answering that?

Socrates: It is clear that the same aspect of anything can neither act or be acted on in opposite ways at the same time and in the same respect. Whenever this happens we will know that what seems to be the same is really different.

Glaucon: That is a good principle to follow.

Socrates: Here is an example. Can the same thing at the same time and in the same respect be both in motion and at rest?

Glaucon: That is impossible.

Socrates: Let's be even more precise in order to avoid misunderstanding later on. Imagine a man who is standing still and moving his hands and his head. If someone were to say that the same person is in motion and at rest at the same time, we could simply reply that part of him is in motion and part is at rest. Do you agree?

Glaucon: Of course.

Socrates: And if the questioner were to point to the example of a top that is both spinning and remaining in the same place and claim that it is the whole top, not only part of it that is moving and remaining in the same place, concluding that the top is in motion and at rest at the same time, we would not agree that this violates our basic principle. The same objection could, of course, be made about anything that revolves on the same spot. But we could again point out that the same parts of the thing are not at rest and in motion. We could say that such things are capable of both a circular motion and a linear motion. When the top moves in a circle, the perpendicular line does not move, but if it also inclines to the left or right, then it is not at rest in any respect.

Glaucon: That is a good way to describe what is happening in such cases.

Socrates: Then no objection of that kind will confuse us or lead us to believe that a single part of the same thing can at the same time and in the same way act or be acted on in contradictory ways. **[437]**

Glaucon: I will never believe such nonsense.

Socrates: In order to avoid examining every such objection and prove that they are untrue, let us accept this basic principle and agree that if it ever turns out to be false, then we will reject the conclusions we inferred from it.

Glaucon: That is a good way to proceed.

Socrates: Don't you think that agreement and disagreement, desire and rejection, attraction and repulsion, are all opposites, regardless of whether they are active or passive, which makes no difference concerning their opposition?

Glaucon: Yes, they are opposites.

Socrates: What about hunger, thirst, willing, and wishing—all desires in general—would you say that the categories we just mentioned apply to them? When people desire something, can we say that they are seeking the object of desire and that they draw toward themselves the thing they wish to possess? When they will that something be given to them, can we say that their mind, in longing to have that thing, signals assent to it, much as if they had been asked a question?

Glaucon: I think that is right.

Socrates: Now what do you think of reluctance and dislike and absence of desire? Do they not belong to the opposite category—to repulsion and rejection?

Glaucon: They do.

Socrates: We have agreed that this is generally true of desire, so we can now single out a particular type of desire. Let's consider the desires that are most prominent among our senses, the ones we call hunger and thirst.

Glaucon: They always seem to be nearby.

Socrates: The object of one is food, and the other is drink.

Glaucon: Yes.

Socrates: Would you agree that thirst desires drink itself, not drink qualified in some way? For example, consider warm or cold, a lot or a little, or any other particular kind. If the thirst is accompanied by heat, then the desire is for a cold drink or if accompanied by cold, then warm drink is desired. If the thirst is excessive, then the drink that is desired will be excessive. On the contrary, if the desire is not great, then the quantity desired will also be small. But if we think about thirst as thirst, it desires only drink, which naturally satisfies thirst, just as hunger itself is only the desire for food.

Glaucon: You are right; in every case the simple desire is for the simple object, but the qualified desire is for the qualified object.

Socrates: Here I would like to guard against a possible objection. **[438]** Someone may claim that nobody merely desires drink or food but good drink or good food. Good is the universal object of desire, so thirst will necessarily be for good drink, and the same applies to every other desire.

Glaucon: That objection does seem to pose a problem for our analysis.

Socrates: However, we can reply that relative terms are related in such a way that when one term is qualified the one correlated with it is also qualified, so that if one term is simple the other is simple.

Glaucon: I don't understand what you mean.

Socrates: Do you understand that what is greater is relative to what is less?

Glaucon: Yes.

Socrates: And is the much greater relative to the much less?

Glaucon: Yes.

Socrates: Is what is sometimes greater relative to what is sometimes less, and is what will be greater relative to what will be less?

Glaucon: Of course.

Socrates: Is it correct to say that in general this applies to all corresponding relative terms, including greater and less, double and half, heavier and lighter, faster and slower, and hot and cold?

Glaucon: That is true in general.

Socrates: This also seems to be the case with scientific knowledge. The object of science in general is knowledge in general, but the object of a particular science is a particular kind of knowledge. For example, the building of a house contains a kind of knowledge that is distinguished from other kinds of knowledge and is called house construction.

Glaucon: Certainly.

Socrates: Is this not because it has a particular nature that distinguishes it from everything else?

Glaucon: Yes.

Socrates: Can we say that this particular form of knowledge has this particular nature because it has an object of a specific kind and that this is true of the other arts and sciences as well?

Glaucon: I think so.

Socrates: Now, if I have finally made myself clear, perhaps you can understand what I originally said about relative terms. I meant that if the first term of a relation is taken alone, then the second is taken alone. If the first term is qualified, then the second is also qualified. Of course, I don't mean that the two are exactly the same. For example, I don't mean that the science of health is healthy, the science of disease is diseased, that the knowledge of good is good, or the knowledge of evil is evil. All I am saying is that because it has health and disease as an object, the science of medicine has a certain nature, and for that reason it is called not merely science but medical science.

Glaucon: Now I understand what you mean, and I agree with you. **[439]**

Socrates: Now we can return to the main point. Perhaps you will also agree that thirst is one of those relative terms. It is what it is in relation to—

Glaucon: Drink!

Socrates: And a certain kind of thirst is relative to a certain kind of drink, but thirst taken alone is not of much or little, good or bad, or any particular kind. It is merely thirst for drink, pure and simple.

Glaucon: I agree.

Socrates: So the soul of a thirsty person, because of the thirst, desires the drink and is attracted to it. Is that right?

Glaucon: That's right.

Socrates: Now suppose something pulls a thirsty soul away from the drink. That would have to be a principle different from the force that draws it like a wild animal to drink. Remember that the same thing cannot at the same time with the same part of itself act in contrary ways concerning the same object.

Glaucon: Acting that way is impossible.

Socrates: That would make no more sense than saying that an archer pushes and pulls the bow at the same time. It is more accurate to say that one hand pushes and the other hand pulls.

Glaucon: Exactly.

Socrates: Might someone be thirsty but unwilling to drink?

Glaucon: Of course. That often happens.

Socrates: What would you say in such a case? Would you not say that there is something in the soul that bids a person to drink and something else that forbids the person to drink, and the one that forbids is stronger than the other one?

Glaucon: Yes, Socrates, I would say that.

Socrates: Would it make sense to say that the principle forbidding the action is spawned by reason and the bidding and attracting forces are associated with passion and disease?

Glaucon: It would.

Socrates: Then I think it would be reasonable to conclude that there are two principles and that they differ from each other. We might call one the rational principle of the soul. The other one, which is associated with some pleasures and satisfactions—the aspect that hungers and thirsts, lusts, and generally is driven by desire—should be termed irrational.

Glaucon: I think that is a reasonable conclusion.

Socrates: Then let's designate these two as primary forms existing in the soul. Now what should we say about spirit, which feels indignation? Is it a third form or one of these two?

Glaucon: I'm inclined to connect it with the emotions of desire.

Socrates: Glaucon, I once heard a story that might help us think this through. Leontius, the son of Aglaion, was coming from the Piraeus. He was under the north wall on the outside when he saw some dead bodies placed on the ground by the executioner. He felt a strong desire to look at the bodies, but he was also disgusted and horrified by the idea of seeing them. For some time he turned away and averted his eyes, but eventually he was overcome by desire. He ran toward the corpses with his eyes wide open and said to his eyes: There, you wretches, take your fill of this lovely sight! **[440]**

Glaucon: I have also heard that story.

Socrates: Don't you think this story indicates that indignation differs from desire and is even opposed to it?

Glaucon: I think it does.

Socrates: Are there not many other cases in which we see people's desires violently prevail over reason and then they criticize themselves and are angry at the violence within them? In this struggle, which resembles the conflict among warring factions within a republic, spirit is on the side of reason. But have you ever seen such spirit side with the desires against reason either in yourself or in anyone else?

Glaucon: I have not.

Socrates: Or suppose that you have done something wrong to someone else. Do you think that the more honorable you are the less you are likely to be indignant if that other person justly causes you to suffer hunger, cold, or some other punishment?

Glaucon: Yes, I think that's right.

Socrates: But if you think you have suffered a wrong inflicted by someone else, then you will boil with anger and indignation. If you are on the side of justice, you will suffer hunger, cold, or some other kind of pain determined to persevere and conquer.

You will persist until you either do or die—unless you hear the voice of reason, like a sheep dog hearing the call of the shepherd.

Glaucon: I like that simile. It reminds me of the comparison we made in our republic between the rulers and their assistants, who are like dogs that hear the voice of their masters.

Socrates: You understand me well. But now I have another point for you to consider.

Glaucon: What is that?

Socrates: Is it true that at first you considered spirit to be a kind of desire, but now you separate them, because you think that when the soul is in conflict, that kind of determination stands on the side of reason?

Glaucon: Definitely.

Socrates: Now you must decide whether it is different from reason or a form of reason. In other words, should we think of the soul as having three aspects or only two—the rational aspect and the desiring aspect? Or is the soul like the republic, in having three aspects—the businesspeople, the warriors, and the leaders? [441] Should we think of the soul as having a third aspect, courageous spirit, which is allied with reason when it is not corrupted by bad education?

Glaucon: Yes, I think there must be a third aspect to the soul.

Socrates: Well, we have shown that being courageous is different from passion and appetite, but we must also show that it is different from reason.

Glaucon: But, Socrates, I think that is obvious if you look at young children. They are full of spirit almost as soon as they are born, but in most people reason develops later—if at all.

Socrates: That's well said, Glaucon. And I think we can see further evidence of the difference in the case of animals. Even Homer, whose words I have already quoted, is a witness when he says—

He smote his breast, and thus rebuked his soul.

In those lines he clearly has in mind the power that reasons about what is better and what is worse, in opposition to the unreasoning and willful indignation that is the subject of the rebuke.

Glaucon: That's entirely true.

Socrates: Now, we have struggled through the argument and have finally reached the shore. We now agree that the same three basic forms existing in the republic also exist in the individual.

Glaucon: Exactly.

Socrates: Then should we not conclude that an individual is wise in the same way that a republic is wise—and because of the same quality?

Glaucon: We should conclude that.

Socrates: Does the same quality that makes a republic courageous constitute courage in the individual? And can we extend that claim to the other forms of goodness as well?

Glaucon: Yes, the same logic applies.

Socrates: So, Glaucon, does that mean that an individual is just in the same way the republic is just?

Glaucon: That follows the same pattern.

Socrates: Don't forget that justice in the republic consisted in having all three basic kinds of citizen do their own work.

Glaucon: How could I forget that?

Socrates: Then we should remember that individuals should do their own work in the republic. And those people will be just in whose soul the three primary forms do their own work.

Glaucon: We should remember that above all.

Socrates: Then is it safe to say that the role of reason is to be wise and care for the entire soul, assisted by the spirit of determination, which follows where it leads?

Glaucon: I would be happy to say that.

Socrates: I think you were also happy to say that the arts and physical training will unify them and bring them into accord, nurturing reason with beautiful words and insight and softening, calming, and civilizing the spirit through harmony and rhythm.
[442]

Glaucon: I have not changed my mind about that.

Socrates: Then these two, thus nurtured and educated, will have learned how to do their own work so that they can rule over the desiring aspect, which in every person is huge and insatiable. They will guard it carefully so that it does not grow too great because of the expansive nature of bodily pleasure and break out of its own sphere. The voracious aspect of the soul yearns to enslave and tyrannize the other aspects over which it has no natural right to rule, throwing all of life into disorder.

Glaucon: No doubt about it.

Socrates: Then these two will defend soul and body from external attack, the one offering good counsel and the other fighting under command of its leader and courageously carrying out its directions.

Glaucon: That's right.

Socrates: How shall we describe the courageous person? Can we say such people are strong and brave and that even in the midst of pain and pleasure they follow what reason prescribes concerning what should or should not be feared?

Glaucon: That is a good description.

Socrates: What about the wise person? Should we call wise those in whom the small aspect that rules and governs is based on knowledge of what is in the interest of all three aspects and what all three have in common?

Glaucon: Yes, let's put it that way.

Socrates: And the moderate person has all three of these aspects in friendly harmony. Would you agree that in moderate people reason rules, and both passionate will and desire agree this is how it should be, and do not rebel?

Glaucon: I would agree with that account not only for the individual but also for the republic.

Socrates: We have characterized the just person several times. Do you still agree with that view?

Glaucon: I do.

Socrates: If we apply the form of justice to the individual, does it retain the sharp outline it had in the republic? Is there any reason that it should not fit both the individual and the republic?

Glaucon: Not as far as I can tell.

Socrates: Is the form of justice different in the individual or is it the same as in the republic?

Glaucon: In my opinion, Socrates, there is no difference.

Socrates: If we still have any doubts, perhaps we can dispel them with a few familiar examples.

Glaucon: What examples do you have in mind?

Socrates: Consider someone who has been given the responsibility of guarding a deposit of silver and gold. Who would think that a just republic, or an individual reared and nurtured according to that model, would be more likely to steal from that treasure than an unjust person? **[443]**

Glaucon: Nobody would think that.

Socrates: Would such a person desecrate holy places, or betray either friends or the republic itself?

Glaucon: Never.

Socrates: Would just people break contracts or agreements?

Glaucon: Not likely.

Socrates: Nor would anyone be less likely to commit adultery, disrespect parents, or fail to perform religious duties.

Glaucon: No one.

Socrates: Can I assume the reason is that each aspect of a just person is doing its own work, whether ruling or being ruled?

Glaucon: Yes, that assumption is true.

Socrates: And are you satisfied that the quality of justice makes both individuals and republics just, or do you think there might be some other quality?

Glaucon: I am satisfied that justice is the cause.

Socrates: Then we have realized our dream. At the very beginning of the task of constructing the republic, some divine power must have led us to our first principle, the form of justice itself. Glaucon, have we confirmed that original intuition?

Glaucon: Definitely.

Socrates: When we discussed the division of labor that required someone who is by nature a carpenter or a shoemaker, as well as the rest of the citizens, to do their own work and not that of someone else—that was useful, but only as a reflection of justice itself.

Glaucon: Clearly.

Socrates: So justice is the reality of which this is a likeness. Justice is not concerned with external things but with the inner person, the true self and its affairs. A just person does not allow the various aspects of the soul to interfere with each other but tends to the order of the inner life. Just people are their own masters. When they have harmonized the three principles within themselves, which may be compared with the high, low, and middle notes of the musical scale as well as the ones between them, then they are at peace with themselves. When they have bound all these together and become a single, moderate, and perfectly integrated unity, then they will be ready to act— whether in acquiring wealth, in the care of the body, or in any public or private business affairs. In all actions of that sort they will call just and good only the ones that preserve and support this internal order. The knowledge that presides over this process is called wisdom. Any action that destroys this order will be called unjust, and the opinion that presides over unjust action will be called ignorance. **[444]**

Glaucon: That is the precise truth, Socrates.

Socrates: Then do we dare to claim that we have found the just person and the just republic and discovered how justice exists in both of them?

Glaucon: I think we can justly make that claim.

Socrates: Is that what you want to say?

Glaucon: It is.

Socrates: Then has the time come to consider injustice?

Glaucon: It has.

Socrates: Given the three aspects of the soul we have discussed, injustice is clearly a kind of rebellion in which one aspect attacks the soul itself by meddling and interfering with the proper function of the other aspects. It is a kind of insurrection, like that of a rebellious subject against a true and natural ruler. The confusion and error caused by this disorder is injustice, excess, cowardice, and ignorance—every conceivable evil.

Glaucon: Exactly.

Socrates: If we know the meaning of justice and injustice, then do we also know the meaning of acting unjustly and being unjust, and of acting justly and being just?

Glaucon: I don't understand the question.

Socrates: It seems that they are like disease and health, but they are in the soul rather than in the body.

Glaucon: I'm still not following you, Socrates.

Socrates: Can we say that what is healthful promotes health, but that which is not healthful encourages disease?

Glaucon: Yes.

Socrates: And do just actions foster justice and unjust actions promote injustice?

Glaucon: Certainly.

Socrates: To produce health is to achieve a natural order of the body in which the proper elements govern, but disease is produced when the parts of the body violate this natural order.

Glaucon: True.

Socrates: This would seem to be equally true of the soul. Would you say that producing justice is establishing a natural order in which the proper aspect governs and injustice is the opposite?

Glaucon: Yes, I would say that.

Socrates: Then goodness is the health and beauty and well-being of the soul, and badness is the disease, weakness, and deformity of the soul.

Glaucon: Yes.

Socrates: Would you say that good practice leads to goodness and bad practice to badness?

Glaucon: Of course.

Socrates: But we have yet to answer our original question about the comparative advantage of justice and injustice. **[445]** Which is more profitable, to be just and act justly and practice goodness, whether seen or unseen by gods and human beings, or to be unjust and act unjustly as long as one is not caught and punished?

Glaucon: Socrates, I would say the question itself has now become ridiculous. If your body is completely ruined, life is unendurable, even if you are treated to every kind of food and drink and have all the wealth and power in the world. How can anyone say that life is worth living if its very essence is undermined and corrupted? Even if you are allowed to do anything you please, what is the point of living if you cannot escape from evil and injustice or are unable to obtain justice and goodness once you know the true nature of justice and injustice?

Socrates: Yes, I agree it is ridiculous. However, we are getting close to the place where we can see the truth with our own eyes, so we should not quit now.

Glaucon: No, let's keep going.

Socrates: Come on, then, let's climb this high point that overlooks the republic. From there we can see the various forms of evil, at least the ones that are worth observing.

Glaucon: I'm following you.

Socrates: From this summit in our argument we can look down and see a single form of goodness but also numerous forms of badness, of which four in particular are worth our attention.

Glaucon: What do you mean?

Socrates: I mean that there seem to be as many forms of the soul as there are of the republic.

Glaucon: How many is that?

Socrates: There are five forms of republic and five forms of soul.

Glaucon: What are they?

Socrates: The first is the one we have been describing, but it has two names: monarchy and aristocracy, depending on whether one person or several are ruling.

Glaucon: Of course.

Socrates: But it is only a single form. Whether the government is in the hands of one person or several—if they are educated as we prescribed—the fundamental laws of the republic will prevail.

Glaucon: That's true.

ENDNOTES

[1] See p. 369.
[2] Homer, *The Odyssey*, i. 351.
[3] See p. 414.

Book Five

Socrates: Ariston's son Glaucon and I had been discussing the best and worst forms of republics and the kind of people who constitute them. I was describing the best kind of republic as one that is most like an individual who is not concerned with external things but with the inner person, the true self and its affairs. A just person does not allow the various aspects of the soul to interfere with each other but tends to the order of the inner life. I suggested that just people are their own master, not the slave of someone else. That kind of republic I would call good and right. I was beginning to discuss the four forms of individuals and republics that fall short of that ideal when I noticed that Polemarchus, who was sitting near Adeimantus, grabbed his collar and started whispering into his ear. I could only hear him say something like "Shall we let him off, or what?" Adeimantus clearly replied "definitely not!" Unable to ignore this disruption, I asked: "What exactly is it that you are not letting off?"

Adeimantus: You!

Socrates: Why? What did I say?

Adeimantus: Socrates, we think you are being lazy and unfair by cheating us out of one of the best parts of the story. You seem to think that you will not be detected when you skip lightly over the important topic of women and children in our republic by simply saying that friends will have all things in common.

Socrates: Isn't that right, Adeimantus?

Adeimantus: Yes, but the word "right" needs to be explained—along with many other things. What sort of community do you have in mind when you say that among friends all things should be held in common? There are many kinds we can think of, and you need to explain which one you mean. We have been waiting for you to tell us about procreation and the rearing of children, and in general about this community of women and children you mentioned. We believe that the right or wrong management of these matters will have a profound effect on our republic for either good or bad. When you set out to talk about several other kinds of republic, we resolved not to let you go on before you give a satisfactory explanation of these matters—as you did with all the other aspects of our republic.

Glaucon: Socrates, I assure you that Adeimantus and Polemarchus are not alone in having that desire. Thrasymachus and I were just conferring, and we are confident that everyone present would like to hear what you have to say about these things. **[450]**

Socrates: My friends, you have no idea of what you are doing by intervening in this way! You are introducing a huge topic just when I was content to put this question of governing a republic to sleep, thinking how grateful I was that you were satisfied with what I said. Now you are trying to stir up a hornet's nest of disputes and get me to start again from the beginning. I saw this trouble coming, and that was why I tried to avoid it. What's that you are muttering, Thrasymachus?

Glaucon: He asked whether you think we came here to look for gold rather than to hear a discussion.

Socrates: Don't you think discussions should have a limit?

Glaucon: Socrates, I think an entire lifetime is the only reasonable limit for a discussion of this kind. So don't worry about it, but please give us an answer. What sort of community should prevail among our guards? How should their children be reared, especially in their early years, which is probably the most difficult period? Tell us how this should be done.

Socrates: I like the sweet simplicity of your request, Glaucon. The answer I am going to give will raise far more doubts than what we have said about your republic so far. Not only will people question the practicality of what I have to say, but even if it could work, many will not believe it should be adopted. For that reason it is a risky undertaking and may turn out to be a mere pipe dream.

Glaucon: Socrates, you should not be afraid, because your audience is not hostile, distrustful, or critical.

Socrates: My good friend, I suppose you are trying to encourage me with those words.

Glaucon: Yes, of course.

Socrates: Then I have to tell you that you are doing the opposite. Your attempt at providing comfort would be effective if I were confident that I knew what I'm talking about. I would feel safe and secure if I were sharing the truth about subjects I love and know with wise people who are friendly toward me. But to carry the argument when you are only a doubting inquirer, as I am, is a dangerous and slippery endeavor. **[451]** I'm not afraid that people will laugh at me—that kind of fear is childish. But at the very moment I ought to be certain of the truth, I dread that I will lose my footing and drag my friends down with me as I fall. I pray to Nemesis, the goddess of justice and retribution, not to punish me for the words I am about to utter. Involuntary manslaughter is less of a crime than deceiving people about what is beautiful, good, and just. I would rather risk deceiving enemies than friends. That is why I respond as I do to your encouragement.

Glaucon: Well, Socrates, if you and your arguments do any serious injury to us, we acquit you beforehand, as if from an accusation of homicide. We declare that you are innocent and not a deceiver! Now have the courage to say what is on your mind.

Socrates: The law says that if you are acquitted, then you are free from guilt, so I will assume it applies also in this case.

Glaucon: So you have nothing to worry about.

Socrates: Then I suppose I should retrace my steps and pick up where I left off. The men have played their role in our drama, so now it is the women's turn, especially because you are so eager to hear their part in the plot. We need to conceive of the place of women and children in a way that is consistent with what we prescribed for the men. As I recall, we determined that the men should be guards and watchdogs for the herd.

Glaucon: That's what we said.

Socrates: Then let's give the women similar training and education and see how that fits our overall design.

Glaucon: What do you mean?

Socrates: Do we separate male from female dogs, assigning only the males the task of hunting and guarding? Do we leave the females at home because we think that bearing and suckling puppies renders them unfit for doing the same work as the males?

Glaucon: No, they share the same tasks. The major difference is between the weak and the strong.

Socrates: But can you use different animals for the same functions unless they are fed and bred in the same way?

Glaucon: You cannot.

Socrates: Then if women are to do the same jobs as men, must they not have the same education? **[452]**

Glaucon: That seems to follow.

Socrates: The men were educated in the arts and given physical training.

Glaucon: Yes.

Socrates: Then should we educate the women in music, give them physical training, and instruct them in the martial arts—expecting them to perform in the same way?

Glaucon: That would be logical.

Socrates: Don't you think that because our proposals are so unusual they would be considered ridiculous, especially if our words became deeds?

Glaucon: I have no doubt about that.

Socrates: For example, one obvious target of ridicule would be the sight of women on the athletic fields, exercising naked alongside the men, especially the older ones. They will not be a vision of loveliness, any more than are the wrinkled old men who currently insist on exercising in public in spite of their unpleasant appearance.

Glaucon: Yes, Socrates, according to our present customs this proposal would seem laughable.

Socrates: Well, we are determined to think this idea through, so we must ignore the jokes and jibes of the comedians who delight in making fun of any kind of innovation. Do you think we should be concerned about how they will respond to women's achievements in the arts and in physical training, and especially about their wearing armor and riding on horseback?

Glaucon: We should pay no attention to their foolish talk.

Socrates: Perhaps we can anticipate their attacks and ask them for once in their life to be serious. We might remind them that not long ago Greeks themselves considered the sight of a naked man to be ridiculous and improper—a view still generally held by most foreigners. I suspect that when the Cretans, and later the Spartans, first introduced naked exercises, the comics of that day also made fun of it.

Glaucon: No doubt.

Socrates: But when experience revealed that exercise is much more efficient without all that covering, the comic effect of what they saw with their eyes vanished in the light of reason. What is really foolish is when a person ridicules anything but what is thoughtless and bad or believes that beauty can be measured by any standard other than goodness.

Glaucon: That is true.

Socrates: In order to determine whether such proposals are possible, whether posed in jest or in earnest, we must first ask about the nature of women. Are women capable of sharing in the activities of men fully, partially, or not at all? **[453]** Can women participate in waging war? Glaucon, would this be the best way to begin our inquiry and possibly even to end it?

Glaucon: It is the best beginning.

Socrates: I propose that we proceed first by presenting the negative case. That way we can make sure that both sides of the argument are fairly presented.

Glaucon: I think that's a good strategy.

Socrates: Then let's present the position of the other side. Our adversary will say something like this:

—Socrates and Glaucon, you do not need an adversary to refute you, because you refuted yourself when you first began constructing your republic. Did you not say that all people should do the work for which they are best suited by nature?

Glaucon: I do recall we adopted that as a basic principle. Why should we not?

Socrates: They will ask:

—Is there not a great difference between men and women?

Of course we will have to reply that there is such a difference. But they will continue the attack:

—Do you not think that men and women ought to be assigned different tasks based on their different natures?

We will have to admit that they should be assigned different work based on their natural differences.

—Then you contradict yourself when you say that men and women, who are entirely different, ought to perform the same actions!

Glaucon, my friend, how can you defend us against someone who offers these objections?

Glaucon: That's not easy to do off the top of my head. Socrates, I beg you to develop the case on our side of the issue.

Socrates: Glaucon, perhaps you now understand the difficulties that made me hesitate to have anything to do with the laws concerning the role of women and the procreation of children.

Glaucon: Yes, there does seem to be a problem.

Socrates: Well, when you are out of your depth, whether you have fallen into a pool or a mighty ocean, you have to swim in either case.

Glaucon: That's true.

Socrates: Then let's swim through this argument and try to find safety. Perhaps we will be able to climb on the back of a dolphin or find some other miraculous rescue.

Glaucon: I'm with you, Socrates.

Socrates: Then let's see if we can find a way out. We have accepted the principle that different natures should engage in different pursuits, and we have agreed that men and women have different natures. But now we seem to be saying that different natures ought to engage in the same pursuits, and for that reason we are accused of inconsistency.

Glaucon: Precisely. **[454]**

Socrates: Glaucon, what a wonderful power exists in the art of arguing on the basis of contradiction!

Glaucon: Why do you say that?

Socrates: Because I believe many people fall into this practice against their will. They think that they are reasoning, but they are really debating. They are unable to define and divide a topic according to its true nature, so they formulate a verbal opposition in order to win the argument. They practice eristic rather than dialectic.

Glaucon: I have often seen that happen, Socrates, but what does that have to do with our present topic and us?

Socrates: It has a lot to do with us, because I think we run the risk of being caught against our will in a verbal dispute.

Glaucon: How so?

Socrates: We have been bravely and contentiously insisting on a claim that is literally true. We rightly said that the people with the same nature should engage in the same pursuits, but we failed to consider what kind of natural difference or sameness we implied. Nor did we think about what we really meant when we assigned different pursuits to different natures.

Glaucon: You are right about that. We never did consider those things.

Socrates: Then it seems appropriate to consider whether there is a difference in nature between bald men and longhaired men or whether they are the same. If we agree that there is a natural difference between them and we find that bald-headed men are shoemakers, would it be right to forbid longhaired men to be shoemakers? Or if longhaired men were shoemakers, should we forbid bald men to follow that pursuit?

Glaucon: That would be absurd.

Socrates: Yes, it would be ridiculous—but why? The absurdity comes from the fact that the original idea of difference of nature relevant to the construction of your republic did not pertain to every natural difference but only to the differences that affect the pursuit in which the individual is engaged. So, for example, a male physician and a female physician may be said to be the same.

Glaucon: True.

Socrates: But a male physician and a male carpenter are different.

Glaucon: They are.

Socrates: Then if men or women seem to differ in their fitness for any craft or other occupation, we should assign them to the ones for which they are suited. But if the only difference between them is that they perform different sexual functions in producing children, that does not prove that women differ from men in the way we are talking about. Therefore, we should continue to insist that men and women have the same pursuits.

Glaucon: I agree.

Socrates: The next step will be to request that our opponent explain exactly how the nature of a woman differs from that of a man in the art of ruling a republic. **[455]** That seems to be fair, but perhaps our adversary will reply, as you did, that to give an instant answer is not easy—such a question requires some reflection.

Glaucon: That is a likely response.

Socrates: Then let's invite those who oppose us to come along with us in the argument so that we can show that there is no special role for a woman in governing the republic.

Glaucon: That's a good idea.

Socrates: Let's begin with this question:

   —When you say that one person has natural talents and another does not, what exactly do you mean? Are you saying that the former acquires a certain skill easily, but that it is difficult for the latter? Will a little bit of learning lead one to discover a great deal, but the other, even after a lot of education and effort, will forget everything? Or do you mean one has a body that serves the mind well, whereas in the other a war is being waged between mind and body? Do you think these are the kind of differences that distinguish a capable person from one who is not?

Glaucon: Socrates, I think our adversary will find it hard to list any other major differences.

Socrates: Can you think of any human pursuit in which the male is not far superior to the female? Or do I need to waste time and talk first about the art of weaving, making cakes, cooking vegetables, and caring for other people, where it would be ridiculous to claim male superiority?

Glaucon: Generally speaking, you are right in stating the inferiority of females, but even if that is the case, I think we must admit that many women are superior to many men in many things.

Socrates: So, my friend, we can rightly conclude that neither a woman, as woman, nor a man, as man, has any special role in governing a republic. Are not natural abilities equally distributed in both sexes? Are not all the pursuits of men also the pursuits of women, even when the women are weaker?

Glaucon: Yes, Socrates, that's true.

Socrates: Then does it make sense to assign all leadership roles to men and none to women?

Glaucon: That makes no sense at all.

Socrates: So you agree that one woman has the natural ability to be a physician and another does not; and that some women have the talent to be a musician, whereas others do not?

Glaucon: I do agree. **[456]**

Socrates: And one woman is naturally inclined toward athletics and military training, whereas others hate physical training and despise war?

Glaucon: Yes.

Socrates: One woman is a lover of wisdom, and another hates philosophy; one is courageous and the next is fainthearted?

Glaucon: That is also true.

Socrates: Then one woman will have the natural qualities to be a guard, and another will not. Didn't we decide to select the male guards on the basis of those same differences?

Glaucon: We did.

Socrates: Then can we say that women are equal to men in the qualities that make good guards, degrees of physical strength in either men or women being the only difference?

Glaucon: I think that's obvious.

Socrates: So, shall we select the women who have those qualities and thus have the same nature to be the colleagues and companions of our guards?

Glaucon: By all means.

Socrates: Because they have the same nature, should they be asked to follow the same pursuits?

Glaucon: They should.

Socrates: Then, to come back to our previous question, would it be unnatural to educate the wives of our guards in the arts and provide them with physical training?

Glaucon: On the contrary, it would be quite natural.

Socrates: So, it seems neither impossible nor a mere pipe dream to enact such legislation, because it is in accord with nature. In fact, should we say that the contrary practice, which prevails today, is unnatural?

Glaucon: I think that's right; it is contrary to nature.

Socrates: As I recall, we asked not only about the possibility but also the desirability of such an arrangement.

Glaucon: That's right.

Socrates: Have we concluded that it is possible?

Glaucon: We have.

Socrates: So now we should inquire about whether it is desirable.

Glaucon: That is the next question.

Socrates: Do you now think that the same education that makes a man a good guard will make a woman a good guard—because they have the same nature?

Glaucon: I do.

Socrates: Now I have another question: Would you say that all people are equally good or that some are better than others?

Glaucon: I would say that some are better than others.

Socrates: In the republic we are imagining, who would be better, the guards who have been educated as we prescribed or shoemakers who have only learned how to make shoes?

Glaucon: Socrates, that's a ridiculous question.

Socrates: I'll take that to be your answer. So does that mean that these guards are our best citizens?

Glaucon: The best by far.

Socrates: And are the women who are among them the best women?

Glaucon: Again, I would say they are the very best.

Socrates: Is there anything better for the interests of the republic than that its men and women should be as good as possible?

Glaucon: Nothing could be better for the republic.

Socrates: Will education in the arts and physical training accomplish this? **[457]**

Glaucon: No doubt.

Socrates: Then may we conclude that our new regulations are not only possible but also desirable to the republic?

Glaucon: We may.

Socrates: Then let the wives of our guards strip for action, wearing goodness as their clothing. In distributing the work, lighter jobs will be given to women with weaker bodies, but otherwise their duties will be the same. As for any man who laughs at naked women engaged in physical training for the sake of the common good, his laughter shows that he has gathered "a fruit of unripe wisdom," and he is ignorant both of what he is laughing at and what he is doing. We will treasure the saying that the useful is good, and the harmful is bad.

Glaucon: Well said.

Socrates: We have successfully escaped one of the difficulties that threatened our legislation about women. The wave that threatened us did not swallow us alive for proposing that the guards of both sexes should have common pursuits. The argument we have examined is the best witness for its possibility and benefit.

Glaucon: Socrates, it was a mighty wave we just escaped.

Socrates: True, but a much bigger one is coming. You won't be so impressed with the size of this wave when you see the next one.

Glaucon: I'm ready. Let's see it!

Socrates: I'm talking about the next law, the one that follows from what we have just said.

Glaucon: I know, and what is it?

Socrates: Here it is: The guards will have all wives in common, their children will also be common, and parents will not know which children are theirs nor will children know which parents belong to them.

Glaucon: That is a larger and more powerful wave than the first one, and both its credibility and its usefulness are much more doubtful.

Socrates: I don't see how anyone could dispute the utility of having wives and children in common, but the possibility of getting it accepted is another matter. I admit that a lot of people would strongly object to it.

Glaucon: I think you will find many objections to both its feasibility and its usefulness.

Socrates: I see, you insist on taking up both of these issues. I had hoped that you would at least find it beneficial, allowing me to escape from one of these objections and only face the problem of whether or not it would work.

Glaucon: You have been caught in your attempt to escape, Socrates, so you will have to defend both of them!

Socrates: I confess, and I will do as you order; but please show some mercy and do me one small favor. Regard me as you would people on a holiday—lazily feasting on dreams while walking alone. **[458]** Before they have figured out a way to realize their wishes—a matter which never troubles them—they find the question of what is possible or impossible rather tiresome and, in pursuing their fantasies, delight in what will happen when their wishes come true, allowing their mind to remain idle. —Glaucon, I'm running out of energy myself, so I request your permission to defer the question of feasibility. For now, please allow me to explore how rulers might work out this plan and, if it were adopted, provide great benefit to the republic and to the guards. If you agree, I would like to have you assist me in considering the advantages of this proposal, and then I promise to consider the matter of its feasibility.

Glaucon: I have no objection to your proposal, and I grant your request.

Socrates: Don't you think that if rulers and their assistants are worthy of their titles, they will be willing to command and obey commands? Even the leaders themselves must obey the laws or follow the spirit of the laws where we have left out the details.

Glaucon: That's right.

Socrates: Glaucon, you are the legislator responsible for selecting the men, so now you should give them women who have the same nature. They will live in common houses and meet at common meals, so there is no need for private property. They will be educated together, exercise together, and generally share a common life. By natural necessity they will be led to mingle with each other. Do you think necessity is the right word?

Glaucon: Yes, if you mean erotic necessity rather than logical necessity. I think this force is more likely to convince and coerce most people.

Socrates: That's true. These affairs, like all the rest, must proceed in an orderly way appropriate to a happy republic. The leaders will not allow profane and indiscriminate intercourse.

Glaucon: It would be wrong to allow any such thing.

Socrates: Then don't you think that marriage should be sacred, and the most beneficial marriages will be the most sacred ones?

Glaucon: I fully agree. **[459]**

Socrates: Now, Glaucon, how can marriages be made most beneficial? I put this question to you, because I have seen more than a few well-bred gamecocks and hunting dogs at your house. Tell me, do you ever pay attention to their mating and their breeding?

Glaucon: What do you mean?

Socrates: I mean that even though they are all first-rate, are some better than others?

Glaucon: Of course.

Socrates: And do you mate them indiscriminately, or do you make sure to breed only the best?

Glaucon: Only the best.

Socrates: Do you select the oldest, the youngest, or those in their prime?

Glaucon: I choose only those who are in their prime.

Socrates: If you did not take care in breeding them, I suppose your dogs and birds would soon deteriorate.

Glaucon: Certainly.

Socrates: Does the same hold for horses and for all animals in general?

Glaucon: It does.

Socrates: Good heavens, my friend! Imagine the kind of skill rulers will need if the same principle also holds for the human species.

Glaucon: Of course the same principle holds, but why is that so remarkable?

Socrates: Because it means rulers will have to employ the kind of medicine we talked about before.[1] You are aware that when patients only need to be given a proper schedule of food, drink, and exercise, then any sort of practitioner will suffice. But when strong medicine needs to be prescribed, then we need a more assertive physician.

Glaucon: That's true, but what are you suggesting?

Socrates: I mean that the rulers will find it necessary to prescribe a large dose of falsehood and deception for the good of the people they are ruling. Did we not say that rulers have a right to use lying as a form of medicine?

Glaucon: We did say that, and we were right.

Socrates: This legal use of lies seems to be especially important in regulating coupling and the procreation of children.

Glaucon: How should we do that?

Socrates: We have already determined that the best of both sexes should be united as often as possible, and the opposite should be the case with the inferior. The offspring of the best should be kept and reared, but not the others. This is the only way to maintain the flock in prime condition. But the rulers must keep this secret to avoid the risk of rebellion by the guards.

Glaucon: That's true.

Socrates: Perhaps we should plan festivals in which the brides and grooms will meet. They will offer the proper sacrifices, and our poets will compose suitable hymeneal songs. **[460]** We can leave the number of weddings to the discretion of our rulers, but their primary goal should be to preserve the optimal population, keeping in mind the effects of war, disease, and similar factors.

Glaucon: That's a good plan.

Socrates: We can devise a clever form of lottery—in which the inferior participants try their luck at each marriage festival—making sure that they lose and blame chance rather than the rulers.

Glaucon: That would be strong medicine, but it should work.

Socrates: At the same time, we can add to the honors and awards given to the bravest and the best warriors the privilege to copulate frequently. Their bravery would be a good pretext for them to generate as many children as possible.

Glaucon: Good.

Socrates: The officers in charge, whether male or female—I assume that women will hold such offices—will be responsible for taking the children of the good parents to a pen in a separate area within the republic and turn them over to nurses who live there. The offspring of the inferior—especially any that are deformed—will be concealed in some secret and unnamed place. Decency will be observed.

Glaucon: That must be done if the breed of the guards is to be kept pure.

Socrates: The nurses will provide for the nurture of the children, bringing the mothers to the fold when they are full of milk, being careful that no mother recognizes her own child. They will provide other wet nurses, as they are needed. They will also make sure that the nursing process does not burden the mothers by having to get up at night; the children will be turned over to the nurses and attendants whenever they bother the mothers.

Glaucon: You are making child bearing an easy task for the female guards.

Socrates: That's how it should be. Now let's proceed with our plan. I think we were saying that the parents should be in the prime of life.

Glaucon: That's right.

Socrates: What is the prime of life? Don't you think it lasts about twenty years for a woman and thirty years for a man?

Glaucon: Which years would you include?

Socrates: Let's say that a woman may begin to bear children to the republic at age twenty and continue until she is forty. A man may begin at twenty-five and continue until fifty-five.

Glaucon: That sounds about right. Both men and women would be at their physical and mental peak during those periods. **[461]**

Socrates: Anyone older or younger who takes part in producing children for the republic will be considered to have done something unholy and unjust. Children conceived in this way will sneak into life under auspices other than those guided by sacrifice and prayer, which will be offered at each festival by priests and priestesses and will involve the entire republic. These ceremonies are designed to assure that each new generation will be even better and more useful than their parents have been. Children bred outside of this arrangement will be considered to be the offspring of darkness and resulting from a terrible lack of self-control.

Glaucon: Right.

Socrates: The same law applies to anyone of the proper age who produces a child with a woman in the prime of life without approval from the rulers. We will say that they are imposing on the republic a bastard that is uncertified and unholy.

Glaucon: I endorse that law.

Socrates: But these laws apply only to people who are within the specified age group. After that, they may have sex with anyone they like, except that a man may not have intercourse with his daughter, his granddaughter, his mother, or his grandmother. Women must avoid sexual relations with their sons, their fathers, their grandsons, or their grandfathers. We will issue strict orders to do everything they can to prevent any such embryo that may come into existence from seeing the light of day. If any of them do survive until birth, it must be made clear that offspring of any such union cannot be reared but must be abandoned.

Glaucon: I think that is a reasonable proposal; but how will they know who are their fathers, daughters and so on?

Socrates: You are right; they will never know specifically who they are, so we need additional regulations. Any man participating in the festival of procreation should regard as his children those born between the seventh and tenth month after that date. He will call all of the male children his sons and all of the females his daughters, and they will call him father. He will call their children's children his grandchildren, and they will call the older generation grandfathers and grandmothers. Those who were born at the same time will call each other brothers and sisters, and they are not allowed to interbreed. But we will not make this an absolute prohibition. If they win in the lottery, and if the Pythian priestess approves, the law will allow brothers and sisters to sleep together.

Glaucon: That's as it should be.

Socrates: Glaucon, this is the design that allows the guards in your republic to have their spouses and families in common. Now we must prove that this arrangement is consistent with the rest of the laws and policies and that it is the best way to deal with such affairs. Is that how you would like me to continue?

Glaucon: Yes, by all means, do proceed that way. **[462]**

Socrates: Then let's begin by asking what we conceive to be the greatest good and the primary aim of the legislator in organizing a republic. Also, what is the greatest evil? Once we have answered those questions, we can assess whether the plan we conceived matches the good or the bad.

Glaucon: That's a good place to begin, Socrates.

Socrates: Can you think of anything worse for a republic than discord and fragmentation where unity ought to prevail? Is there any greater good than the bond of unity?

Glaucon: No.

Socrates: Perhaps you would say that there is unity when there is common pleasure and common pain—I mean when all the citizens are happy or sad on the same occasions?

Glaucon: Yes, I would say that.

Socrates: Doesn't a republic tend to unravel when feeling is not common but only private? If one half were to rejoice and the other half grieve when the same events take place in the republic and the same things happen to its citizens, wouldn't that tear it apart?

Glaucon: Of course.

Socrates: Differences of that sort seem to arise when people disagree about what they call "mine" and "not mine."

Glaucon: Exactly.

Socrates: And it is the same with things that are foreign.

Glaucon: Clearly.

Socrates: So do you think the best republic is achieved when the greatest number of people apply the terms "mine" and "not mine" in the same way to the same thing?

Glaucon: Absolutely.

Socrates: Then perhaps you would approve of an analogy with the body. When a finger is injured, the pain reaches the soul—the ruling power—and the entire organism sympathizes with the affected part. That's why we say that it is the person that has a pain in the finger. In general we use the same expression whenever there is a pain or pleasure caused by suffering or relief from suffering.

Glaucon: I do agree with that analogy. The best ordered republic is one that most fully achieves the kind of common feeling you describe.

Socrates: Do you mean that when any of the citizens experiences either good or bad, the entire republic will either rejoice or grieve with that person?

Glaucon: That is exactly what I mean—if the republic is well governed.

Socrates: Now Glaucon, I think it is time to return to your republic and see whether it best embodies these principles of good order.

Glaucon: That's a good idea.

Socrates: Can we say that your republic, like all the others, has those who rule and those who are ruled?

Glaucon: Yes. **[463]**

Socrates: And so they all call each other citizens.

Glaucon: Of course.

Socrates: But what name do people give to their rulers in other republics?

Glaucon: They often call them masters, but in democratic republics they call them rulers.

Socrates: Other than calling them citizens, what do the people call the rulers of your republic?

Glaucon: They call them protectors and defenders.

Socrates: And what do the rulers call the people?

Glaucon: Supporters and providers.

Socrates: What do they call them in other republics?

Glaucon: Slaves.

Socrates: What do the rulers call each other in other republics?

Glaucon: Fellow rulers.

Socrates: And in yours?

Glaucon: Fellow guards.

Socrates: Have you seen examples of rulers in other republics that speak of one as a friend and another as an adversary?

Glaucon: Of course, that is extremely common.

Socrates: I suppose the friend is considered to be a person sharing a common interest, whereas there is no common interest with an adversary.

Glaucon: Exactly.

Socrates: Glaucon, would any of the guards in your republic speak of one of their colleagues as a friend and another as an adversary?

Glaucon: Certainly not, because everyone they meet will be considered to be a brother or sister, father or mother, son or daughter, or a grandparent or grandchild.

Socrates: That's a splendid answer. But now I would like to ask you another question. Will you be satisfied simply to give them the names of family relationships, or should they conform to these names in all their actions? For example, in using the word "father," would caring for that person as a father be implied along with filial reverence and duty as commanded by law and custom? And should anyone who violates these bonds be regarded as an unholy and unrighteous person who is unlikely to be well treated either by the gods or by other human beings? Is this what children will hear from all the citizens about their parents and other family members when they are pointed out to them? Or will they hear something else?

Glaucon: They will hear only that. What could be more ridiculous than for them to speak the names of family relationships only with their lips without acting accordingly?

Socrates: Then in this republic the language of harmony and agreement will be heard more often than any other. So, as we indicated before, when anyone in the republic is successful or fails in some endeavor, everyone will say with them "this success is mine" or "that failure is mine."

Glaucon: That's true. **[464]**

Socrates: Didn't we say that this way of thinking and speaking would result in common pleasures and pains?

Glaucon: That's what we said.

Socrates: Then this republic, more than any other, will have a common interest that they will call their own and this is the cause of the common feeling of pleasure and pain?

Glaucon: Yes, they will have a greater community of feeling than any other republic.

Socrates: And in addition to their general constitution, do you think that the reason for this is that in this community women and children are shared?

Glaucon: Yes, I think that is the reason.

Socrates: And the conclusion that this unity of feeling is the greatest good was implied in our comparison of a well-ordered republic to a body and its various parts as they are related to pleasure and pain?

Glaucon: Yes, we arrived at that conclusion, and we were right in doing so.

Socrates: Then you think that having spouses and children in common is the source of the greatest good in the republic.

Glaucon: I do.

Socrates: This agrees with the principle that the guards should not have private houses, private lands, or any other property of their own. Their pay should be their maintenance, which they receive from the other citizens and share alike.

Glaucon: Exactly.

Socrates: Then this common property and common family membership tends to make them true guards. Rather than tearing the republic into pieces over differences about what is "mine," with each person hauling acquisitions into a private house with a separate spouse and separate children and private pleasures and pains, everyone will be affected as far as possible by the same pleasures and the same pains. They agree about what is near and dear to them and therefore work toward a common goal.

Glaucon: You have said it well.

Socrates: They have nothing but themselves that they can call their own, so they will not initiate lawsuits and disputes about property. They will be free from quarrels about money, custody of children, and other family members.

Glaucon: That follows naturally, and they will be rid of all of that.

Socrates: We would expect that equals would defend themselves against equals and would declare this to be fair and right, and for that reason they should keep themselves in good condition, but we would not expect to see them involved in trials for slander or bodily assault.

Glaucon: That would be good. **[465]**

Socrates: An additional advantage of this law is that if someone offends another person, the resentment can be satisfied without letting it get out of hand.

Glaucon: A definite advantage.

Socrates: The older people will be responsible for ruling and correcting the younger ones.

Glaucon: Of course.

Socrates: Younger people will certainly not strike or do any other violence to an elder, unless the rulers command it. Nor will the young be disrespectful in any way. Shame and fear will guard against such actions, keeping people from attacking those who serve the role of parents. They will fear that brothers, sons, and fathers will aid anyone injured in this way.

Glaucon: That's true.

Socrates: In every way these laws will help the citizens maintain peace with each other.

Glaucon: There will be great peace.

Socrates: Because the guards will never quarrel among themselves, there is no danger that the rest of the republic will be divided either against them or against each other.

Glaucon: No danger at all.

Socrates: I hesitate to elaborate on the trivial troubles this will eliminate, because they are hardly worth mentioning. For example, poor people flattering the rich, all the pains and difficulties that accompany bringing up a family, finding the money needed to run a household, borrowing and then trying to evade debts, and scraping up the funds that are to be managed by women and slaves. These petty pains are obvious and not worthy of attention.

Glaucon: You don't need eyes in order to see that.

Socrates: They will be free from all this and will live a life more blessed than that of the victors at Olympia.

Glaucon: How can that be?

Socrates: Because the people who win in the games are considered happy when they receive only part of what is enjoyed by our citizens whose victory is greater and who have won complete support at public cost. The victory they achieve is the salvation of the entire republic; they and their children wear the crown of a fulfilled life; they receive the highest rewards while living; and when they die they are given an honorable burial.

Glaucon: These are glorious rewards.

Socrates: Glaucon, earlier in our conversation somebody—I don't recall who—rebuked us for not making the guards happy, saying that they have nothing when they might possess everything! **[466]** We replied that we might consider the question in more detail later, but at that point we were satisfied with making the guards into true guards. We were not attempting to make any particular group happy but seeking the happiness of the republic as a whole. Do you remember that?

Glaucon: Yes, I remember it clearly.

Socrates: Then what do you say now that the lives of our protectors are seen to be far better and worthier than that of Olympic victors? Do you think that we need to compare their lives with those of shoemakers, other craftspeople, or farmers?

Glaucon: Certainly not.

Socrates: It is probably worth repeating that if any of our guards should foster the adolescent notion that being a guard promises a kind of happiness that would make it impossible to continue to be a guard, becomes discontent with the secure and harmonious life that is clearly the best, and seeks to dominate the republic and its resources, that person will have to learn the lesson from Hesiod that it was a wise person who said "Half is better than the whole."

Glaucon: If that person were to consult me, I would recommend staying put and enjoying that life.

Socrates: Then would you conclude that women and men ought to have a way of life such as we recently described—common education, common children, common responsibility for the welfare and safety of the republic—whether that means remaining at home or going to war? Are you ready to say that they should guard together, hunt together like dogs, women sharing every task with men? Do you affirm that this is the best alternative for them, one that does not violate the nature of females as compared with males or undermine their natural relationship?

Glaucon: Yes, Socrates, I affirm all of that.

Socrates: Then we finally come to the question of whether that kind of community would be possible among human beings as it is among other animals. And, if it is possible, how should it be done?

Glaucon: I was just about to ask that question.

Socrates: Well, concerning war, there seems to be little difficulty in how this will be managed.

Glaucon: How will they wage war?

Socrates: Of course they will go together on campaigns, taking along any of the children who are strong enough. As in the crafts, the children will observe the work they will do when they are grown. But they will not only watch, they will be useful by assisting and serving their fathers and mothers in war. [467] Have you ever noticed how the children of potters look on and help, long before they touch the wheel?

Glaucon: I have.

Socrates: Would you expect potters to take greater care than the guards in educating their children, giving them ample experience through observing their proper work?

Glaucon: That would be ridiculous.

Socrates: You should also consider the effect on the parents. Don't you think all animals fight more bravely in the presence of their young?

Glaucon: That's true, Socrates, but if the guards are defeated—which often happens in war—the danger for the young people would be immense. The children, as well as their parents, would be lost and the republic would never recover!

Socrates: True, but would you try to prevent them from taking risks?

Glaucon: That's not what I'm saying.

Socrates: Then if they are going to take risks, should it not be in ventures that, if successful, promise to improve them?

Glaucon: Certainly.

Socrates: Do you think it makes little difference and is not worth the risk whether future military personnel do or do not see war when they are young?

Glaucon: I think it is quite important.

Socrates: Then we should provide an opportunity for the children to observe war, and if we can also provide for their safety all will be well.

Glaucon: Yes.

Socrates: May we assume that the parents will understand the risks of war and will know which battles are safe and which are dangerous?

Glaucon: We may assume that.

Socrates: So we can expect them to take the children on safe campaigns and try to avoid the dangerous ones?

Glaucon: True.

Socrates: And can we suppose that they will arrange for commanders who are experienced veterans and able to be leaders and teachers for the children?

Glaucon: That would be the right way to do it.

Socrates: But nobody can anticipate all the risks in a war.

Glaucon: Not even the most experienced warriors!

Socrates: Then to guard against the unexpected, the children should be given wings so that they can fly away and escape.

Glaucon: What do you mean?

Socrates: I mean we should put them on horses and teach them to ride as early as possible. Then we can take them to see the war, not on spirited war-horses, but on the most gentle yet the fastest steeds we can find. In that way they can get a good look at their future work, but if they are in danger they can follow their leaders and escape. **[468]**

Glaucon: I think that's the right way to do it.

Socrates: Now what about the conduct of your military personnel as they relate to each other and to the enemy? I would like to offer some suggestions.

Glaucon: What are they?

Socrates: I propose that if they discard their weapons, desert their post, or commit any other act of cowardice, they should be immediately downgraded and become a farmer or a craftsperson.

Glaucon: By all means.

Socrates: And any who allow themselves to be taken alive by the enemy will be given as booty to their captors, who will be allowed to do with them as they please.

Glaucon: That's an appropriate punishment.

Socrates: How shall we treat warriors who distinguish themselves in battle? What do you think of the idea of having all of their young comrades take a turn in placing a crown on their heads?

Glaucon: I approve.

Socrates: And what about receiving the right hand of friendship?

Glaucon: Of course.

Socrates: I fear you will not agree with my next proposal.

Glaucon: What is it?

Socrates: That they should kiss and be kissed by them.

Glaucon: That is an excellent idea and I would add to it. Nobody they wish to kiss should be allowed to refuse for as long as the campaign lasts. That way, if there is anyone present that they love, whether male or female, they will be all the more eager to win the prize for valor in battle.

Socrates: That's a good arrangement. We have already said that a brave man should mate more often than the others do and should have first choice, so that he may have as many children as possible.

Glaucon: We did agree to that.

Socrates: We learned from Homer the custom of honoring brave people. He tells how Ajax, after he had excelled in battle, was rewarded with the best cut of meat. That seems to be an appropriate reward for a hero in the prime of life, because it is not only a tribute honoring him but it also further strengthens his body.

Glaucon: That's a good point.

Socrates: We will take Homer as our teacher and at sacrifices and similar occasions will honor the brave with hymns—

> And seats of precedence, and meats, and flowing goblets;

honoring men and women alike and training them for goodness.

Glaucon: Excellent!

Socrates: And when anyone performs gloriously in war, we will say that person belongs to the golden race.[2]

Glaucon: Definitely.

Socrates: Should we believe Hesiod when he affirms that when they are dead—

> They are holy spirits upon the earth, authors of good, averters of ill, guardians of speaking men?[3]

Glaucon: We should believe him. **[469]**

Socrates: Let's also ask the god how we are to perform the funeral rites for divine and heroic people and do as he says.

Glaucon: We should be sure to do that.

Socrates: In future ages we will celebrate their memory in ways appropriate for heroes with ceremonies at their monuments and graves. And we will also provide the same honors to all those who have bravely served the republic, whether they die of old age or in some other way.

Glaucon: That is only proper.

Socrates: Next, we should deal with the issue of how our warriors should treat enemies. What do you think about that?

Glaucon: What aspect of treatment do you have in mind?

Socrates: I'm asking whether they should become slaves. Do you think that Greeks should enslave Greeks or allow other people to do so if they can prevent it? Or should they adopt the policy of sparing Greek cities in light of the danger that someday barbarians may enslave us all?

Glaucon: I think it is definitely better to spare them.

Socrates: Then they will not be allowed to own Greek slaves. Not only will they follow that rule, but they will urge other Greeks to adopt it as well.

Glaucon: Certainly. That will unite them against the barbarians and keep their hands off each other.

Socrates: Now what about the enemies killed in battle? Should the victors take anything but their armor? The practice of stripping the dead often provides an excuse for cowards to avoid the battle while pretending to fulfill a duty. But many armies have been lost because of this love of plunder.

Glaucon: That often happens.

Socrates: Don't you think it is greedy and avaricious, lowly and weak, to rob a corpse and treat a dead body as an enemy, when the real enemy has already departed, leaving only the instruments of fighting? Isn't that like dogs growling at stones rather than the person throwing the stones?

Glaucon: That's a good analogy.

Socrates: Then they should refrain from plundering corpses and preventing their burial.

Glaucon: Yes, they should avoid those practices.

Socrates: If we intend to preserve good relations with other Greeks, should we allow offerings of weapons and armor taken from Greeks at the temples of the gods? **[470]** Or do we have reason to think such offerings would bring desecration unless the god commands it?

Glaucon: We should be careful to avoid that.

Socrates: What about destroying Greek territories and burning houses? What should be the practice?

Glaucon: I would appreciate hearing your opinion.

Socrates: Both should be forbidden. The most they should take is the annual harvest. Would you like to know why I say that?

Glaucon: Very much.

Socrates: If we distinguish between the words "hostility" and "war," we reveal a difference in nature between conflict that is internal and domestic and the kind that is external and foreign. We might call the internal kind "hostility" and the external form "war."

Glaucon: That is a proper distinction.

Socrates: Should we add that ties of blood and friendship relate the Greeks to each other, whereas barbarians are foreign and strange?

Glaucon: We should.

Socrates: Therefore, when Greeks fight against barbarians and barbarians fight against Greeks, you could say that this is a natural conflict which we call war. But when Greeks fight against each other, although being friends by nature, you might say that the Greek world is suffering from disorder and discord. That kind of conflict should be called hostility.

Glaucon: I agree with that analysis.

Socrates: Now consider what happens when such hostility takes place and a republic is divided. When both parties destroy the lands and burn the houses of the other, imagine how vicious that clash appears. How can either be considered to be patriotic when they tear apart their nurse and mother? They might justify taking the current harvest of the people they have conquered, but they should treat them as people with whom they will soon make peace, not as enemies in a perpetual war.

Glaucon: That way of thinking is much more civilized.

Socrates: Glaucon, is this republic you are founding intended to be a Greek republic?

Glaucon: Of course.

Socrates: Then they should be good and gentle.

Glaucon: Definitely.

Socrates: Will they be lovers of Greece and think of Greece as their own land, sharing common temples with their compatriots?

Glaucon: Certainly.

Socrates: So any conflict that takes place among them will be mere hostility—not war but a quarrel among friends. **[471]**

Glaucon: Exactly.

Socrates: They will quarrel as people who someday intend to end their quarrel.

Glaucon: Unquestionably.

Socrates: That means they will chastise them by bringing them to their senses rather than seeking to enslave or destroy them like enemies.

Glaucon: That's right.

Socrates: Because they are Greeks, they will not seek to destroy Greece by ravaging lands or burning houses. Nor will they consider the entire population of a republic—including all men, women, and children—to be their enemies. They know that only a few people are responsible for starting conflicts, whereas most of the people are their friends. That is why they will not waste their lands and tear down their dwellings but confine their hostility to last only until the many innocent victims compel the guilty few to make reparation.

Glaucon: Socrates, I agree that this is how our citizens ought to confront their Greek opponents, but in their war with barbarians, the current way Greeks treat each other will serve as a guide.

Socrates: Then let us also give this command to the guards: They should neither devastate the soil nor burn houses.

Glaucon: Yes, we will make that a law, and we can safely say that this as well as our previous legislation is excellent. But it seems to me, Socrates, if we let you continue talking about these details, I'm afraid that you will never return to the question you deferred at the beginning. I mean the issue of whether this plan is possible to implement and, if so, how it could be done. If it is possible, I am ready to endorse it as having all kinds of advantages. I can even think of some you did not mention. For example, our warriors will be extremely brave, constantly encouraging each other and calling each other by their names—fathers, brothers, and sons. They would never desert their positions. Then if you imagine the women as part of their forces, whether in the front ranks or in the rear, either to terrorize the enemy or as reinforcements in case they are needed, this would make them invincible. There are also many other domestic advantages that could be added to the ones you mentioned. But even though I applaud all these benefits and am willing to praise many others you could add, please leave it there and move to the question of whether and how this republic could be realized.

Socrates: Glaucon, now you suddenly attack my presentation and show no mercy for my reluctance. I barely escaped the first and second waves, and you seem to be unaware that you are conjuring up the largest and most dangerous of the breakers. **[472]** When you have seen it and heard its roar, then you will sympathize with my natural fear and hesitancy, especially once you grasp the incredible nature of the proposal I have in mind.

Glaucon: The more you delay, the more determined we are to hear you tell us how to bring about a republic of the sort we have been describing. So stop procrastinating and explain your proposal!

Socrates: Then I will begin by reminding you that we found our way to this point as we were searching for justice and injustice.

Glaucon: True, but why do you want to start there?

Socrates: Because I was going to ask whether, once we have found justice, we will demand that a just person must be perfectly just. Or would you be satisfied if the just person manifests justice as fully as possible when compared with others?

Glaucon: We would be satisfied with that.

Socrates: When we were seeking justice and the perfectly just person, as well as injustice and the entirely unjust person, we were actually looking for a paradigm that we could use to judge our own happiness and unhappiness. We should compare ourselves to them in order to evaluate our lives—not with the expectation that they might actually exist.

Glaucon: That is true, Socrates.

Socrates: Would we criticize an artist who painted a picture of the most beautiful human being in great detail and then was unable to prove that any such person could ever come into existence?

Glaucon: Of course not.

Socrates: What would you say about us? Have we not been creating in words the paradigm of a good republic?

Glaucon: That's exactly what we have been doing.

Socrates: Does it diminish the value of our words if we cannot prove that such a republic could actually be founded?

Glaucon: Not at all.

Socrates: Then let's accept that as true. But if I am to respond to your request and explain how we might come as close as possible, then I ask for your agreement.

Glaucon: What agreement? **[473]**

Socrates: I want to know whether you think that words surpass actions and that it is natural for practice to fall short of reality. In spite of popular opinion, do you agree with that view or not?

Glaucon: I do agree.

Socrates: Then don't insist that an actual republic, as realized in human action, will correspond exactly to what we have created with words. But if we are able to discover how a republic might come as close as possible to achieving what we have imagined, then will you admit that we have found the possibility you requested? I would be content with that, but will it satisfy you?

Glaucon: That would satisfy me as well.

Socrates: Next, we should explore what is responsible for bad government in existing republics and discover how much change is required that would allow them to achieve the best possible form. Ideally we would identify a single change, or perhaps two, achieving our goal by making only a slight alteration.

Glaucon: That's a good plan.

Socrates: Glaucon, I can think of one change that would bring about the transformation we are seeking; but even though it is possible, it is neither easy nor slight.

Glaucon: What is it?

Socrates: I am about to encounter the greatest of the waves, but I am determined to speak even if it means being deluged and washed away by laughter and ridicule. So listen carefully.

Glaucon: I'm listening.

Socrates: Until philosophers rule in the republic or kings and rulers seriously and successfully pursue wisdom—unless political power and the love of wisdom unite and those people who follow only one of them are categorically excluded—neither republics nor the entire human race will ever be free from corruption. Until that happens, the republic we have been creating will never come to life and see the light of day. Glaucon, this is what I wanted to say all along but feared to utter, because it is difficult to admit that there is no other way to achieve happiness either for individuals or for communities.

Glaucon: Socrates, I hope you realize the strong response such a speech will elicit! The words you have spoken will provoke many people, some with great influence, to strip for action and grab any weapon at their disposal, and attack you full force, intending to do you great harm. **[474]** If you don't quickly prepare an answer, they will oblige you to pay the penalty of public scorn and ridicule.

Socrates: Glaucon, you are the one who got me into this.

Glaucon: And it was a good thing I did. However, I will also do what I can to get you out of it, but all I can offer is goodwill and encouragement and perhaps by my answering your questions more carefully than others might. Now, with such an assistant, perhaps you can show the skeptics that you are right.

Socrates: Your generous offer of assistance means I must give it a try. If there is a chance of our escaping the attacks you describe, I think we must begin by explaining who these philosophers are that we dared to say ought to rule the republic. We might be able to defend ourselves by showing that some people by nature are suited for pursuing wisdom and for leading in the republic, whereas others should follow rather than lead.

Glaucon: Then I think this would be a good time to produce your definition.

Socrates: Follow me, and I will do my best to give a satisfactory explanation.

Glaucon: Lead on.

Socrates: Do you remember, or must I remind you, that a lover who is worthy of the name shows love not only to some aspects of an object of love but to the whole?

Glaucon: It looks as though you will have to remind me, because I really don't understand.

Socrates: Glaucon, I'm surprised to hear that response from you of all people! A lover like you should not forget that all who are in the flower of youth arouse your desire, pierce your heart, and are worthy of your attention. Is that not your response to all young beauties? One you will praise for having a snub nose that you will call charming, another with an aquiline nose you will commend for having a royal look, while yet another has neither a snub nor an aquiline nose that you will say has the grace of regularity. A dark complexion is perceived as vigorous, and those with light skin are children of the gods. The term "honey-pale" was surely dreamed up by a lover who has no aversion to a pallid cheek as long as it belongs to one who is young. In other words, you will use any excuse and invent any phrase to avoid passing over a single flower in full blossom. **[475]**

Glaucon: If it pleases you to have me play the part of the lover to make your point, I will agree for the sake of the argument.

Socrates: Now consider lovers of wine. Don't they do the same thing? They welcome any excuse to drink any wine.

Glaucon: True.

Socrates: The same holds for ambitious people who love honor. If they cannot be generals, they will be captains. If great and important people do not honor them, they are glad to be honored by common people. But honor of some kind they must have.

Glaucon: Exactly.

Socrates: Now I will ask my question again. When we say someone desires something, does that person desire all or only part of it?

Glaucon: All of it.

Socrates: And we will say that a philosopher loves wisdom— not this or that part of it, but all of it.

Glaucon: Definitely.

Socrates: But people who dislike learning—especially when they are young and cannot explain why something is or is not worthwhile—should not be called lovers of wisdom any more than we would say that people who have no appetite and refuse to eat are hungry for food. We would probably call that person a bad eater.

Glaucon: And we would be right to say that.

Socrates: But a person who has a taste for every kind of knowing and who is curious to learn and never gets too much of it, may justly be called a philosopher. Is that right?

Glaucon: Socrates, if curiosity is what makes a philosopher, you will find many strange creatures claiming that name. Everyone who loves any kind of spectacle delights in figuring things out and would have to be included. And surely people who crave being part of an audience simply to hear something new would be out of place among philosophers, because the last thing they can endure is a serious discussion. They rush to all the Dionysiac festivals, whether in town or in small villages, as if they were under contract to hear every chorus. Are you claiming that all such people and any others with similar tastes—along with all who dabble in arts and crafts—are philosophers?

Socrates: Certainly not. They only resemble philosophers.

Glaucon: Then who would you say are the real philosophers?

Socrates: Those who are eager to see the truth.

Glaucon: Right. But how do you explain what you mean by that?

Socrates: I might have trouble explaining it to someone else, but I'm sure you will agree with what I am about to say.

Glaucon: What is that?

Socrates: That beauty is the opposite of ugliness. They are two, not one.

Glaucon: Of course.

Socrates: And being two, each of them is one. **[476]**

Glaucon: Yes.

Socrates: This is also true of justice and injustice, goodness and badness, and every other form or kind. Taken singly, each is one, but because of their communion with actions, physical bodies, and with each other, they manifest themselves in different ways and appear to be many.

Glaucon: That's right.

Socrates: Then this is how I distinguish the lovers of spectacle— the dilettantes and those who crave action—from those who alone deserve to be called lovers of wisdom.

Glaucon: How do you distinguish them?

Socrates: Those who love sounds and spectacle delight in pretty tones, colors, and shapes, as well as the various objects made from them, but their mind is powerless to grasp and embrace the nature of beauty.

Glaucon: That is true.

Socrates: Only a few are able to encounter and behold beauty.

Glaucon: Very few.

Socrates: Consider the life of a person who delights in beautiful things but does not recognize beauty and is unable to follow when guided to understand it. Would you say such a person is awake or living in a dream? Don't you think that a dreamer, whether awake or asleep, is someone who mistakes a likeness for the thing itself?

Glaucon: I would definitely say that.

Socrates: Now consider the opposite case, someone who recognizes beauty and is able to distinguish it from the things that manifest it—neither mistaking them for it nor it for them. Is that the life of a dreamer?

Glaucon: I would say that person is clearly awake.

Socrates: Wouldn't it be right to say that one of them knows how to think, whereas the other merely supposes and has an opinion?

Glaucon: That would be a good way to put it.

Socrates: What if someone who holds such an opinion becomes angry, quarrels with us and denies what we say? Is there some way to conceal our doubt about the soundness of that individual's thinking and yet to pacify and gently convince that person?

Glaucon: There must be a way.

Socrates: Then let's think of something to say. We should begin by making clear that we do not resent anything that person may know. On the contrary, we would welcome it and rejoice about any such blessing. Next, we would ask a question. (Glaucon, perhaps you can answer for our hostile friend.) When people know, do they know something or nothing?

Glaucon: They know something.

Socrates: Something that is or is not?

Glaucon: Something that is. How could what is not ever be known? **[477]**

Socrates: Then are we certain that even if we considered the matter from every point of view, what exists completely is entirely knowable and what does not exist at all is completely unknowable?

Glaucon: Nothing could be more certain.

Socrates: Good. But suppose there is something that both is and is not. Would that not exist in an intermediate way, between what exists absolutely and what does not exist at all?

Glaucon: Yes, it would be between them.

Socrates: Therefore, if knowledge belongs to what is and ignorance to what is not, it is necessary to find an intermediate between knowledge and ignorance, if there is such a thing.

Glaucon: Certainly.

Socrates: Can we say that there is something called opinion?

Glaucon: We can.

Socrates: Is it the same as the power of knowing?

Glaucon: It is different from knowing.

Socrates: Then we can assign opinion and knowledge to different categories, each belonging to a different power of the mind.

Glaucon: Yes.

Socrates: And knowing relates to the category of what exists. And now we need to make yet another distinction.

Glaucon: What distinction?

Socrates: Let's begin by saying that powers such as seeing and hearing enable us and other beings to act and do whatever we do. Do you understand this distinction?

Glaucon: Yes, I understand.

Socrates: Then listen to how I think about such powers. I am unable to see them, so the distinctions of color, shape, and other qualities by which I notice differences in many other things do not apply to them. When I think about these powers, I consider only their purpose and what they do. Anything that has the same purpose and performs the same function I call the same power, but anything that has a different purpose and a different function is a different power. Does that describe your experience as well?

Glaucon: It does.

Socrates: Now we can return to the main point. Is knowing a power or something else?

Glaucon: Knowing is definitely a power, the most vigorous one of all.

Socrates: Is forming an opinion also a power?

Glaucon: Certainly. It is what allows us to have an opinion.

Socrates: But a little while ago you said that knowledge and opinion are not the same. **[478]**

Glaucon: Of course I said that. How could any reasonable person equate a power that is infallible with one that is fallible?

Socrates: Well said! Then we clearly agree that knowing and having an opinion are different powers of the mind.

Glaucon: We do.

Socrates: And because they are, by their very nature, distinct powers, they have different purposes?

Glaucon: Necessarily.

Socrates: Knowing aims at understanding what is.

Glaucon: Yes.

Socrates: But forming an opinion is simply having an opinion.

Glaucon: Yes.

Socrates: Then if knowing is about being, opinion must be about something else.

Glaucon: Yes, it must be about something else.

Socrates: Let's think this through. When someone has an opinion, must it not be about something? Is it possible to have an opinion that is an opinion about nothing?

Glaucon: That would be impossible.

Socrates: Can we say that a person who has an opinion has it about one thing?

Glaucon: Yes.

Socrates: But what is not, is—strictly speaking—not one thing but nothing.

Glaucon: True.

Socrates: So we should say that ignorance relates to what is not, and knowledge to what is.

Glaucon: Exactly.

Socrates: Then opinion relates neither to what is nor to what is not.

Glaucon: Correct, not to either.

Socrates: Then opinion is neither knowledge nor ignorance.

Glaucon: That's right.

Socrates: So we must look elsewhere. Could it be more distinct than knowledge or more obscure than ignorance?

Glaucon: Neither.

Socrates: Then I suppose you think opinion is darker than knowledge but brighter than ignorance.

Glaucon: That is what I think.

Socrates: It lies between the other two.

Glaucon: Yes.

Socrates: Can we say that it is intermediate?

Glaucon: No doubt.

Socrates: As I recall, we said earlier that if something appears to be the kind of thing that both is and is not, then it exists in an intermediate way, between what exists absolutely and what does not exist at all. And the power that relates to it is neither knowledge nor ignorance but will be found in the interval between them.

Glaucon: That is what we said.

Socrates: In that interval we have discovered something we call having an opinion.

Glaucon: True.

Socrates: So we must still find that which takes part both in what is and what is not and cannot rightly be called a pure form of either one. If it does appear, we would be right to call it opinion, assigning extremes to extremes and what is between to the middle. Do you agree?

Glaucon: I do. **[479]**

Socrates: Given these hypotheses, I have a question for our fine friend who believes that there is no beauty—no unchanging idea of beauty itself—the one who does believe in many beautiful things and who is a lover of beautiful sights yet cannot bear to be told that the beautiful is one, or the just is one, or anything else is one. I will put the question this way: My friend, of all the many beautiful things, is there one that will not also appear ugly? Of all the just things, is there one that will not also appear unjust? And among holy things, is there one that will not also appear unholy?

Glaucon: No, in some way they will always appear to be both beautiful and ugly, and the same goes for the other qualities you mentioned.

Socrates: What about the many double things? Will they not also appear to be halves—doubles of one thing and halves of another thing?

Glaucon: That is inevitable.

Socrates: And large things will be called small, light things will be called heavy, depending on your point of view.

Glaucon: Either term can always be attached to all of them.

Socrates: Can anything that is called by a specific name be said to be what it is rather than its opposite?

Glaucon: They are like the riddles with double meanings that jokers pose at dinner parties, and they resemble the children's puzzle about a eunuch [a man who is not a man] who aimed at a bat [a bird that is not a bird] with a pumice stone [a stone that is not a stone]. They all have more than one meaning, and it is impossible to fix them in your mind as being one or the other, both or neither.

Socrates: Then what should you do with them? Can they find a better place than between what is and what is not? Obviously they are not in greater darkness nor exist less than what is not, nor are they more full of light and existence than what is.

Glaucon: I agree.

Socrates: So we seem to have found that the conventional meanings of terms like beauty that are used by many people are bouncing around in a region that is intermediate between pure existence and total non-existence.

Glaucon: That is what we have found.

Socrates: And we agreed earlier that anything of this sort we might find should be described as opinion, not knowledge. It is an intermediate flux that is caught and detained by an intermediate power of the mind.

Glaucon: We agreed on that.

Socrates: Then those people who look at many beautiful things but who neither see nor can be taught to see beauty, who see many just acts but not justice, and so on, can be said to have opinion but not knowledge about many things.

Glaucon: Yes, that follows.

Socrates: But those who observe the things themselves, which are eternal and immutable, may be said to know rather than merely have an opinion.

Glaucon: That cannot be denied.

Socrates: Then we can say of those people that they love and embrace knowledge, whereas the others love and embrace opinion. **[480]** I'm sure you will remember that the ones in the second group listened to sweet sounds and gazed upon fair colors but would not accept the existence of beauty.

Glaucon: Yes, I do remember.

Socrates: Then would it be inappropriate to call them lovers of opinion rather than lovers of wisdom? Will they be angry with us if we describe them that way?

Glaucon: I will tell them that they should not be angry about a description of themselves that is true.

Socrates: But those who embrace being we will not call lovers of opinion but lovers of wisdom.

Glaucon: Absolutely.

ENDNOTES

[1] See p. 389.
[2] See p. 415.
[3] Hesiod, *Works and Days*, 110.

Book Six

[484] *Socrates:* Glaucon, our dialogue has gone a long and tiring way, but it has finally shed light on who are and who are not lovers of wisdom.

Glaucon: That's true, Socrates, but I don't think we could have found an easier path.

Socrates: I suppose not, but I think this matter could be made even clearer if there were not so much ground still to cover as we try to understand the difference between a just and an unjust life.

Glaucon: Then where do we go now?

Socrates: To the next destination. Philosophers are able to grasp what is eternal and unchanging, but those who wander among what is changing and fluctuating are not philosophers. Therefore it is natural to ask next which of these two should rule in the republic.

Glaucon: What would be the most appropriate way to answer that question?

Socrates: We should determine which kind is better able to protect the laws and practices of the republic. They should be our guards.

Glaucon: That sounds right.

Socrates: Can there be any doubt that someone assigned to keep guard ought to have keen eyesight rather than be blind?

Glaucon: No doubt at all.

Socrates: Glaucon, how do blind people differ from those who do not know reality? Are people not blind who lack a paradigm of beauty, goodness, and justice in their mind to which they can look and, like painters, cherish and preserve that order here and now?

Glaucon: They are alike; both are missing something important.

Socrates: Should we select them to be our guards if there are others who not only equal them in experience and the various forms of goodness but who also know reality?

Glaucon: Assuming they are equal in other respects, it would be absurd to choose the ones who do not know rather than the ones who do. That's the most important factor. **[485]**

Socrates: Then I suppose we should determine whether it is possible for people to combine knowledge with these other qualities.

Glaucon: Definitely.

Socrates: We should begin, as we said before,[1] by determining their basic nature. Once we agree about that, then if I am right, we can agree that this combination of qualities is possible. Only those people should rule the republic. Do you agree that by nature philosophers love to know what endures, the essence of things, rather than wandering between what comes into existence and passes away?

Glaucon: Yes, I agree about that.

Socrates: Then can we also agree that they love all of reality and that they are unwilling to relinquish any part of it, whether great or small or more or less important? We have already illustrated this point with examples of various kinds of lovers.[2]

Glaucon: They will not settle for only a part.

Socrates: Then let's consider another quality that must be part of their nature.

Glaucon: What quality?

Socrates: Truthfulness. They love truth and hate falsehood, which they refuse to accept.

Glaucon: Yes, we may add that quality.

Socrates: My friend, I think you should say "must" rather than "may," because anyone who is amorous by nature cannot help loving everything that belongs to or is related to the object of that love.

Glaucon: You are right, Socrates.

Socrates: Is anything more closely related to wisdom than truth?

Glaucon: Nothing.

Socrates: Can the same person naturally love wisdom and naturally love lies?

Glaucon: That is impossible.

Socrates: Then a lover of learning, from childhood on, yearns for the whole truth.

Glaucon: Certainly.

Socrates: But a person whose desires lead firmly in one direction tends to be weaker in others—like a stream that has been diverted into a different channel.

Glaucon: True.

Socrates: Those people whose desire flows toward various forms of learning will be fully occupied with the pleasures of the mind and will pay little attention to bodily pleasure. I'm talking about true lovers of wisdom, not those who pretend to be philosophers.

Glaucon: That's how it happens.

Socrates: Such people are moderate and never greedy. The incentives that have other people grubbing for money are lacking in them.

Glaucon: That's right. **[486]**

Socrates: There is another quality we should consider in identifying the nature of a genuine philosopher.

Glaucon: What do you have in mind?

Socrates: Small-mindedness. It has no place in the soul of a person who is yearning for the whole of human and divine reality.

Glaucon: That's for sure.

Socrates: Then do you think that a mind accustomed to thinking about being and about what endures throughout time is preoccupied with human life?

Glaucon: Impossible.

Socrates: Would such a person be frightened by death?

Glaucon: Of course not.

Socrates: Can cowardly and small-minded natures take part in true philosophy?

Glaucon: Not at all.

Socrates: Can a harmonious soul that is not in love with money, not petty, not boastful, and not a coward ever be unjust or ruthless in making deals?

Glaucon: No.

Socrates: In identifying lovers of wisdom even when they are young, you should notice whether they are civilized and gentle or antisocial and savage.

Glaucon: True.

Socrates: There are other signs.

Glaucon: What are they?

Socrates: Is a person quick or slow to learn? You would not expect people to be fond of an activity that produces great pain or one in which they make little progress even after a lot of effort.

Glaucon: That would be unlikely.

Socrates: Do they retain or quickly forget what they have learned? If they cannot hold on to knowledge, how can they avoid being empty-headed?

Glaucon: They cannot.

Socrates: And by laboring in vain, will they not wind up hating both this fruitless activity and themselves?

Glaucon: No doubt.

Socrates: Then we will not include forgetful souls among lovers of wisdom. A philosopher must have a good memory.

Glaucon: Definitely.

Socrates: Can we say that a person who is a stranger to the arts and who is naturally clumsy lacks harmony and gracefulness?

Glaucon: Yes, we can say that.

Socrates: Do you think truth is closer to harmony or to excess?

Glaucon: To harmony and right proportion.

Socrates: Then we should also look for a harmonious and graceful mind that by nature is easily led to the essential form of everything that exists.

Glaucon: Certainly.

Socrates: Then can we affirm that all these qualities go together and that they are necessary for a soul that seeks to participate fully and completely in reality?

Glaucon: They are absolutely necessary. **[487]**

Socrates: Can you find any flaw in a study that can be pursued only by someone who has a good memory, learns quickly, is noble, gracious, and a friend and companion of truth, justice, courage, and moderation?

Glaucon: Not even Momus, the god of censure and blame, could find fault with such a study!

Socrates: Then only those people, when they are mature and educated, should be trusted to lead the republic.

Adeimantus: Socrates, nobody can refute you, but the people who hear you talk this way have a strong feeling that they are being led astray bit by bit at each stage of the argument. They lack skill in asking and answering questions, and these small concessions accumulate so that by the end of the discussion they find that they have turned around completely and contradict what they said at first. They are like novices playing checkers against an expert, eventually outmaneuvered by their opponent with no place to move. In the present game, where words are the pieces, they are eventually silenced and have nothing to say. But that does not mean they are wrong. I say this because of what we have just heard. At this point, we might say that even though we cannot contradict you at each step of the argument, the fact is that people who devote themselves to philosophy are a strange breed, if not downright evil. I'm not talking about the ones who amuse themselves with it while young and then give it up when they mature, but the ones who cling to it too long. The result is that even the best of them are rendered useless to society by the very kind of study you propose.

Socrates: Well, Adeimantus, do you think you would be wrong in saying that?

Adeimantus: I don't know, but I would like to hear your opinion.

Socrates: I think the objection is justified.

Adeimantus: But how can you say that corruption and evil in republics will never cease until philosophers rule and also admit that philosophers are useless?

Socrates: That question can only be answered indirectly by using an analogy.

Adeimantus: But of course you are not in the habit of speaking indirectly and never use analogies!

Socrates: First you get me to take on an impossible proof and then you make fun of me! Now you are going to hear an analogy that will show the weakness of my imagination. **[488]** The way society treats the best people is so atrocious that it is impossible to compare it with a single thing, so in order to defend them I must create an image out of many things, the way painters do when they combine goats and stags into one picture. Imagine a fleet of ships or even a single one with a captain who is taller and stronger than any of the crew but who is a bit deaf, near-sighted, and has knowledge of navigation comparable to his sight and hearing. The sailors are quarreling with each other about who should steer the ship. They all insist on taking the helm in spite of being unable to indicate when they learned how to navigate or name their teacher. They even claim that the art of navigation cannot be taught, and they are ready to cut to pieces anyone who says it can. They crowd around the captain and do everything possible to gain control of the helm. If they fail and others succeed, they kill them and throw them overboard. Then they disable the noble captain with drugs or strong drink and take command of the ship, consume the ship's supplies by eating and drinking whatever they wish, and continue the voyage in the way you would expect from such a crew. The person who was most successful in helping them gain control of the ship, whether by persuasion or by force, they honor with titles such as "skillful navigator," "pilot," and "master mariner." They denounce anyone who lacks such skill as being useless. They have no idea that a true pilot in order to qualify for commanding a ship must pay attention to the time of the year and the different seasons, the sky and the stars, the winds, and whatever else belongs to the art of navigation. The true pilot does not believe that there is an art related to grabbing control either by force or persuasion and thinks it is impossible to combine such a practice with the art of navigation. How would such sailors regard the true pilot on such a ship? Would they not use terms such as "stargazer," "useless idler," and "babbler"? **[489]**

Adeimantus: They would use those terms and even worse ones.

Socrates: I assume that you understand this analogy, so I do not need to explain how it relates to the plight of the true lover of wisdom in society.

Adeimantus: The meaning is clear.

Socrates: Then you should use it to instruct anyone who is surprised at finding philosophers without honor in society. Please explain that it would be much more remarkable if they were honored.

Adeimantus: I will do that.

Socrates: Tell them it is true that the best philosophers are useless to the multitude. However, this is not because there is something wrong with those who love wisdom but because people do not know what to do with them. It would be unnatural for the captain to plead with the sailors to be put in command or for wise people to beg at the doors of the rich—whoever came up with that saying has it wrong. The truth is that sick people, whether they are rich or poor, must go to the doctor rather than expect the doctor to come to them, just as those who need a leader must seek out the person who knows how to lead. If rulers are to be genuinely useful, they cannot go around asking to be put in charge. They are not at all like our current politicians, who resemble the mutinous sailors in our analogy and who call the true pilots useless stargazers.

Adeimantus: That's right.

Socrates: Adeimantus, under these conditions it is easy to understand why those who choose the opposite way of life have no respect for the noblest pursuit. But the greatest and most severe attack on philosophy comes from the very people who pretend to practice it. I'm talking about the ones the critic of philosophy had in mind in saying that the majority of them are downright evil and the best of them are useless. Perhaps you recall that I agreed with them.

Adeimantus: Yes, I remember.

Socrates: Have we adequately explained why the best ones are considered useless?

Adeimantus: We have.

Socrates: Should we also explain what leads the majority of them to go bad and show why we should not blame the love of wisdom for this any more than for its uselessness?

Adeimantus: Definitely.

Socrates: Then we should ask and answer in our usual way, beginning with the good and noble nature of the person who always follows the truth in all matters. Anyone who does not follow that guide or boasts about the truth is an imposter and has nothing to do with the genuine love of wisdom. **[490]**

Adeimantus: That is what we said.

Socrates: But isn't this a long way from the popular opinion about philosophers?

Adeimantus: Yes it is.

Socrates: We should begin our defense by saying that it is natural for true lovers of knowledge to pursue reality, never being satisfied by a multitude of personal beliefs. They will never be satisfied, diluted, or lose the passion for knowing until their love of wisdom has grasped every essence with a kindred power in their soul. Through that power they approach and have intercourse with being itself, generating mind and truth and in that way genuinely knowing, living, and growing. Only then will their labor pains come to an end.

Adeimantus: I can think of no better plea on behalf of lovers of wisdom.

Socrates: Will such people love lies or hate them?

Adeimantus: They will hate them.

Socrates: And when truth leads the chorus, should we expect evil to follow?

Adeimantus: How could we!

Socrates: But we might expect to find a just and sound character, tempered by moderation.

Adeimantus: That's right.

Socrates: Adeimantus, I assume there is no reason for me to enumerate the other members of the philosophical chorus. You will surely recall that courage, generosity, quickness to learn, and good memory are part of the ensemble. But then you raised an objection. You said that nobody could refute my words but that in fact some of the people described by those words are useless and most are downright evil. This led us to examine the reason why so many of them are bad, and that, in turn, brought us to examine and define the nature of true lovers of wisdom.

Adeimantus: Exactly.

Socrates: Now we must consider the reasons why this nature is corrupted, why so many go bad, and so few escape being spoiled—I mean the ones you call useless rather than evil. **[491]** After that, we will consider the nature of those souls who imitate a pursuit that is too much for them and for which they are not well suited. As you said, those people produce many false notes and create a disharmony that damages the reputation of all philosophers.

Adeimantus: Socrates, what is the source of their corruption?

Socrates: I will try to explain it to you. Don't you think everyone would agree that a true philosophical nature of the sort we described seldom comes into existence and will be found in only a few people?

Adeimantus: I definitely think such people are rare.

Socrates: And think of the many forces that tend to destroy those rare few.

Adeimantus: Which forces?

Socrates: The strange thing is that the very qualities of their nature we have been praising—courage, moderation, and all the rest—tend to corrupt the soul and lure it away from philosophy.

Adeimantus: That is strange.

Socrates: Equally strange is that what are supposed to be good things can also destroy and distract—beauty, wealth, bodily strength, and influential family connections. I suppose I need not dwell on them in detail.

Adeimantus: I know the goods you mean; but what do you want to say about them?

Socrates: If you grasp the truth as a whole and in the right way, you will have no trouble understanding my meaning, and it will not seem so strange.

Adeimantus: How should I do that?

Socrates: Think about any seed or living being, whether animal or vegetable. When it lacks proper food, a favorable environment, or good soil, then the more vigorous it is the more it suffers, because what is bad is more opposed to what is good than to what is not so good.

Adeimantus: That's right.

Socrates: So people with the best nature will be damaged more by hostile conditions than those with an inferior nature, because the contrast is greater.

Adeimantus: Yes.

Socrates: Then, Adeimantus, may we say that the most gifted minds, when they are badly educated, become the worst? Is it not true that great crimes and pure evil spring out of a vigorous nature ruined by bad education, rather than from deficiency? Can people with weak natures bring about either the greatest good or the greatest evil?

Adeimantus: Socrates, you are right about that. **[492]**

Socrates: The same would be true of the philosophical nature. Like a plant that is properly nurtured, it will grow and achieve excellence; but if it is sown or planted in hostile soil, it becomes the most obnoxious of all weeds—unless some god rescues it. Or do you agree with those people who say that young people are corrupted by sophists? Do you really think that individual sophists who teach privately can do that much harm? Is it not the people who say such things that are the worst sophists, the ones who indoctrinate all alike—whether young or old, male or female—and mold them in their own image through popular opinion?

Adeimantus: When do they do that?

Socrates: When they sit crowded together in a legislature, a law court, a theater, a military camp, or any other large gathering where they approve or disapprove of what is said or done with a loud uproar. They exaggerate their praise or blame by shouting and clapping, augmented by the echo from the rocks or the acoustics of any place where they are gathered. Will this not cause young people's hearts to leap within them? How can even the best individual education withstand the flood of applause or condemnation and not be swept away by the current? Will this not instill in them the same opinions as the general public about what is good and what is bad, leading them to do what the crowd does and be like the others in every respect?

Adeimantus: Yes, Socrates, necessity will compel them.

Socrates: And there is an even greater necessity to be mentioned.

Adeimantus: What is that?

Socrates: The actions these new sophists use when their words fail to persuade. Are you familiar with the kind of public educators who levy fines, take away civil rights, and impose the death penalty?

Adeimantus: I know them all too well.

Socrates: So what words spoken in private by any other sophist could prevail against them?

Adeimantus: None.

Socrates: And it would be foolish even to try, because there is not, has never been, and can never be another kind of character or excellence brought into existence by training opposed to them. Of course, I am talking only about human beings. As the proverb says, conventional rules never apply when we are speaking of the divine. You would not be far off in saying that whatever is saved and turns out to be good in the midst of the rotten governments that now prevail is saved by divine intervention. **[493]**

Adeimantus: I cannot disagree.

Socrates: Then there is another point on which I would like your agreement.

Adeimantus: What is it?

Socrates: That every one of those hired teachers which current rulers call sophists and consider to be their rivals only teaches the common opinions of the majority as they are expressed in public meetings. This is what they call wisdom. You might compare them with someone raising a mighty beast studying its moods and desires, learning how to approach it, handle it, and determining when and how it is hostile or friendly. They must discover the meaning of the various noises it makes and discern what sounds soothe or infuriate it when made by someone else. By constantly living with the beast, they acquire this lore, which they call wisdom. Then they organize it into a system and turn it into a craft that they teach to others. They have no idea of what they are teaching or whether the desires and decrees of the huge brute are good or bad, just or unjust, fair or foul, so they call whatever delights the beast good and whatever annoys it bad. Having never observed what is truly just and beautiful, they have no way to judge or explain their nature or the vast difference between what is good and what is necessary. Don't you think these people are strange educators?

Adeimantus: Strange indeed!

Socrates: Adeimantus, do you think there is any difference between them and the people who believe that wisdom consists of discovering the passions and delights of the capricious multitude, whether in painting, music, or in politics? Will you agree that those who consort with the crowd and exhibit for its judgment a poem or some other work of art or an act of political service will also experience the fatal necessity of producing whatever it praises? But if they try to explain why such preferences really are beautiful or good, have you ever heard anything but nonsense?

Adeimantus: No, and I doubt that I ever will.

Socrates: With that in mind, consider whether the multitude will ever embrace the existence of beauty itself rather than many beautiful things or accept anything itself rather than the various instances of it? **[494]**

Adeimantus: Never.

Socrates: Then can the multitude ever be a lover of wisdom?

Adeimantus: That is impossible.

Socrates: Then it is inevitable that the multitude will scorn those who pursue the love of wisdom.

Adeimantus: There is no way to avoid it.

Socrates: And will those individuals who follow the crowd and try to please it also scoff at philosophers?

Adeimantus: Of course they will.

Socrates: Is there any way that a philosophical nature can be preserved and the love of wisdom sustained over the course of a lifetime? Do you recall that we said it is natural for such people to be courageous, learn easily, have a good memory, and be generous?

Adeimantus: I remember.

Socrates: Won't such people, even when they are young, be first in all things, especially if their body resembles their mind?

Adeimantus: Yes.

Socrates: But as they get older won't their relatives and fellow citizens want to use them for their own purposes?

Adeimantus: No doubt.

Socrates: The others will flatter and praise and honor them to get their hands on the power that will one day be theirs.

Adeimantus: That's often how it happens.

Socrates: What will they do under such circumstances, especially if they are citizens of a great republic and are rich, noble, tall, and attractive? Will they not be full of lofty aspirations, thinking that they are capable of managing the affairs of Greeks and barbarians alike? And isn't this likely to fill them with false pride, vanity, and empty arrogance?

Adeimantus: It would be easy to give you some examples.

Socrates: Now, what if someone quietly approaches and frankly points out this person's lack of the good sense needed for a decent life, claiming that it cannot be obtained without working like a slave. Do you think someone in that frame of mind and under such bad influences would be inclined to listen to such talk?

Adeimantus: That's not likely.

Socrates: But let's suppose that there are a few who are naturally receptive to such words and attracted to the love of wisdom. What happens when their friends and relatives think they are going to lose the benefits they were expecting to reap? To stop the influence of such teaching, won't they say and do anything, including secret plans and public prosecutions?

Adeimantus: They would use any means necessary. **[495]**

Socrates: Is there any way for a person in such circumstances to pursue the love of wisdom?

Adeimantus: That would be impossible.

Socrates: Then we were not wrong in saying that the very qualities that comprise the philosophical nature may serve to divert a poorly educated person from pursuing the love of wisdom, as do wealth and the other so-called good things of life that go with it.

Adeimantus: We were quite right in saying that.

Socrates: Adeimantus, my friend, this is what causes the downfall of the natures best adapted to the noblest of all pursuits. And, as we said, such natures are rare even in the best of times. From this group come the people who cause the greatest harm to republics and individuals, but it is also the source of those who do the greatest good when the tide carries them in that direction. But we should not expect weak characters to do anything great either to individuals or to republics.

Adeimantus: How true!

Socrates: When those who are best suited for philosophy depart, leaving her unwed and abandoned, they will end up leading a false life that is unworthy of them; and she—like an orphan abandoned by her family—is defiled by unworthy suitors and accused of the faults of her votaries, some being useless and most of them deserving everything bad that happens to them.

Adeimantus: Yes, that is what people say.

Socrates: Well, what else would you expect when you consider the puny creatures that see this open space and are attracted by the fancy names and impressive titles? They are like escaped prisoners who take sanctuary in a temple. The ones who have been most successful in their trivial pursuits leap into philosophy. Even in this sorry state, philosophy maintains a dignity not found in other occupations and attracts many people with unworthy natures, their souls diminished and weakened by meaningless occupations, just as their bodies are deformed by backbreaking labor. Don't you think this is inevitable?

Adeimantus: I do.

Socrates: Do you see any difference between such a person and a balding little metalworker that has been released from jail and come into some money? He has a bath, gets some fancy clothes and dresses like a bridegroom about to marry the boss's daughter who has been disinherited and left without support.

Adeimantus: That's a good comparison. **[496]**

Socrates: What will come from such a marriage? Will it not be base and vile?

Adeimantus: No doubt.

Socrates: When people who are not suited for education approach philosophy and form an inappropriate alliance with her, what kind of thoughts and opinions are likely to be generated? Will they not be sophisms that are appealing to the ear but lacking anything true and not even being close to genuine wisdom?

Adeimantus: That's absolutely right, Socrates.

Socrates: So, Adeimantus, there is only a small remnant of worthy students of philosophy. Perhaps a person with a noble nature who has been properly brought up under favorable circumstances in the absence of temptation, possibly isolated by exile, remains faithful to philosophy. Or maybe a lofty soul is born in a small town and refuses to be drawn into petty politics. Or there may be a few with a gift for the arts who leave their lesser occupation for the love of wisdom. Some may resemble our friend Theages, who had many reasons to avoid philosophy, but the bridle of ill health kept him out of politics. The case of my own divine sign is probably not worth mentioning, because seldom, if ever, has such a guide been reported by anyone else. Those who belong to this small group have tasted the sweetness of the love of wisdom and know what a sacred possession it is. They have observed the madness of the multitude and they know that present political practice is corrupt, unsound, and unjust. There is nobody who can come to the rescue of those who fight for justice. Anyone who tries would be like a person who has fallen among wild beasts. Unwilling to join in the evil deeds of the others, they would be unable to resist their fierce nature and would be useless to the republic or to their allies. They would throw away their life in vain without doing any good to themselves or to other people. As they reflect on all this, they will keep quiet and mind their own business—like someone who takes shelter under a wall seeking protection against dust and rain driven by the wind. When they see other people overflowing with lawlessness, they are content to live their own life and avoid being unjust or unholy, departing in peace with good will and high hopes.

Adeimantus: That would be no small achievement before leaving this life. **[497]**

Socrates: Yes, it would be a great accomplishment, but not the greatest. Better yet would be to find a republic suited to their nature where they could flourish and save both themselves and their community. But I think we have said enough about why philosophy has such a bad name and why it is undeserved. Now, Adeimantus, is there anything else you would like to say?

Adeimantus: I have nothing more to say, but I would like to hear which of the existing republics is conducive to philosophy.

Socrates: None of them! That is precisely the source of my complaint. Not a single one of them is suitable to a philosophical nature, and so they are twisted and warped. They are like an exotic seed that has been sown in foreign soil, which loses its natural qualities and adapts to the local conditions. Instead of maintaining its character, it becomes something else. But if the philosophic nature ever finds an excellent republic to match its own excellence, then it will be recognized as something divine and all other natures and ways of life as merely human. Now, of course, you are going to ask which form of government that is.

Adeimantus: No, Socrates, you are wrong about that. I was going to ask a different question—whether this is the form of government we have described in founding our republic or if you have some other one in mind.

Socrates: It is in many respects, but remember we said earlier that there must be someone in the republic who will hold fast to the principles that guided you, the legislator, in formulating the laws.

Adeimantus: Yes, we did say that.[3]

Socrates: But we did not explain it sufficiently. You frightened us with objections and demands that made it clear that the discussion would be long and difficult. Even now what remains is far from easy.

Adeimantus: What do you mean?

Socrates: We must determine how a republic should engage in the study of philosophy so it will not be destroyed. Everything great is filled with risk. As the saying goes: "hard is the good."

Adeimantus: Even so, please complete the investigation by clearing up that point and answering that question.

Socrates: I will not be hindered by a failure of will but perhaps by lack of ability, and you can see my zeal yourself. Notice how bold I am in proclaiming that a republic ought to conduct the study of philosophy in a way totally different from current practice.

Adeimantus: What do you have in mind? **[498]**

Socrates: Those who study philosophy now do so while young, in the period before they get involved with making money and managing a household. They barely begin the most difficult part—I mean the study of speaking with rational justification—when they consider themselves to be sufficiently educated and turn their attention to something else. When they grow older, they find it a major achievement if they can listen to a serious discussion conducted by other people, considering philosophy to be a kind of hobby. As the years pass, the light is quenched more completely than Heraclitus' sun, because the fire is never rekindled.

Adeimantus: How should it be done?

Socrates: Just the opposite way. When they are children and young adults, their studies should be appropriate to their tender age. They should take proper care of their bodies during the period when they are growing, providing a reliable means for philosophy to do its work. As their intellect matures, they should focus on the soul, and their mental exercise should be more rigorous and more challenging. Finally, when their strength wanes and their military and civic duties are completed, then they should be allowed to roam freely as they pursue the love of wisdom without any other serious demands. That way they can live the best possible life here and attend to their future destiny.

Adeimantus: Socrates, you really do seem to be quite zealous about this, but I suspect that your listeners will be even more earnest in opposing you and will never be convinced—least of all Thrasymachus.

Socrates: Don't try to stir up a quarrel between Thrasymachus and me now that we have become friends—though we were never enemies. I will make every effort until I either convince him and the others or at least help prepare them for the day when we converse in this way again in a future life.

Adeimantus: Clearly you are not thinking about the short term!

Socrates: It's really quite brief when you compare it with eternity. But it is no wonder that the multitude is unconvinced by what I have said because they have never seen anything like it. All they have experienced is artificially crafted and constructed words, quite unlike these that spontaneously come together of their own accord. Nor have they ever seen a human being who is perfectly formed in word and deed to manifest goodness and to lead a republic that is also good. Or do you disagree? **[499]**

Adeimantus: No, I agree completely.

Socrates: They have seldom heard the beautiful and free words of people whose sole purpose is to seek the truth for the sake of knowledge—keeping their distance and scorning the clever and refined debate that aims only at conflict and contest, whether in lawsuits or in private conversation.

Adeimantus: They are strangers to the kind of dialogue you have in mind.

Socrates: We anticipated this when truth forced me, in spite of my trepidation, to say that there is no chance that either republics or individuals will be free of corruption until that small group of true lovers of wisdom is charged with taking care of the republic—not the ones who are perverse but the ones who are currently called useless. Or perhaps the people who currently rule, or their children, will be inspired by the true love of wisdom. I do not believe that these alternatives are impossible; if they were, we might be rightly ridiculed for engaging in wishful thinking. Am I right about that?

Adeimantus: Quite right.

Socrates: Then whenever the most ardent lover of wisdom is compelled to take charge of a republic—whether in the countless ages of the past, in some unknown place at present, or at some time in the distant future—we are ready to insist that something like our republic has existed, exists, or will exist whenever the philosophic Muse takes charge. It is not impossible for that to happen, though we admit that it is difficult.

Adeimantus: I agree with you.

Socrates: But I suppose you will also say that most people would not agree.

Adeimantus: Exactly.

Socrates: My dear friend, do not have such a low opinion of people. They will surely change their mind if you approach them gently and try to calm them by redeeming the bad name of the love of learning. If you explain to them that the true nature and vocation of the philosopher is what we just described, then they will understand that you are not talking about the people they have in mind. **[500]** If they view philosophy in this light, they will surely change their mind. Or do you suppose that most people will respond with hostility and maliciousness to someone who is gentle and without malice? Adeimantus, I will answer for you. There may be a few who are like that, but not the majority.

Adeimantus: I can't disagree with what you say, Socrates.

Socrates: And do you also agree about why many people have a bad attitude toward philosophy? It is because of intruders, who force their way in from the outside—like a band of revelers—and proceed to quarrel, abuse the guests, and gossip about everyone else. Is that proper conduct for those who love wisdom?

Adeimantus: It is completely inappropriate.

Socrates: That's right, Adeimantus, because those who fix their mind on what is true and real have no time for such petty human affairs. They have no desire to be filled with envy and hatred toward others and to fight with them. Their eyes are directed toward fixed and unchanging principles that neither do nor suffer injustice. Instead, they follow a regular order that moves according to reason, which they emulate and to which they conform as much as possible. Can people help emulating what they admire?

Adeimantus: Impossible.

Socrates: Lovers of wisdom keep company with the divine and unchanging order and thus become part of it as far as human nature allows. However, hostility is everywhere and hard to avoid.

Adeimantus: That's true.

Socrates: And if they are required to form not only themselves but also humankind—as individuals and as republics—into what they see there, do you think that they will lack skill in creating justice, moderation, and the common good?

Adeimantus: On the contrary, they will be most skillful in that task.

Socrates: And if the majority understands that we are telling the truth about the lover of wisdom, will they be angry with philosophers? Will they refuse to believe us when we tell them that only a republic sketched by artists who make use of this divine pattern can ever be happy? **[501]**

Adeimantus: They will not be angry if they understand. But what do you mean about the artist's sketch?

Socrates: I mean that they will approach both the republic and the human character as a blank slate that they have wiped clean. This is not easy to do, but it is what distinguishes ours from every other legislator. They will not touch either the individual or the republic, and they will make no laws until they have either found or created a clean surface.

Adeimantus: That would be the right way to do it.

Socrates: Next, they would proceed to make an outline of the constitution. Does that sound right?

Adeimantus: It does.

Socrates: As they paint their picture, I assume they will constantly look in both directions, first at the nature of justice, beauty, and moderation, and then at the human image they are trying to produce, mixing and blending the various tones to create a true human form. They will create according to the other image which, when it exists in human form, Homer called godlike—the divine form.

Adeimantus: That's a good description.

Socrates: And time and again they will paint a feature and erase it and paint over it until they have made the human character as godlike as possible.

Adeimantus: That would be the way to make the most beautiful picture.

Socrates: Now do you think we are beginning to persuade those people you said would be ready to attack us with full force? Are we convincing them that this painter of constitutions we have been praising should replace the one who infuriated them? Are they growing calmer because of what they hear?

Adeimantus: If they have any sense, they will be much calmer.

Socrates: On what grounds could they still object? Would they doubt that a philosopher is a lover of truth and reality?

Adeimantus: That would be absurd.

Socrates: Or that the philosopher's nature, as I described it, is the best kind?

Adeimantus: They cannot doubt that either.

Socrates: Then will they say that a nature of that kind, if properly educated, will not be as good and wise as any that ever existed? Or would they prefer the ones we have rejected?

Adeimantus: Surely not.

Socrates: Will they still be angry when we say that until philosophers rule in republics neither republics nor individuals will ever be free from evil nor will our mythical republic of words ever be realized?

Adeimantus: I think they will be less angry.

Socrates: Rather than less angry perhaps we can say that they would be quite gentle because they have been convinced and have come around to our side, even if only out of shame? **[502]**

Adeimantus: Of course.

Socrates: Then let's assume that we have won them over. Now will anyone deny that children of kings or other leaders might be born with a philosophical nature?

Adeimantus: No one will doubt that it is possible.

Socrates: And once they have come into existence, will anyone say that they will necessarily be corrupted? Even we have agreed that it would be difficult; but is it impossible that in the whole course of time one of them might be rescued?

Adeimantus: How could they deny that?

Socrates: One of them would suffice. If even one republic were to follow such a person, what now seems incredible could be accomplished.

Adeimantus: Yes, one would be enough.

Socrates: If the ruler sketched such laws and practices, it is possible the citizens might be willing to enact them.

Adeimantus: Yes, that would be possible.

Socrates: And would it be impossible or miraculous for other people to share our opinion about this?

Adeimantus: Not at all.

Socrates: Have we adequately shown that all of this is for the best?

Adeimantus: Yes, Socrates, I think we have.

Socrates: Then we can conclude that the laws, if implemented as we described, would be best; and even if it would be difficult to implement them, it would not be impossible.

Adeimantus: I agree.

Socrates: Now that we have addressed this difficult task, we should attend to the question of how to educate these people who might be able to save the republic and its constitution. We need to discuss the studies and practices to which they should apply themselves, and at what age that should be done.

Adeimantus: Yes, those are important issues.

Socrates: Earlier I tried to avoid the difficult questions of how to acquire wives, produce children, and appoint rulers, knowing they would generate jealousy and be difficult to manage. But my cleverness did not help much, because I had to deal with them anyway. I have said enough about the matter of women and children, but now I must examine the question of the rulers, beginning at the beginning. As you may recall, we said that by administering pleasure and pain we should test their love of the republic and their loyalty, which should not be diminished by hard work, fear, or any change of circumstances. **[503]** The ones who failed such tests were to be rejected, but those who emerged pure, like gold tried in the fire, should become rulers and receive honors both in this life and after death. That is the kind of thing we were saying when the argument veiled her face and stepped aside, afraid of stirring up the very difficulty we are now facing.

Adeimantus: I do remember—and what you say is true.

Socrates: I shied away from making the bold claim I have since had the audacity to utter: If we want guards in the complete sense of the term, we should appoint lovers of wisdom.

Adeimantus: Yes, we have now told that to the whole world.

Socrates: It is natural that there will be only a few of them, because the essential qualities rarely come together, usually emerging in bits and pieces.

Adeimantus: What do you mean?

Socrates: Quickness in learning, a good memory, good sense, shrewdness, and similar qualities are seldom found in people who prefer to live orderly, peaceful, and stable lives. The same is true of those who are high-spirited and generous. They tend to be impetuous, ignoring sound judgment.

Adeimantus: That's right.

Socrates: On the other hand, steadfast and settled natures you can count on not to be afraid and run away in a battle are equally immovable when they have to learn something new. They are often drowsy and are likely to yawn and go to sleep when confronted with intellectual work.

Adeimantus: How true!

Socrates: But both sets of qualities are necessary for those who are to be educated as leaders and who will hold any office or command.

Adeimantus: I agree.

Socrates: Don't you think such people will be hard to find?

Adeimantus: I do.

Socrates: Then they must be tested not only in the tasks and dangers and pleasures we discussed before, but there must be another ordeal we neglected to mention. They must practice many kinds of learning to see whether they are capable of the highest ones—or if they will run away from them as cowards do in physical contests. **[504]**

Adeimantus: Yes, that's how we should test them. But what do you mean by the highest forms of learning?

Socrates: Do you remember that we distinguished three aspects of the soul and then identified the qualities of moderation, courage, wisdom, and justice as they relate to the soul?

Adeimantus: If I have forgotten that, I don't deserve to hear any more!

Socrates: Then you remember what preceded that discussion?

Adeimantus: What was it?

Socrates: As I recall, I said that the more precise way of inquiry would be longer and harder, but that it would provide a full view of reality to those who follow it. But you said that following the shorter road of providing examples would be good enough for you, and so the inquiry proceeded in what I thought was an imperfect manner. But it's up to you to say whether you were satisfied with that approach.

Adeimantus: Yes, I thought that it gave a fair measure of truth, and the others who are here thought so as well.

Socrates: But, my friend, a measure that falls short of reality, even to a small extent, is no measure at all. What is incomplete is never a true measure—even though people are often content with it and think that they do not need to search further.

Adeimantus: That's because so many people are lazy.

Socrates: But this is not a condition we would care to see in the leader of our republic and its laws.

Adeimantus: True.

Socrates: Then our leaders should be required to take the longer road and work at learning as much as physical training. Otherwise, they will never reach the height of knowledge, which is their proper goal.

Adeimantus: Do you mean that there is a higher form of knowledge than justice and the others we have been considering?

Socrates: Yes, there is, and here we must not settle for looking at a mere sketch, as we have been doing, but strive for complete precision. When we take great pains to elaborate little things so that they may be clear and exact, it would be ridiculous to think that the most valuable matters are not worthy of the greatest precision.

Adeimantus: That would be absurd. But, Socrates, do you think that we will fail to ask you about the nature of this highest study?

Socrates: You are welcome to ask, but I'm sure you have often heard the answer. So either you don't remember right now or you are simply trying to cause trouble for me again. I'm inclined to think it is the second alternative, because you have heard many times that the good is the highest form of knowledge and that everything else is just or useful only in relation to it. **[505]** You must be well aware that I'm going to talk about this and that I will point out that we know little about it; yet without it no other knowledge and no other possession will be worth anything. Do you think that possessing anything else is of any value without the good, or that knowing everything else is worthwhile without knowing the beautiful and the good?

Adeimantus: Of course not.

Socrates: And I'm sure you know that most people believe that pleasure is the good, whereas those who are more refined think the good is knowledge. But when they are asked to explain the nature of this knowledge, they wind up saying that it is knowledge of the good.

Adeimantus: That's funny!

Socrates: Yes, it is. First they chide us for our ignorance; then they tell us the good is knowledge of the good, assuming that we knew the meaning of the term in the first place.

Adeimantus: Quite true.

Socrates: And what about the ones who define goodness as pleasure? Are they any less confused? When you question them, they are forced to admit that there are bad pleasures as well as good ones.

Adeimantus: They cannot avoid that conclusion.

Socrates: Then they have to concede that the exact same thing is both good and bad.

Adeimantus: Yes.

Socrates: So, there can be little doubt about the disagreements that arise over this question.

Adeimantus: No doubt at all.

Socrates: And isn't it obvious that many people are willing to settle for the appearance of justice or beauty in what they possess, in how they act, or in the opinion people have of them? But when it comes to possessing what is good, nobody is satisfied with the mere appearance. They seek what is really good and scorn what only seems to be good.

Adeimantus: That is clear.

Socrates: We all pursue this goal and do everything for its sake, having a kind of intuition that goodness exists, but we are also unsure about it, not knowing its nature or having a clear proof, as with other things. **[506]** But that also takes away our assurance about the benefit of those other things. Adeimantus, do you think that the best people in our republic, to whom we entrust everything, ought to be in the dark about such an important matter?

Adeimantus: Certainly not.

Socrates: People who do not know how the beautiful and the just are also good will not be able to guard what is beautiful and just. But I suspect they do not know beauty and justice either.

Adeimantus: That is a shrewd suspicion!

Socrates: Then we will have proper order only in a republic governed by a guard who has such knowledge.

Adeimantus: That's correct. But, Socrates, I wish you would tell us whether you think this highest principle of goodness is knowledge, pleasure, or something else.

Socrates: What a man! Adeimantus, you have been making it clear for some time that you will not be content with the thoughts of other people.

Adeimantus: That's true, Socrates, and I don't think it is right for you always to repeat the opinions of others and never present your own—especially because you have been thinking about these things for such a long time!

Socrates: Do you think it is right for people to pretend to know what they do not know?

Adeimantus: No, I don't believe that's right, but at least you ought to tell us your opinion.

Socrates: But don't you know that opinions are awful and useless—that the best of them are blind? Would you deny that people who hold a correct opinion without understanding are like blind people who find their way along a straight road?

Adeimantus: I cannot disagree with you.

Socrates: And would you prefer to observe what is blind, obscure, and ugly when it is possible to hear about what is bright and beautiful?

Glaucon: Socrates, I beg you not to turn back just as you are about to reach the goal! We will all be satisfied if you simply explain goodness as you have already explained justice, moderation, and the other virtues.

Socrates: Glaucon, that would satisfy me too, but I'm afraid I will fail, and my excessive zeal will make me look foolish. No, my friends, let's not ask about the nature of goodness itself right now; that goes far beyond my present ability. But I am willing to talk about the child of the good that most nearly resembles it—or would you rather let the whole matter drop?

Glaucon: No, don't quit now. We will take the child as interest on the loan, but you will still owe the principal. **[507]**

Socrates: I do wish I could pay the full debt now, giving you the parent rather than the child, but as I deliver the child please make sure that I don't give a false account.

Glaucon: We will take every precaution, but do go ahead.

Socrates: I will proceed, but only after I remind you about what we have agreed on several times in the course of this discussion and in others.

Glaucon: What do you have in mind?

Socrates: That there are many beautiful things and many good things, each one existing by itself and designated by a specific word.

Glaucon: Yes, we have agreed about that.

Socrates: And we give a single name to the beautiful itself and the good itself and all the others we called many, recognizing each as a single form that indicates what it is.

Glaucon: We do.

Socrates: And is it fair to say that the many discrete things can be seen but not thought, whereas the forms can be thought but not seen?

Glaucon: Exactly.

Socrates: And with what do we see visible things?

Glaucon: With our eyesight.

Socrates: And with our hearing we hear and with the other senses we perceive the various objects of sense.

Glaucon: True.

Socrates: But have you ever considered how extravagant the maker of our senses was in fashioning the power of sight?

Glaucon: No, I've never thought about it.

Socrates: Think about it. Do hearing and sound attach themselves to some other kind of thing in order to hear and be heard?

Glaucon: They need no such thing.

Socrates: The same is true of most of the other senses. Can you think of any that have such a need?

Glaucon: No.

Socrates: But notice that without such an addition there is no seeing or being seen.

Glaucon: What do you mean?

Socrates: I mean that your eyes may have the power to see, and things may contain color, but unless there is something else that is naturally suited for this specific purpose, your eyes will see nothing and the colors will be invisible.

Glaucon: What do you mean?

Socrates: I'm talking about light.

Glaucon: Of course. **[508]**

Socrates: Then it seems that the link between the power of seeing and what is visible is far more valuable than the bond between the other senses and their objects, at least if light is not worthless.

Glaucon: It is far from worthless.

Socrates: Now which of the heavenly gods would you say rules over this link? Whose light allows the eye to see and the visible to appear?

Glaucon: That's obvious. You and everyone else would attribute this power to the sun.

Socrates: Now we can describe the relationship between sight and this god.

Glaucon: How would you do that?

Socrates: Neither sight itself nor the eye is the same as the sun.

Glaucon: True.

Socrates: Can we say that of all our organs, the eye is most like the sun?

Glaucon: The most by far.

Socrates: And can we also say that the power the eye possesses is a kind of overflow from the abundance of the sun?

Glaucon: Exactly.

Socrates: Then the sun is not sight but the cause of sight and is also seen by sight.

Glaucon: Yes.

Socrates: This is what I mean by the child of the good, which the good produced as analogous to itself. The sun is to sight and the objects of seeing what the good is to mind and the objects of thinking.

Glaucon: Socrates, can you explain that a bit more?

Socrates: Think of your eyes when you direct them toward colors of objects, no longer in daylight but in moonlight or starlight. Then they see dimly and are nearly blind, seeming to be without clear vision.

Glaucon: True.

Socrates: But when you direct them toward objects on which the sun shines, don't those same eyes see clearly?

Glaucon: They do.

Socrates: The mind is like the eye. When it settles on what is illuminated by truth and being, then it clearly thinks and understands, and we see that it has knowledge. But when it turns toward what comes into existence and passes away, then its sight dims and, lacking understanding, it holds on to opinions—first this one, then that one.

Glaucon: That's how it is.

Socrates: Then we can say that the form of the good provides truth to what is known and the power of knowing to the knower. It causes knowledge and truth, and in that sense, we can think of the good as knowable. And you would be right to consider goodness as even more beautiful than truth and knowledge. As in our previous discussion, light and sight can be said to be like the sun but not to be the sun, so in this analogy knowledge and truth can be considered to be like the good but not to be the good. The good has even greater value than they have. **[509]**

Glaucon: You are praising an extraordinary beauty that produces both truth and knowledge and is even more beautiful than they are. But I suppose you will deny that the good is the same as pleasure.

Socrates: Don't even think that! Instead, let's continue to consider the similarity in another way.

Glaucon: How?

Socrates: I think you would say that the sun is both the source of visibility in all visible things and also the cause of generation, growth, and nourishment. But it is not the process of generation itself.

Glaucon: Of course.

Socrates: In the same way, we find that goodness is not only the source of learning in everything that is known, but it is also its existence and nature. Goodness itself is not existence, but it surpasses existence in dignity and power.

Glaucon: By the god Apollo, is that the most you can say about the superiority of the good?

Socrates: Well, it's your fault for forcing me to express my opinion!

Glaucon: Don't stop now, especially if there is anything you omitted in making your analogy with the sun.

Socrates: I left out a great deal.

Glaucon: Then let's hear everything, no matter how small.

Socrates: I'll do my best, but I suspect a great deal will have to be omitted.

Glaucon: I hope not.

Socrates: Then imagine that there are two ruling powers, one assigned to what is intelligible and the other to what is visible. Do you have these two forms clearly in mind—what can be seen and what can be thought?

Glaucon: I have.

Socrates: Now think of a line that has been divided into two unequal parts, and then divide each of those parts in the same way. The two main divisions correspond to what is visible and what is intelligible. Now let's compare the subdivisions from the standpoint of clarity and obscurity. The first segment of the visible contains two kinds of images—shadows and reflections. **[510]** The reflections can be in water, from smooth, polished surfaces, or anything else of that kind. Are you following me?

Glaucon: Yes I am.

Socrates: In the second segment of the visible, place the things of which the first segment contains the images—animals, plants, and all the natural and artificial objects.

Glaucon: I understand.

Socrates: Would you agree that from the standpoint of what is true and what is not true, a likeness is related to the object it copies as guessing is related to knowledge?

Glaucon: Yes, I agree with that analogy.

Socrates: Now let's consider how to divide the intelligible.

Glaucon: What do you suggest?

Socrates: Remember, there are two subdivisions. In the first one, the mind uses as images the things that were imitated in the visible realm. This inquiry can only be hypothetical, proceeding to a conclusion based on assumptions, rather than going to a first principle. In the second subdivision of the intelligible, the mind dispenses with hypotheses, makes no use of images, and inquires only by means of the forms themselves.

Glaucon: I don't quite understand what you mean.

Socrates: Then I'll try again. Perhaps you will understand it better after this introduction. I suppose you know that students of geometry, arithmetic, and related disciplines assume concepts such as odd and even, various kinds of geometrical figures, the three kinds of angles, and many others. These are assumptions that everyone is supposed to know and which they take for granted, never explaining them either to themselves or to others. They begin with these concepts and on that basis proceed logically until they arrive at their conclusion.

Glaucon: Yes, I do know that.

Socrates: And do you also know that even though they use and reason about visible shapes, they are not thinking about them but about what they resemble? They are not thinking about the figures they draw, but of the square itself, the diagonal itself, and so on. They make use of the shapes they draw or mold, which also have shadows and reflections in water, but they are really searching for the ideas themselves, which can be seen only with the mind.

Glaucon: That's true. **[511]**

Socrates: I talked about this kind as intelligible, even though the mind is required to use hypotheses, because it cannot get beyond making assumptions and proceed to first principles. At this stage, the mind uses the objects of which the shadows are resemblances as images. When compared to shadows, they are more tangible and more highly prized.

Glaucon: I understand. You are talking about geometry and the arts related to it.

Socrates: Now in speaking of the other aspect of the intelligible, please understand that I mean the knowledge that reason itself attains through the power of dialectic, using assumptions not as first principles, but as hypotheses—as ways of access and points of departure—so that it can go beyond assumptions and apprehend the first principle of the whole. Holding fast to that first principle and then proceeding to what depends on it, it descends without the aid of any visible object, moving from ideas to ideas and ending in ideas.

Glaucon: I understand you, Socrates, though not fully, because you are talking about an overwhelming task. I think you mean that dialectic searches for knowledge and reality. In that quest it provides greater clarity than what we call the arts and sciences, because they are based only on hypotheses. These hypotheses are grasped by understanding rather than sense perception. Because they proceed from assumptions and do not reach a first principle, those who contemplate them do not use the higher form of reason on them. But when a first principle is connected to them, then they can be known by reason. The way of thinking used by geometry and similar sciences you would call understanding, not reason, because it is intermediate between opinion and reason.

Socrates: Glaucon, your explanation is correct. Now, think of four states of mind corresponding to those four segments of the line. Reasoning is at the top, understanding is second, believing is third, and guessing is last. Finally, organize them on a scale with the four states of mind so that they display clarity to the same degree that their objects possess the truth.

Glaucon: I understand and agree, so I will arrange them as you say.

ENDNOTES

[1] See p. 474.
[2] See pp. 474–475.
[3] See p. 412.

Book Seven

[514] *Socrates:* Now, Glaucon, let's think about the ignorance of human beings and their education in the form of an allegory. Imagine them living underground in a kind of cave. The mouth of the cave, which is far above, is as wide as the cave itself and opens to the light outside. These people have been here since childhood. Their legs and necks are chained so that they cannot move. They can see only what is in front of them, because the chains are fastened in a way that keeps them from turning their heads. A fire burns at some distance behind them. If you look carefully, you can see a wall between the fire and the prisoners, like a curtain that hides puppeteers showing their puppets.

Glaucon: I can see that.

Socrates: Can you also see people passing behind the wall, carrying all kinds of objects above their heads so that they show over the wall? They are carrying statues of humans and animals made of wood, stone, and other materials. Some of them are talking and others are silent. [515]

Glaucon: That's a strange image, Socrates, and these are strange prisoners.

Socrates: They are like us. They see only the shadows the light from the fire throws on the wall of the cave in front of them—their own shadows or those of the objects passing behind the wall. Do you think they could actually see themselves?

Glaucon: How could they see anything but shadows if they are unable to move their heads?

Socrates: And what about the objects being carried by the people behind the wall?

Glaucon: They would see only the shadows.

Socrates: If the prisoners were able to talk with each other about these shadows, wouldn't they believe that they were discussing reality?

Glaucon: That's right.

Socrates: Suppose sounds echoed off the wall of the cave. Wouldn't the prisoners imagine that what they heard came from one of the shadows?

Glaucon: No doubt.

Socrates: So, it's obvious that for these prisoners the truth would be no more than the shadows of objects.

Glaucon: That seems to be inevitable.

Socrates: Now let's consider how they might be released and cured of their ignorance. Imagine that one man is set free and forced to turn around and walk toward the light. Looking at the light will be painful; the glare will be dazzling and make it impossible to see the objects that previously appeared as shadows. Then imagine someone telling him that what he previously saw was an illusion, but as he approaches, what is real and true will become visible. How would the prisoner respond? What if someone points to the objects as they pass and asks their names? Won't he experience great difficulty, considering the familiar shadows to be more real than the objects he sees now?

Glaucon: Much more real.

Socrates: And if the prisoner is forced to look at the light, won't the pain to his eyes cause him to take refuge in the shadows, which are easier to recognize than what is now shown to him?

Glaucon: That's true.

Socrates: Next imagine that he is dragged up the rough, steep path to the mouth of the cave and not released until he is in the presence of the sun itself. Don't you think that he would be pained and outraged at being treated this way? **[516]** And when he is in full sunlight, won't he again be blinded and unable to see any of the things that we would now say are real?

Glaucon: He wouldn't be able to see them right away.

Socrates: He would have to get used to seeing the world outside the cave. First he will recognize the shadows, then the reflections of people and other objects in the water, and finally he could see the objects themselves. Then he will gaze at the night sky, still better able to see the light of the moon and the stars than the sunlight or the sun.

Glaucon: That's probably how it would be.

Socrates: But at last he would be able to see the sun in its proper place, rather than its reflection in the water or somewhere else. Then he will be able to consider its true nature.

Glaucon: Yes.

Socrates: He would infer that the sun produces the seasons and the years, that it rules over everything visible and is, in some way, the cause of everything that he and his fellow prisoners used to see.

Glaucon: Clearly that's the way he would learn.

Socrates: And when he remembers where he used to be, and what passes for wisdom in the cave among his companions, don't you think he would feel sorry for them and be happy about the change that has taken place in himself?

Glaucon: There's no doubt about it.

Socrates: Let's suppose that the prisoners were in the habit of conferring honors and awards on those who are the quickest in seeing and remembering and predicting the appearance of the shadows, in saying which came first and which came later and which appear together. Do you think he would seek such honors or envy those who won them? Or wouldn't he say with Homer that it's "better to be the poor servant of a poor master"[1] and endure anything, rather than think as they do and exist in their condition?

Glaucon: Yes, I think he would put up with anything rather than live that kind of life.

Socrates: Now imagine what would happen if he returned to his old place in the cave. If he suddenly came out of the sunlight, wouldn't his eyes be overcome by darkness?

Glaucon: At first he wouldn't see anything.

Socrates: It might take some time before his eyes adjusted, so if the prisoners were holding a contest and he had to compete with them in measuring shadows while his eyesight was still weak, wouldn't he look stupid? **[517]** People would say that he went out of the cave and then returned without his eyes, so it is foolish to even consider such a risk. If someone were caught trying to release the other prisoners and lead them up to the light, that person would probably be killed.

Glaucon: I'm sure you're right.

Socrates: Glaucon, my friend, you may now connect this allegory with what we were saying before. What we normally see with our eyes can be compared with the prison where the people dwell, and the fire can be related to the power of the sun. Consider the journey out of the cave and seeing the things there to be the ascent of the soul to the realm of what is knowable. This is my belief, which I have shared at your request. It would take a god to know whether it is right or wrong. But regardless of whether it is true or false, I believe that in the realm of what is knowable the idea of the good appears last of all and can be seen only with great effort. Once we see it, we understand it to be the cause of all things that are right and beautiful, the origin and ruler of light in this world, and the ultimate source of truth and reason beyond it. This must be understood by anyone who wishes to act rationally and effectively either in public or private life.

Glaucon: I agree with what you say, as far as I can understand it.

Socrates: Then I hope you will agree with me on another matter. You shouldn't be surprised if the people who learn to think this way are unwilling to be caught in everyday human affairs or—to continue with the symbolism from our allegory—if their souls naturally long for the realm outside the cave.

Glaucon: I agree that this would be quite natural.

Socrates: And should we be surprised if a person who passes from contemplating divine things to viewing human affairs behaves in a ridiculous way? For example, while still adjusting to the darkness with blinking eyes, such a person might be forced into law courts, or anywhere else, to dispute about the images of justice, or even the shadows of images of justice, and meet the expectations of those who have never seen justice itself.

Glaucon: There's nothing surprising about that.

Socrates: Anyone with common sense knows two different ways and causes that can confuse the eyes—either by coming out of the light or by going into the light. **[518]** This is true of the mind's eye as well as the body's eye. If you remember this when you encounter someone whose vision is perplexed and weak, you will not be too quick to laugh. First you will ask whether that soul has come out of a brighter life and is unable to see because of the darkness or—having turned from darkness to daylight—is dazzled by the brightness. You would consider the one who comes from the light to be in a happy state, but you would pity the other one. And if you were inclined to laugh at them, you would find more reason to laugh at the one looking at the light than laughing at the one returning to the cave.

Glaucon: That's a good way to put it.

Socrates: But if this is true, then those people are wrong who claim that they can educate by putting knowledge into an empty mind, like putting vision into a blind eye.

Glaucon: I have heard them make such claims.

Socrates: According to our account, the power to know is already in every soul. But just as the eye cannot turn from darkness to light without turning the whole body, when the mind's eye is turned around, the whole soul must turn from becoming to being and must be able to endure seeing its brightest form, which we call the good.

Glaucon: That is our account, and I think it's true.

Socrates: There must be an art that expedites this change as easily and completely as possible, not by implanting vision, which the eyes already have, but by turning them in the right direction, which they lack.

Glaucon: Yes, there must be such an art.

Socrates: What people call the other virtues of the soul are more like the qualities of the body. They are not innate, but are instilled by habit and exercise, whereas understanding comes from the gods and has an eternal power. But, depending on which way it is turned, it can either be useful and beneficial or useless and harmful. **[519]** Surely you've noticed the cunning intelligence flashing from the eye of a clever villain—how eager and clear such a paltry soul is in finding the way to achieve its ends. Far from blind, its keen eyesight serves evil, and the greater the intelligence, the greater the crime.

Glaucon: Very true.

Socrates: Now consider sensual pleasures, such as those that come from excessive eating and drinking, that naturally drag people down into the realm of shadows like lead weights. What if those weights were cut off in childhood? If people were released from such impediments and turned in the opposite direction, the same soul in the same people would then see the truth as keenly as it sees the shadows toward which it is now turned.

Glaucon: That's likely.

Socrates: Yes, and there is something else that is likely, possibly even a necessary inference from what we have said. People without education and without experience of the truth will not be able to govern a republic, because they will lack the single purpose that could rule their private and public actions. And others who never bring an end to their education will never act at all, except under compulsion, imagining that they are already in the Islands of the Blessed.[2]

Glaucon: I think that's right.

Socrates: Then it is our responsibility as founders of the republic to compel the best minds to attain the knowledge we have called the greatest. They must climb to that height and arrive at the good. When they have done that and have seen enough, we must not allow them to do as they do now.

Glaucon: What do you mean?

Socrates: I mean that we must not allow them to remain in the realm outside the cave. They must be compelled to descend again among the prisoners in the cave and participate in their labors and their honors, whether these honors are worth having or not.

Glaucon: Wouldn't that be unjust? Should we give them an inferior life when they might have a superior one?

Socrates: My friend, you have forgotten the primary aim of the lawmaker. The goal of the law is not to make an individual or a group happier than the rest but to make the whole republic happy. Legislators try to create harmony among the citizens by persuasion and force, encouraging them to benefit the republic and, in that way, benefit each other. The lawmaker does not cultivate such people so that they can go their own way but uses them as instruments to bind together the republic. **[520]**

Glaucon: You're right. I had forgotten that.

Socrates: Then, Glaucon, you can see that it is not unjust to force our philosophers to care for and look after other people. We will explain that in other republics, people like them are not required to take part in civic life, because they arise spontaneously and are not welcomed by the government. They are self-taught, so they have no obligation to compensate for an education they never received. But to our rulers we will say: "We have brought you into the world to rule, to be sovereigns over yourselves and other citizens. You have been educated far better and more fully than they have, so you are able to participate in both kinds of life. When it is your turn you must each go back down where the others dwell and acquire the habit of seeing in the dark. Once you adjust, you will see ten thousand times better than the others. Because you have seen beauty, justice, and goodness, you will know both the shadows and the things themselves." Therefore, Glaucon, the order of our republic will be a waking reality, not a dream, as it generally is in other republics. In most of them people fight with one another about the shadows and struggle for power, which they think is a great good. But the truth is that a republic in which the rulers are most reluctant to govern is the best, whereas the one in which they are most eager to rule is the worst.

Glaucon: I completely agree with you, Socrates.

Socrates: And do you think that when they hear this, our students will refuse to take their turn and do their part in the work of the republic, when they are allowed to spend the lion's share of their time with each other in the pure world of ideas?

Glaucon: That's impossible! They are just people, and our commands are just. I have no doubt that every one of them will consider holding office to be a necessity, unlike those who currently rule in republics.

Socrates: Yes, my friend, that's the whole point. [521] If you can discover a better life for your future rulers than governing, then you might have a well-governed republic. Only in that kind of republic will people rule who are really rich, not in gold and silver but in goodness and wisdom—the true blessings of life. But if they go into the administration of public affairs, poor and hungry for their personal advantage, believing that to be the way to the good life, there will never be order. They will spend their time fighting for power, and the conflicts that arise will ruin them along with the entire republic.

Glaucon: That's true, Socrates.

Socrates: And it is only the life of true philosophy that scorns the life of political ambition. Can you think of any other?

Glaucon: No, I can't.

Socrates: The people who govern should not love their task, because if they do, they will fight with rival lovers.

Glaucon: No question about it.

Socrates: Who should be urged to take charge of the republic other than those who are wisest about public affairs and who, at the same time, love higher honors and have a better life than a political one?

Glaucon: These are the people I would choose, no one else.

Socrates: Then should we consider how such leaders might come to exist, how we might bring them from darkness into the light—and how some, as we are told, have ascended from the world below to the gods?

Glaucon: We should consider that.

Socrates: Well, it is not child's play. It's not like the game in which children flip an oyster shell to produce dark or light, depending on which side comes up. We're talking about the turning of a soul from the daylight, which is no better than night, to the true day, the ascent to true being made possible by philosophy. What kind of learning has this power? Shall we consider that question?

Glaucon: Of course.

Socrates: Then we must determine what kind of knowledge would draw the soul from becoming to being. And something else just occurred to me. Do you remember what we said about our guards—that, in their youth, they should be good warriors and athletes?

Glaucon: Yes, I remember that clearly.

Socrates: Then this new kind of knowledge must include another quality.

Glaucon: What quality?

Socrates: Usefulness in war.

Glaucon: Yes, I suppose so.

Socrates: We identified two studies in the educational program we discussed before, didn't we?

Glaucon: That's right.

Socrates: There was gymnastics, which has to do with growth and decay by watching over the development and decline of the body.

Glaucon: Yes.

Socrates: But that's not the kind of knowledge we are looking for. **[522]**

Glaucon: No.

Socrates: What about the arts? How did they figure in our educational program?

Glaucon: They were the counterpart of gymnastics. Their purpose was to instill proper habits in the soul, not as a science would, but by providing a kind of harmony and rhythm both in music and in words, unconcerned with truth and falsehood. But such artistic knowledge is not the kind that produces the good you're looking for now.

Socrates: Your memory is excellent, Glaucon. There was no knowledge of that kind in our earlier curriculum. But, my friend, what branch of knowledge is there of the sort we are seeking? We rejected the practical arts as crude.

Glaucon: Yes, but if we reject gymnastics and both the fine arts and the practical arts, then what is left?

Socrates: Perhaps there is nothing left. But then where can we find something that has universal application?

Glaucon: What do you have in mind?

Socrates: I mean something that all forms of thought, including the arts and sciences, use in common. It's something everyone learns as part of elementary education.

Glaucon: What is it?

Socrates: The simple ability of distinguishing one, two, and three. Let's call it number and calculation. Is this not a form of knowledge shared by all the arts and sciences?

Glaucon: I can't deny that.

Socrates: And would you say that the art of war also uses it?

Glaucon: Certainly.

Socrates: Think of Palamedes. Whenever he appears in one of the tragedies, he shows how unfit Agamemnon is to be a general. Haven't you noticed how Palamedes claims to have invented mathematics, numbering and arranging the ranks of the army at Troy? This implies that they had never been numbered before. It also indicates that Agamemnon, being ignorant of mathematics, was unable to count his own feet. And if that were true, what kind of general could he be?

Glaucon: He would be a strange one.

Socrates: Then can we say that a warrior, in addition to military skill, must have knowledge of arithmetic?

Glaucon: That's for sure, at least if a general wants to know anything about arranging the troops. I would even say that knowledge of arithmetic is necessary for any human being.

Socrates: Then I'd like to know whether you have the same idea as I have about this discipline.

Glaucon: What is it?

Socrates: I believe that this is the kind of study we are seeking, one that naturally arouses thinking. **[523]** But people ignore its proper use, which is to lead us to being.

Glaucon: Socrates, I don't understand what you mean.

Socrates: I'll try to explain, but I need your help as I try to think this through. Please think along and agree or disagree as I try to figure out the proper ways to reach that goal and whether this is one of them.

Glaucon: You point the way.

Socrates: Let's consider our sense perceptions. There are two kinds: those we accept without thinking further about them and another group that make us think because we mistrust our senses.

Glaucon: I suppose you mean perceptions of things that are far away, and paintings that deceive the eye.

Socrates: No that's not quite what I have in mind.

Glaucon: Then what do you mean?

Socrates: I mean that some sense perceptions do not lead to their opposites, so they provoke no further thought; but other perceptions, regardless whether they are near or far away, lead us to think equally about an idea and its opposite. Let's take an example. Look at these three objects—my little finger, middle finger, and index finger.

Glaucon: I see them clearly.

Socrates: They are quite close to us, but that's not the point.

Glaucon: What is the point?

Socrates: Each of them is equally a finger, no matter where it is located, whether it is black or white, thick or thin. This kind of perception would not normally lead us to think that a finger is anything but a finger.

Glaucon: True.

Socrates: So there is nothing in this case that would lead us to give it further thought.

Glaucon: No, there isn't.

Socrates: Now is this also true when we consider whether the fingers are large or small? Can simply seeing a finger by itself adequately tell us? Or does it matter that one is located in the middle and another at the end? And what about our sense of touch? Can touching a single finger indicate whether it is thick or thin, hard or soft? **[524]** And what about the other senses? Can they provide full information about such matters? On the contrary, it seems that the senses give only relative answers, sometimes judging the very same thing to be hard and soft. The sense that reveals what is hard also reveals what is soft.

Glaucon: I think that's right.

Socrates: Then it seems that our mind would be puzzled by encountering both hard and soft. And what can light and heavy mean if what is light indicates what is heavy and what is heavy indicates what is light?

Glaucon: Yes, such indications are strange and have to be explained.

Socrates: It is this kind of puzzle that forces the mind to summon reason and calculation to help decide whether it is dealing with one object or two.

Glaucon: I agree.

Socrates: And if there are two objects of perception, then each would be different from the other and yet one.

Glaucon: Certainly.

Socrates: So if each is one and both are two, we will think of them as separate, because if they were inseparable, we could only think of them as one.

Glaucon: That's right.

Socrates: And the eye, as we said earlier, saw both large and small, but only in a confused way, and was unable to distinguish them.

Glaucon: Yes.

Socrates: But the thinking mind, trying to bring clarity to this chaos of sense perception, was forced to reverse this process and see large and small as separate and not confuse them with each other. Isn't this how we first begin to inquire into what we really mean by large and small?

Glaucon: I agree; that's how such inquiry begins.

Socrates: Is this how we arrive at the distinction between what is visible and what is intelligible?

Glaucon: Yes it is.

Socrates: That's what I had in mind when I said that some experiences promote thinking and some do not. The ones that lead us to think are the ones that confront us with a contradiction.

Glaucon: I understand what you are saying, and I agree with you.

Socrates: Good. Now how would you classify unity and number?

Glaucon: I don't know.

Socrates: If you think about it, you can find the answer in what we just said. If a person could perceive unity itself, by sight or by any other sense, then, as we said about the finger, there would be nothing to lead the mind toward being. But when a contradiction arises, in which one is also the opposite of one and also more than one, then the mind is bewildered and thought is awakened. Trying to come to terms with it, we ask: "What is unity itself?" **[525]** This is how studying the nature of one has the power to turn the soul around and lead it to contemplate true being.

Glaucon: That happens especially when we look at one, because the same thing can be seen as one and at the same time as infinitely many.

Socrates: Yes, and if this is true of one, it must be no less true of all number.

Glaucon: That's right.

Socrates: Can we say that arithmetic and calculation are entirely concerned with number?

Glaucon: We can.

Socrates: And they lead us to truth?

Glaucon: Yes, they do that to an amazing degree.

Socrates: Then this is the kind of knowledge we were seeking. It has a double use, both military and philosophical. The warrior must learn the art of number in order to arrange the troops, and the philosopher, as true mathematician, needs it in order to emerge from generation and change and grasp true being.

Glaucon: Well said.

Socrates: Will the person who guards our republic be both a warrior and a philosopher?

Glaucon: That's right.

Socrates: Then we should legislate this kind of knowledge for the leaders of our republic. We must convince them not to learn arithmetic as amateurs do; but to study it until they grasp the nature of number itself with the mind alone. Nor should they simply use calculation as merchants and traders do, with the goal of buying and selling, but should focus on its military use. Above all, this study should nurture the soul itself, providing an easy way to progress from change to truth and being.

Glaucon: Those are excellent words, Socrates.

Socrates: Yes, Glaucon, this discussion recalls the elegance of mathematical reasoning and suggests the many ways it can be used for our purpose when we pursue it philosophically and not just for business.

Glaucon: I'm not sure what you mean.

Socrates: I mean that arithmetic elevates the soul, forcing it to consider number itself and resist the mere counting of visible bodies. You know how experts in the field reject and ridicule anyone who tries to divide the one into parts. If you divide, they multiply, making sure that one will not stop being one and become lost in fractions.

Glaucon: Yes, I have heard such discussions.

Socrates: Let's imagine someone challenging them by asking, **[526]** "My friends, what are these wonderful numbers about which you are reasoning, each one being the kind of unity you demand: equal, unchanging, and indivisible?" How would they respond?

Glaucon: I suppose they would say they are talking about numbers that are manifested only in thinking, unable to be grasped in any other way.

Socrates: Then can you see why this kind of knowledge is necessary? Does it not require the use of pure thinking in the search for truth itself?

Glaucon: Yes, I can see that.

Socrates: Have you noticed that people who are naturally good in arithmetic are also quick in other kinds of study, and that even people who lack such natural talent can improve by being educated in arithmetic?

Glaucon: Yes, Socrates, I have noticed that.

Socrates: You won't find many studies as difficult or more demanding.

Glaucon: No, you won't.

Socrates: So, for these reasons we should not neglect the study of arithmetic for the best people.

Glaucon: I agree.

Socrates: Then let's require it as one of the subjects in our curriculum. Now let's consider the study related to it.

Glaucon: Do you mean geometry?

Socrates: Yes.

Glaucon: The part of geometry that is useful in war is of obvious value. It is needed for pitching camp, taking up a position, closing or opening the ranks of an army, and similar military maneuvers, whether in battle or on a march. A military leader who knows geometry will surely be better.

Socrates: True, but a little geometry or arithmetic is enough for that purpose. The question is whether the higher study of geometry is needed, the kind that fosters our ultimate goal—I mean beholding the form of the good. This tendency is found in all activities that force the soul to turn its gaze toward the full perfection of being, a vision the soul must attain by any means.

Glaucon: I fully agree, Socrates.

Socrates: Then should we say that if geometry forces us to behold the essence, it concerns us; if it deals only with what changes, it doesn't concern us?

Glaucon: Yes, that's a good way to put it. **[527]**

Socrates: But currently the language used by people who practice geometry contradicts its true nature, as anyone who is acquainted with the subject will admit.

Glaucon: How so?

Socrates: They speak of finding the side, of squaring, applying, and adding, as if they were actually doing something that has practical consequences. But the real object of geometry is knowing, not doing.

Glaucon: That's true.

Socrates: Can we agree on another claim?

Glaucon: What claim?

Socrates: Do you agree that geometry aims at eternal knowledge, not at what is constantly changing?

Glaucon: I do agree; geometry seeks knowledge of what is always true.

Socrates: Then, my friend, geometry draws the soul toward truth, fostering philosophical thinking, elevating what is currently allowed to descend.

Glaucon: What can do that better?

Socrates: Then you should do a good job at teaching geometry to the inhabitants of your beautiful republic. You should also keep in mind the indirect benefits of learning geometry.

Glaucon: What kind of benefits?

Socrates: You have already mentioned the military benefits, and we know from experience that people who have studied geometry are better able to understand other subjects as well.

Glaucon: Yes, there is a world of difference between someone who has studied geometry and those who have not.

Socrates: Then let's establish this as the second subject our future leaders should study.

Glaucon: Agreed.

Socrates: What do you think about making astronomy the third subject they should study?

Glaucon: I think it's a good idea. Understanding the seasons and the passing of months and years is useful not only for farming and sailing but also to the military.

Socrates: Glaucon, you amuse me with your fear of what people will think if you prefer studies that have no use. I know it's difficult to convince them that every soul has a function that is cleansed and enlightened by these studies and dulled and blinded by other activities. The eye of the soul is far more precious than ten thousand of the eyes you have in your head. Only this one is able to see the truth. There are two kinds of people: one group will agree and be enlightened by these words, but the other will have no idea of what you are talking about. To them such studies seem to be nonsense, a worthless waste of time. **[528]** You should decide now which group you have in mind. Or perhaps you are not talking about either one but are simply following the argument for your own sake—which doesn't mean you would object if someone benefits from what you say.

Glaucon: I would prefer to carry on the argument for my own sake.

Socrates: Then we need to go back, because we made a mistake about which science comes next.

Glaucon: What was the mistake?

Socrates: After plane geometry we considered revolving solids, but we should have examined solids by themselves, moving from two dimensions to three, studying cubes and whatever else has depth.

Glaucon: That's true, Socrates, but I don't think that these subjects have yet been developed.

Socrates: There are two reasons for that. In the first place, they are difficult and no government supports them, so there is little interest in studying them. The second reason is that students cannot learn them unless they have a teacher, and such teachers are hard to find. Even if one could be found, the people who pursue these subjects are so conceited that they wouldn't pay any attention to such a teacher. Things would be different if the entire republic would respect and support them. Then they would listen, serious research would be conducted, and new discoveries would be made. Even now, when they are largely ignored and their worth and use are little known, they still make their way because of their natural appeal and may emerge into the light.

Glaucon: I agree that they are attractive subjects. But I still don't fully understand the change in the order of these studies. First you began with geometry of plane surfaces.

Socrates: Yes.

Glaucon: You placed astronomy next but then stepped back.

Socrates: That's right; the more haste the less speed. The unfortunate state of solid geometry made me pass over it and proceed to astronomy, the motion of solids.

Glaucon: Yes, that's what happened.

Socrates: So, let's assume that solid geometry will be developed once it is encouraged by the government, and then our future leaders can go on to astronomy as the fourth subject to be learned.

Glaucon: Now I understand the natural order of study, and I am ready to applaud your method of inquiry, and I will not praise astronomy simply for being useful. **[529]** I think everyone must agree that astronomy requires the soul to look upward, leading us from down here to up there.

Socrates: Everyone but me, because I think that those who confuse astronomy with philosophy make us look down rather than up.

Glaucon: What do you mean?

Socrates: You seem to have too broad a concept of what it means to know higher things. I suppose you think that throwing your head back and studying the decorations on the ceiling would count as using your mind and not just your eyes. You are probably right, and I am foolish, but I think that only the knowledge of being and what is invisible leads the soul to look upwards. Whether a person gapes at the heavens or squints at the ground in an attempt to study by sensing particular things, nothing can be learned, because we cannot know things of that kind. Whether you lie on the ground or float on your back in the water, your soul looks down, not up

Glaucon: You are right to scold me. I'm the one who is being foolish. But I would still like to know how astronomy can be learned so that it contributes to the knowledge we are seeking.

Socrates: Let me explain it this way. The embroidery of the heavens is stitched on a visible cloth, and even though it is the most beautiful and perfect among visible things, it is inferior to the reality of absolute velocity and absolute slowness that are relative to each other and carry within themselves the true number and true figure of everything they produce. We must apprehend them by reasoning and thinking, not by seeing. Do you disagree?

Glaucon: No, I agree with you.

Socrates: Therefore, we should use the embroidery of the starry sky as a model for the kind of knowledge we are seeking. Its beauty is like the beauty of sketches or drawings we might find from the hand of a great artist like Daedalus. Anyone who knows geometry would appreciate their exquisite skill but would never dream that we could find in them what is really equal or double or any other true proportion. **[530]**

Glaucon: No, that would be ridiculous.

Socrates: Do you believe that a genuine astronomer would think the same way about the movements of the stars, imagining that they are formed by their maker in the best possible way? The genuine astronomer will seek the true order, remembering that the ratio of night to day, or of day and night to the month, the month to the year, or the motion of the stars to all of them and to each other are all visible and material. The astronomer would never make the mistake of supposing that they are eternal and without deviation—that would be absurd—but will use all possible means to discover the truth about celestial motion.

Glaucon: When you put it that way, Socrates, I completely agree.

Socrates: Then if astronomy is to become a real part of education it should be taught like geometry—through problem-solving—not simply by observing what is in the sky. That way it will improve the natural use of reason.

Glaucon: Your approach is far superior to the method of present astronomers.

Socrates: Yes, and there are many other studies that should change in the same way if our legislation is to be effective. Perhaps you can give an example.

Glaucon: Not off the top of my head.

Socrates: Motion has many forms, not just one. Two of them are obvious, and there are others, but we can leave those to wiser heads than ours.

Glaucon: What are the two?

Socrates: We have already named one of them, but there is a second that corresponds to it.

Glaucon: What is it?

Socrates: One of them is for the ears, and the other for the eyes. Just as our eyes are able to look up at the stars, our ears can hear harmonious motion of another kind. According to the Pythagoreans, they are sister sciences. Shall we agree with them?

Glaucon: That sounds right to me.

Socrates: But music is a difficult subject, so we would be better off learning it from them. They can tell us whether there are any other applications of these sciences. But we must not lose track of our primary goal.

Glaucon: What goal do you have in mind?

Socrates: We are seeking perfect knowledge, and our students should aim for that end. We agreed that today's astronomers fall short of such knowledge. The way our students currently study music is equally empirical. **[531]** The sounds and harmonies they analyze are only the ones that they can hear, so their labor is worth no more than that of present astronomers.

Glaucon: Yes, it's amusing to hear them talk about what they call "condensed notes," and to watch them strain their ears as if they were listening to their neighbors. One group claims that they have found the smallest interval and propose that it should be taken as the unit of measurement. Another maintains the opposite theory and insist that there is no difference between the two sounds. Both groups value their ears more than their minds.

Socrates: I suppose you mean those people who tease and torture the strings and rack them on the pegs of the instrument. I could extend the metaphor and speak of the blows the plectrum gives, and the charges against the strings of being silent or of lying on the stand; but I'll abandon the image and say that these are not the people I mean. I'm talking about the Pythagoreans, the ones I just said we should ask about music. But they also make the same mistake as the astronomers; they investigate the numbers of the harmonies they hear, never reaching the stage of problem-solving to reveal the natural harmonies of number and determine why some numbers are harmonious and others are not.

Glaucon: Socrates, I think you are talking about a divine achievement.

Socrates: I would rather say it is useful, because it seeks the beautiful and the good, though it is useless for any other purpose.

Glaucon: That makes sense.

Socrates: But Glaucon, it is only when these studies reach the point of unity and connection with each other and reveal their mutual affinity that they will serve our purpose; otherwise they have no value.

Glaucon: I think that's right, Socrates, but you're describing a major project.

Socrates: Are you talking about the prelude or the song itself? Surely you know that what we have been talking about is merely the prelude to what lies ahead of us; I can't believe that you would consider mathematicians to be dialecticians.

Glaucon: Certainly not—only a few people I have known think that way.

Socrates: Do you think that those who are unable to justify their ideas and understand a justification when they hear it will have the knowledge we require? **[532]**

Glaucon: Again I would say no; our students must be able to justify their ideas.

Socrates: Glaucon, I think we have come at last to the song that dialectic sings—a mental performance the power of sight can only imitate. In our allegory we imagined looking at real animals, the distant stars, and finally at the sun itself. In this way a person begins to use dialectic, seeking to discover reality by thinking—not by relying on sense perception—and by settling for nothing less than goodness itself. This journey leads to the limit of what we can think, just as leaving the cave led to the limit of what we can see.

Glaucon: That's a good way to put it.

Socrates: Don't we call this journey dialectic?

Glaucon: Yes, that's what we call it.

Socrates: Then the release of the prisoners from their chains, their turning from the shadows to images and then to the light, their ascent from the cave to the sun while their eyes are still weak and they are unable to look at animals and plants and the light of the sun but are able to see divine images in the water and shadows of reality—rather than shadows of images cast by the firelight, which is itself only the image of the sun—this process of studying and pursuing the arts we recently described has the power to lift what is best in the soul to contemplate what is best in reality, just as the most lucid of the senses reveals what is brightest in the visible world.

Glaucon: I agree with what you are saying. Even though it is hard to believe, from another point of view it is even harder to deny. But whether or not it has been proved, let's assume it is true—I'm sure we will discuss it again on another occasion. Let's proceed from the prelude to the song itself and describe it in the same way. Tell us the nature of dialectic, its various aspects, and the paths that lead to the end of our journey. [533]

Socrates: My dear Glaucon, I'm afraid that you cannot follow me any farther, though I am quite willing to lead. Instead of presenting an image through allegory, I would have to disclose the truth itself as it appears to me. I'm not sure that what I see is true, but I am confident that there is truth to be grasped and that we should settle for nothing less. Don't you agree?

Glaucon: Of course.

Socrates: Can we also say that only the power of dialectic can reveal it to someone who has learned the subjects we were just discussing?

Glaucon: We can definitely say that.

Socrates: And nobody can establish that there is any other way of inquiry specifically designed to understand reality itself. All the other arts are concerned with human desire and opinion, cultivated for producing and nurturing things that grow or building and tending what is constructed. We did agree that mathematical studies such as geometry have some power to grasp reality, but they only dream about being, never able to capture it while fully awake. They work only with assumptions that they take for granted and cannot justify. When a person does not know first principles and cannot give an account of the conclusions and the reasoning leading to that conclusion, how could we possibly call such arbitrary agreement genuine knowledge?

Glaucon: That would be impossible.

Socrates: Then dialectic is the only form of inquiry that goes to the source, eliminating hypotheses and seeking the certainty of first principles. When the eye of the soul is buried in the muck of Hades,[3] dialectic releases it and turns it up toward the light, assisted by the studies we have been discussing. We are in the habit of calling those studies sciences, but they should have some other name, indicating greater clarity than opinion and less clarity than knowledge. This is what we previously called understanding.[4] But let's not quibble about names when we have matters of such importance to consider.

Glaucon: No, the particular name doesn't matter as long as it clearly distinguishes the state of mind we are discussing.

Socrates: Then we will be satisfied, as we were before, to make four distinctions, two for thought and two for opinion. We will call the first knowing, the second understanding, the third believing, and the fourth guessing. Opinion is concerned with what changes, but thinking pertains to being. **[534]** So, we can offer the following proportion:

> As being is to change, thought is to opinion.
> As knowing is to faith, understanding is to conjecture.

But that's enough about these distinctions concerning the objects of opinion and intellect. To treat it fully would be a long process, many times longer than this one.

Glaucon: I agree with you as far as I understand you.

Socrates: Do you also agree that the dialectician is the one who comprehends in thought and word the essence of each thing? And would you say that the person who is unable to comprehend and share the essence fails to know?

Glaucon: How could I deny that?

Socrates: Would you say the same about goodness? Would you say that until a person is able to identify the idea of the good and can meet all objections, able to refute them not by appeal to opinion but to existence, never faltering in the argument—would you say that unless a person can do that, it is not knowledge of goodness or any of its forms but the shadow cast by an opinion that leads such a person to dream and slumber in this life, never waking up here but descending to Hades and falling asleep there?

Glaucon: I would certainly say all of that.

Socrates: Nor would you allow the children of the republic we are nurturing and educating in words—if it should ever become real—to become rulers and take control of the most important matters if they are as irrational as the diagonal lines in a square.[5]

Glaucon: Certainly not.

Socrates: Then you will make it a law that they should have an education that will teach them to become proficient in asking and answering questions.

Glaucon: Yes, I will do that, but only with your help.

Socrates: Then I think that we can safely say that dialectic is the capstone of education for our future leaders. No other study can be placed higher than dialectic, which completes our educational program.

Glaucon: I agree. **[535]**

Socrates: Now we still have to decide who should learn these things and how these studies should be assigned.

Glaucon: Yes, that's clear.

Socrates: Do you remember how we previously decided to choose our leaders?

Glaucon: Of course I do. How could I forget?

Socrates: I assume that we should still choose the people with the same natures: we should select the most reliable, the bravest, and, if possible, the most attractive. Because of their nobility and strength, they should also have the natural qualities that foster their education.

Glaucon: What qualities do you have in mind?

Socrates: I think they should have a passion for study and the ability to learn quickly, because people are more likely to avoid hard thinking than rigorous physical exercise. The reason for that is that the pain of intellectual labor is closer to home, being proper to the mind and not shared with the body.

Glaucon: I think that's right.

Socrates: They should also have a good memory, be persistent, and should love to work; otherwise they will never endure the challenges to both mind and body.

Glaucon: The people we select should have those qualities as part of their nature.

Socrates: The current mistake is to allow people to study dialectic who have little aptitude for the subject, and that's why philosophy has fallen on hard times.[6] Only her true children should pursue philosophy.

Glaucon: What do you mean?

Socrates: I mean that our students should not be half-hearted in their approach. For example, some people like athletics, hunting, and all other physical activities, but they dislike learning, listening to discussions, and thinking. Others have the opposite problem, loving mental work but ignoring their bodies.

Glaucon: I agree fully with what you are saying.

Socrates: Concerning the truth, isn't a soul crippled that hates intentional lies in itself and in others and yet accepts unintentional lies and is not ashamed of being discovered wallowing like a pig in the mire of ignorance?

Glaucon: There's no doubt about that.

Socrates: Or consider moderation, courage, and generosity and every other aspect of goodness. **[536]** Here again we should take care to distinguish the legitimate from the illegitimate child, because whenever republics or individuals fail to recognize these qualities, they unconsciously make friends with those who are lame or deficient and even choose them to be rulers.

Glaucon: I've seen that happen too many times.

Socrates: Justice herself will praise those we nurture with our educational system if they are physically and mentally sound, and we will preserve the republic; but if they are the opposite, then our republic will collapse, and we will bring an even greater flood of ridicule on philosophy.

Glaucon: That would be a disgrace.

Socrates: It would, but now I'm afraid that I'm the one who is being ridiculous.

Glaucon: How so?

Socrates: I started taking our imagined republic much too literally and spoke with too much passion. When I saw philosophy dragged through the mud, I was carried away by my anger against the people who are responsible for her disgrace.

Glaucon: As I listened to you, I thought your anger was justified.

Socrates: Well, that's how I felt when I was speaking. Now we should remember that earlier, when we were selecting our rulers, we chose older people,[7] but that won't do now. Solon made a mistake when he said that as people age they learn many things. Old people can no more learn than they can run; youth is the proper time for great and significant work.

Glaucon: That's for sure.

Socrates: Therefore, mathematical reasoning and the other forms of education that prepare them for dialectic should be presented to them when they are children, but not under compulsion.

Glaucon: Why not?

Socrates: Because a free person ought to be free in acquiring knowledge. It does no harm to force people to exercise the body, but knowledge acquired under coercion will not last.

Glaucon: I suppose that's right.

Socrates: Glaucon, my good friend, don't use force but let their early education be a form of play; this will allow you to find out their natural inclinations. **[537]**

Glaucon: That sounds reasonable.

Socrates: Do you remember that we said young children should be taken on horseback to see battles, and when it is safe to take them close enough, to acquire a taste for blood like young hounds?

Glaucon: I do remember that.

Socrates: We should approach these other labors, lessons, and dangers in the same way. The name of anyone who excels in these ventures should be put on a list.

Glaucon: At what age?

Socrates: As soon as they have finished their compulsory physical training. That period of two or three years is useless for any other purpose because exercise and sleep are not conducive to learning. But it is an important test for young people to determine who is the best athlete.

Glaucon: I can't object to that.

Socrates: After that we will select the best twenty-year-olds and promote them to the highest rank. The subjects they learned as children, without any special order, will now be integrated, showing their connection to each other and to the nature of things.

Glaucon: Yes, that is the only kind of knowledge that lasts.

Socrates: And this is the point at which we can determine who has the potential for dialectic and who doesn't, because the ability to see how things are connected is the mark of the dialectician.

Glaucon: I agree.

Socrates: Keeping all this in mind, the next step is to select from those who excel in dialectic, who are the best students, the best soldiers, and adept in the public service required by law. When they are thirty years old, you will cull out the best from this second group and elevate them to an even higher rank, testing them through dialectic to determine which ones are able to dispense with sight and the other senses and can grasp being itself. But now we must be extremely careful.

Glaucon: What's the danger?

Socrates: Haven't you noticed the evil that comes from such inquiry as it is now practiced?

Glaucon: I'm not sure what you mean.

Socrates: I'm talking about the anarchy promoted by those who question everything.

Glaucon: That is a problem.

Socrates: Do you think we should be surprised by their actions? Rather than blame them, perhaps we should sympathize with them.

Glaucon: Why should we do that?

Socrates: Consider this analogy. Imagine a child who is switched with another one at birth and who is brought up in a large and wealthy family and by many flatterers. Eventually this child learns about the change but is unable to find its real parents.

[538] How would such a person respond to the substituted parents both during the period of not knowing of the switch and then after finding out the truth? Would you like to hear what I think?

Glaucon: Yes, tell me how you think such a person would act.

Socrates: I would guess that while ignorant of the switch, such a person would respect both father and mother more than the flatterers, would be willing to obey them, would provide for their needs, and would not be likely to do or say anything evil against them.

Glaucon: I too would expect that kind of behavior.

Socrates: But once the truth about the parents is known, I think that honor and respect for them might decrease and that the influence of the flatterers would increase. Perhaps they would become constant companions and the flatterer's way of life would be adopted; and lacking an unusually good character, the changeling would forget about parents and the rest of the family.

Glaucon: I suppose so, but I don't see how this applies to people who learn how to question and argue.

Socrates: Here's how. You know that we have convictions about what is just and good that we were taught as children. We were brought up under their authority, obeying and honoring them like parents.

Glaucon: That's right.

Socrates: And we are also attracted by practices that counter these beliefs—pleasures that flatter and lure our soul—but these pleasures will not influence people who have a strong sense of what is right and who continue to honor and obey the principles taught by their parents.

Glaucon: True.

Socrates: Now imagine a person in this condition who is confronted by someone who asks about the meaning of justice and goodness. Answering with the convictions learned at home is not enough, because the questioner refutes those answers with clever arguments, leading to the conclusion that nothing is any more right than wrong and destroying all the time-honored beliefs taught by the law and by parents. Do you think that this person will still honor and obey as before?

Glaucon: No, it is more probable that such a person would lose respect for those early convictions and no longer follow their direction.

Socrates: If these beliefs are no longer considered to be honorable and natural, who would pursue any way of life other than the one that flatters and pleases? **[539]**

Glaucon: Most people would choose the life of pleasure and flattery.

Socrates: So, one who observes the law would be transformed into an outlaw.

Glaucon: No doubt.

Socrates: As I said, we should not be surprised if people who learn to argue will begin to act this way—we might even extend our sympathy to them.

Glaucon: I think we might even pity them.

Socrates: To avoid such feelings of pity for your thirty-year-olds, you must be careful when you teach them how to reason.

Glaucon: Now I understand the danger, and I agree with you.

Socrates: As a precaution, could we make sure they don't learn it while they are too young? You have probably noticed that when young people get their first taste, they tend to argue for amusement, as if it were a game—always contradicting and refuting, copying those who refute them. They are like puppies that delight in tearing and pulling everyone who comes near.

Glaucon: Yes, they do seem to take great delight in tearing things apart.

Socrates: When they have won many battles and have often been defeated by others, they quickly get in the habit of violently rejecting everything that they believed before. The result is that both they and philosophy acquire a bad reputation.

Glaucon: That's the truth.

Socrates: But mature people have nothing to do with such madness. They follow the example of the dialectician who is seeking the truth, not the debater who contradicts for the sake of amusement. Through reason and moderation, they will bring honor both to themselves and to the art of dialectic.

Glaucon: Those are wise words, Socrates.

Socrates: We already prepared for this when we said that dialectic should be taught only to people who are orderly and stable, not to just anyone who comes upon argument by chance, as is now the practice.

Glaucon: We were right to make that rule.

Socrates: Do you think it will be enough to spend twice as many years on the serious study of dialectic as were devoted to bodily exercise?

Glaucon: Would that be four or six years?

Socrates: Let's say five years. After that they should be sent back into the cave and required to hold a military position or any public office for which they are qualified. This will give them substantial life experience, and they will have a chance to show whether they will be pulled in all directions by temptation or whether they will stand firm. **[540]**

Glaucon: How long should they be required to stay there?

Socrates: Fifteen years. When they have reached the age of fifty, those who still survive and have distinguished themselves both by what they have learned and by what they have done, are able to turn their mind's eye to the universal light that illuminates all things, seeing goodness itself. According to this pattern, they will bring order to the republic and to individual lives, especially their own. Philosophy will be their primary concern, but they must also take their turn toiling in political office and working for the common good. They will do this not as if it were some great thing but out of necessity. When they have nurtured others like themselves and left them to govern the republic, they will depart to the Islands of the Blessed and dwell there. The republic will honor them with monuments and public rituals and—if the oracle agrees—treat them like demigods, or at least as blessed and holy people.

Glaucon: Socrates, you are a sculptor, and you have made the men who rule our republic perfect in beauty.

Socrates: Yes, Glaucon, and also the women who rule, because what we have been saying applies both to the men and women who have such natural qualities.

Glaucon: You are right about that; since they are to have all things in common, women are to have the same opportunities as men.

Socrates: Now, Glaucon, would you agree that what we have said about the republic and its government is not mere fantasy? Although it would be difficult, it might be possible, yet only in the way we have imagined—when true philosophers rule in the republic. They would reject worldly honors as worthless, valuing only what is right and seeking only the honor that comes from doing what is right. They would consider justice to be the greatest and most important of all things, serving it and fostering it as they bring order to their own republic.

Glaucon: And how will they do that, Socrates? **[541]**

Socrates: Glaucon, let's propose that they send everyone more than ten years old out into the fields, taking possession of the younger children so that they will not acquire the habits of their parents. Then they could train them with their own habits and laws—I mean the ones we have just established. This is how the republic and the constitution we spoke about would be able to succeed most quickly and most easily. Such a republic would be truly happy and benefit its people greatly.

Glaucon: Yes, it certainly would be the quickest way. And, Socrates, I think you did describe superbly how such a constitution might come into existence.

Socrates: Then, have we said enough about the ideal republic and of the ruler who corresponds to that republic? It is now clear what kind of person that should be?

Glaucon: Yes, it is clear, and I agree that we have said quite enough.

ENDNOTES

1. Homer, *Odyssey*, xi. 489.
2. In Greek mythology, the Islands of the Blessed are a kind of paradise in which good people dwell forever.
3. See *Plato's Republic*, 363, where this is described as one of the punishments of evil people in Hades.
4. See *Plato's Republic*, 511.
5. Cf. *Plato's Meno*, 84–86, in which a young boy follows Socrates' dialectical lesson about the geometry of squares.
6. Cf. *Plato's Republic*, 495.
7. See *Plato's Republic*, 412.

Book Eight

[543] *Socrates:* Well, Glaucon, we have so far agreed that in our perfect republic women and children should be common to all, that everyone should learn the arts of war and peace, and that those who have become the best philosophers and the bravest soldiers should be their leaders.

Glaucon: Yes, Socrates, we have agreed on that.

Socrates: And we have also agreed that once the rulers take charge they should house the soldiers together the way we said, allowing nobody to own a private house. Do you also remember what we decided about their other property?

Glaucon: Yes, as I recall none of them was to have the possessions of ordinary people. Instead they were to be athletes, warriors, and guards. The other citizens were to provide support for their basic needs, and in return, they were to take care of themselves and the rest of the republic.

Socrates: That's right. Now that this part of our job is done, let's go back to the point where we digressed, so that we can return to our original path.

Glaucon: That should be easy. At that point you seem to have finished describing the republic, and you said that such a republic is good, and that the person corresponding to that form of the republic is also good. But you also had a lot more to say about both the republic and the person. **[544]** And you said that if this is the proper form of the republic, the others are flawed. I think you said that there are four major forms of them, and that it is worth examining not only their imperfections but also the flaws of the individuals that correspond to them. Once we have considered all of them and agreed about the best and the worst, then you said that we might determine whether the best is also the happiest and the worst the most miserable. But when I asked you about those four forms of government, Polemarchus and

Adeimantus jumped into the discussion and you started from the beginning, finally arriving where we are now.

Socrates: You remember well, Glaucon.

Glaucon: Then, you must put yourself in the same position, as a wrestler would, and let me ask the same questions as before, making sure that you answer the same as you would have answered then.

Socrates: I will if I can.

Glaucon: I am especially interested in hearing about the four flawed forms of government you had in mind.

Socrates: That's not hard to do. To the extent that those four governments have distinct names, the first is called timocracy. It has existed in Crete and Sparta and it is widely praised. Next is oligarchy, which is not so well respected and has many evils. Third is democracy, which naturally follows oligarchy, though it is quite different. Finally comes high-born tyranny, the fourth and most diseased form a republic can take. Glaucon, can you think of any other kind of constitution that has a distinct form? Of course there are dynasties and kingships that are bought and sold as well as some other intermediate forms of government found both among Greeks and non-Greeks.

Glaucon: Yes, I have heard that there are many strange forms of government in existence.

Socrates: Are you aware that there are as many basic forms of government as there are kinds of human character? Or do you suppose that republics spring from oaks and rocks rather than from human nature which, like a weight added to scales, tips the balance?

Glaucon: I agree that republics resemble human beings; they grow out of human character.

Socrates: Then if there are five forms of republic, there must be five kinds of individual soul.

Glaucon: That's right.

Socrates: We have already said that the type corresponding to aristocracy is just and good. **[545]** Now we have to describe the inferior kinds, such as those who follow the Spartan model and love competition and seek honor. We should also examine the character of the oligarch, the democrat, and the tyrant. Let's place the most just and the least just side by side and compare their relative happiness or misery. This will complete our investigation, allowing us to determine whether we should seek injustice, as Thrasymachus advises, or seek justice, as our present argument suggests.

Glaucon: That is obviously how we should proceed.

Socrates: Then let's follow the same plan as before, first looking at the republic and then proceeding to the individual. Let's begin with the government based on the love of honor—I don't know what to call it other than timocracy—and then consider the character of the individual who corresponds to it. After that we will consider oligarchy and the oligarch, democracy and the democratic person, and finally we will inspect tyranny and look into the tyrant's soul. Then we can make our final decision.

Glaucon: That's a reasonable way to view and judge in such an important matter.

Socrates: First let's think about how aristocracy yields to timocracy, assuming that political change arises from divisions among the ruling powers; but if the government remains united, no matter how small it is, it cannot be altered.

Glaucon: I agree with that assumption.

Socrates: Then how will change take place in a republic, and in what way will the rulers and their assistants come to disagree among themselves? Shall we follow Homer and pray to the Muses, asking them to tell us how conflict was first kindled?[1] Shall we imagine them, in tragic style, treating us like children, pretending to be serious and enchanting us with solemn words?

Glaucon: What would they say? **[546]**

Socrates: Something like this:

Formed in this way, a republic can hardly be shaken; but considering that everything that has a beginning also has an end, even this constitution will in time perish and come to dissolution. This is how the dissolution will take place. In plants that grow in the earth, as well as animals which move on the surface, fertility and sterility of soul and body occur when cycles are completed, short-lived for those whose existence is brief and long-lived for those whose existence is long. But the wisdom and education of your rulers will not attain full knowledge of human fecundity and sterility. The laws that regulate them will not be discovered by computation based on sense experience, but will escape them, and they will bring children into the world even when they should not. Everything that has a divine birth has a period that is contained in a perfect number; but human birth is regulated by a number in which first increments—created by involution and evolution—having been given three intervals and four terms of approximating and differentiating, and, at times, increasing and waning numbers—make everything agreeable and commensurable. The base of these, with a third added, when joined with a figure of five and raised to the third power, produces two harmonies. The first—a square—is a hundred times as great; and the other—a figure having one side equal to the former—taken one way, is equilateral, but considered another way, is oblong, consisting of a hundred numbers squared upon rational diameters of a square, the side of which is five, each of them being less by one or less by two perfect squares of irrational diameters and a hundred cubes of three. Now this number represents a geometrical figure that has control over the good and the evil of births. When our leaders are ignorant of the right seasons and unite bride and bridegroom out of due time, then the children will not be good or happy. And though the best of them will be appointed by their predecessors, still they will be unworthy to hold their places; and when they come to power as leaders, they will soon fail in taking care of us. Valuing us, the Muses, far less than they should, first by undervaluing music and then by neglecting athletics, our young people will be less cultivated. In the succeeding generation, rulers will be appointed who have none of the qualities of leaders who can test the metal of your different races, which, like Hesiod's, are of gold, silver, brass, and iron. **[547]** *Iron will be mingled with silver, brass, and gold, and hence there will arise* *inequality and irregularity, which always and in all places are causes of enmity and war. Such is the origin of conflict, wherever arising.*—

This is the answer of the Muses to us.

Glaucon: Yes, and we may assume that they answer truly.

Socrates: Of course, because they are Muses.

Glaucon: What do the Muses say next?

Socrates: They continue this way:

When conflict arises, the races are pulled in different directions. The races of iron and brass begin to acquire money, land and houses, gold and silver. But the gold and silver races, having the true riches in their own nature, incline toward goodness and the ancient order of things. When the races begin to compete with each other, they start using force against each other. At last they agree to divide their possessions and assign their lands and houses to individuals. They enslave their former friends and counselors, whom they had protected as free people, making them their subjects and servants, while they themselves are occupied with war and with watching over the others.

Glaucon: Socrates, I think that adequately explains the origin of the change.

Socrates: Yes, and the new government that arises in this way will take on a form midway between oligarchy and aristocracy.

Glaucon: That sounds right.

Socrates: After this transformation takes place, let's consider their way of life. Clearly the new republic will have the qualities of oligarchy and of aristocracy, along with some of its own.

Glaucon: That's true.

Socrates: It will resemble the perfect republic by honoring its rulers; by keeping the military from working in agriculture, manual labor, and the business of making money; by providing common meals; and by requiring athletic and military training.

Glaucon: Those are important elements that should be preserved.

Socrates: But they would fear putting wise people in power, because the wise are subtle and complex rather than literal and earnest. They would prefer passionate and direct characters, who are by nature suited for war rather than peace. They would value military strategy and planning and concentrate on making war—the distinguishing feature of this form of government. **[548]**

Glaucon: I can think of many examples of such governments.

Socrates: People of this kind lust after money, as do those who live in oligarchies, longing to hoard gold and silver which they will hide in dark places. They will have banks and treasuries where they will deposit and conceal their wealth. They will build walls around their houses, which they will use as private nests where they will spend lots of money on their wives and anyone else they please.

Glaucon: That's true, Socrates.

Socrates: They cannot be open about how they got the money they love so much, so they will be stingy with it; but they will gladly spend other people's money, stealing their pleasures and running away from the law like children from their father. They have been trained by force, not educated by persuasion. They ignore the true Muse of thinking and philosophy and prefer athletics to music and poetry.

Glaucon: I think we can safely say that this form of government is a mixture of good and bad elements.

Socrates: Yes, there is a mixture, but one aspect dominates the others—the spirit of competition and the drive for success, which spring from the willful and high-spirited aspect of the soul.

Glaucon: You're absolutely right.

Socrates: This is the origin and nature of timocracy; but we have given only an outline of it. We need not elaborate on this sketch, because we have said enough to show the nature of the just and the unjust. It would be an endless job to go through every possible form of republic and all the different types of human character in order to cover all aspects.

Glaucon: I agree.

Socrates: Now we must examine the kind of person who corresponds to this type of government. How did such a person come into being, and what qualities does that person have?

Adeimantus: I think that in loving combat and competition such a person is a lot like Glaucon.

Socrates: Adeimantus, I think they are similar in that respect, but they differ in other ways.

Adeimantus: In what ways?

Socrates: I think that such a person would be more obstinate and less accomplished in music and poetry than Glaucon, but would still be a lover of the Muses and, even though a careful listener, would not be a good speaker. **[549]** A person of this sort would be rough with slaves, unlike an educated person who is too dignified for that, would be courteous with equals, and would readily submit to superiors. Such people love power and honor, claiming the right to rule not because of the ability to speak well or any similar quality but because of being an accomplished soldier who is good with weapons. That kind of person also loves athletics and hunting.

Adeimantus: I think you have well described the character of timocracy.

Socrates: When young, such a person will despise wealth, but as time passes will become a lover of money. This person will not faithfully follow goodness, having lost the best safeguard against a greedy nature.

Adeimantus: What is that?

Socrates: Reason, tempered by the arts, is the best way to nurture and protect goodness throughout life.

Adeimantus: I agree, Socrates.

Socrates: This is the timocratic person who resembles the timocratic republic.

Adeimantus: You are right.

Socrates: That is where such a person comes from. Often he is the son of a courageous father who dwells in a poorly governed republic. The father declines the honors and offices offered to him, hesitates to file lawsuits, and is sometimes willing to waive his rights in order to avoid trouble.

Adeimantus: How does the son develop?

Socrates: The son's character begins to form when he hears his mother complaining that her husband is not one of the rulers, causing her to be snubbed by other women. And when she sees that her husband is not eager to make money, and when she sees that he is not interested in battling and brawling in public meetings or private lawsuits, taking such things with a grain of salt; and when she observes that he ignores her and is absorbed in his own thoughts, she is extremely annoyed and tells her son that his father is much too easy-going and is not a real man, along with a number of similar complaints that such women love to utter.

Adeimantus: Yes, I have heard many such attacks, each with its own particular style.

Socrates: And, as you know, Adeimantus, long-time servants of the family who are expected to be loyal talk privately to the son in the same way. When they learn that someone owes money to their father or is doing something wrong to him and he fails to prosecute them, the servants tell the son that when he grows up he must retaliate and be more of a man than his father. **[550]** When he leaves the house, the son observes the same sort of thing. Those who mind their own business in the republic are considered to be foolish and are not respected, but the ones who stick their nose into everybody's business are honored and applauded. The young man, seeing all these things and hearing his father's words, takes a close look at his father's way of life and compares him with the others. As a result he is pulled in opposite directions. His father fosters and nourishes the rational principle in his soul, and the others encourage his passions and appetites. He does not have a basically bad nature, but fallen into bad company, he is brought by their mutual influence to the point where he surrenders his soul to the principles of competition and passion, becoming proud and ambitious.

Adeimantus: I think you have accurately described the development of such a person.

Socrates: Then we have accounted for the second kind of government and the second type of character.

Adeimantus: We have.

Socrates: Next shall we follow Aeschylus and look at another kind of person posted at another gate, or, following our plan, shall we begin with the type of government?

Adeimantus: Let's follow our plan.

Socrates: I think the next form is oligarchy.

Adeimantus: What kind of government do you mean by oligarchy?

Socrates: It is one that rests on the value of property; the rich have power and the poor do not.

Adeimantus: I understand.

Socrates: Shall I explain the transformation from timocracy to oligarchy?

Adeimantus: Please do.

Socrates: Well, even a blind person can see how that change takes place.

Adeimantus: How does it happen?

Socrates: The pile of money they have hoarded causes the problem and leads to the demise of timocracy. First they create legal loopholes when spending money on themselves, but eventually they and their wives ignore the law completely.

Adeimantus: That sounds about right.

Socrates: When one sees another do this, they become rivals in such evasion, and soon the entire population joins in.

Adeimantus: Yes, it is likely to happen that way.

Socrates: The more success they have in business, the more they value it and the less they value goodness. When riches and goodness are placed on the scales of a balance, the one rises as the other falls.

Adeimantus: That's true. **[551]**

Socrates: So, as wealth and wealthy people are honored in a republic, goodness and good people are dishonored.

Adeimantus: Clearly.

Socrates: And what is honored is cultivated, and what has no honor is neglected.

Adeimantus: That's right.

Socrates: And finally, instead of loving competition and glory, people become lovers of business and money. They honor and worship the rich, putting them in office, but they despise the poor.

Adeimantus: That's exactly how it happens.

Socrates: Then they set up laws requiring a certain amount of money to qualify for citizenship. Depending on how exclusive the oligarchy is, the sum is larger or smaller. They forbid anyone who lacks a specified amount of property to participate in the government, enforcing these changes in the constitution with military power if intimidation does not work.

Adeimantus: True.

Socrates: In general, this is how oligarchy comes about.

Adeimantus: I agree, but what are the main features of this form of government? Also, we said that oligarchy has many evils. What are its flaws?

Socrates: Let's begin with the requirement for citizenship. Consider what would happen if pilots were selected according to the amount of money they own, and a poor person, who is a better pilot, were rejected.

Adeimantus: I don't think I would like to take that trip.

Socrates: Can we apply this principle to all forms of leadership?

Adeimantus: Yes, I think we can.

Socrates: What about the governing of a republic—is that an exception?

Adeimantus: Not at all; it is especially true in governing republics, because governing is the most difficult and most important of all.

Socrates: Then this is the first major defect in oligarchy.

Adeimantus: Clearly.

Socrates: There is another flaw that is about as bad.

Adeimantus: Which one do you have in mind?

Socrates: Such a republic will always be divided, being not one but two—one of the poor and the other of the rich. They dwell together, but they will always be plotting against each other.

Adeimantus: Yes, that is just as bad as the first defect.

Socrates: Another problem is that they would find it difficult to wage war against an external enemy, because they are more afraid of arming the population than of the enemy. But if they do not arm the people, then they will indeed be oligarchs—few to fight and few to rule. Nor can they hire mercenaries to fight for them; they love money so much, they refuse to raise taxes.

Adeimantus: They do have a problem.

Socrates: And what about our earlier objection to such a government—that the same people are responsible for everything, being farmers, business people, and soldiers all at the same time? [552] Do you think that is a good way of doing things?

Adeimantus: Of course not; we have rejected that arrangement several times.

Socrates: There is one more evil, perhaps the greatest of all.

Adeimantus: What's that?

Socrates: For the first time we have a political order in which one might forfeit one's entire property to someone else and continue to dwell in the republic without really being part of it, neither doing business, working in the arts, nor serving in the military. In such a republic you could become poor and completely helpless.

Adeimantus: Yes, that happens in this form of government.

Socrates: There seems to be no defense against that in an oligarchy. It is a republic of both extremes: great wealth and utter poverty.

Adeimantus: I'm afraid you are right.

Socrates: Let's think again about the person. If you were wealthy and spending your money freely, would you be one bit more valuable to the republic than if you were living on the streets? Or would you seem to be a leader but in reality you would be only a consumer?

Adeimantus: I think you said it well, Socrates. Such a person only seems to be a ruler but is really just a spender.

Socrates: Perhaps we can say that such a person is a drone, a pest in the republic, who functions much as does the drone in a hive.

Adeimantus: That's a good analogy.

Socrates: Adeimantus, the god has made flying drones without stingers, but also walking ones that have dreadful stingers. In their old age the kind that lack stingers become beggars, whereas criminals spring from the ones with stingers.

Adeimantus: That's where they come from.

Socrates: So, when you see beggars in a republic, criminals such as thieves, pickpockets, and temple robbers will be hiding nearby.

Adeimantus: No doubt.

Socrates: So we find beggars in oligarchies?

Adeimantus: Nearly everybody is a beggar who is not a ruler.

Socrates: May we be so bold as to suppose that there will be lots of criminals in such a republic, armed with stingers, who the police must restrain by force?

Adeimantus: We may.

Socrates: And can we trace the existence of such people to lack of education, poor training, and an inferior form of government in the republic?

Adeimantus: We can.

Socrates: Then this is the form of government called oligarchy, and these are some of the evils it contains. There may be others.

Adeimantus: Socrates, I think you have described it well. **[553]**

Socrates: Let's put aside the form of government in which rulers are selected for their wealth and proceed to consider the nature and origin of the kind of individual who corresponds to it.

Adeimantus: Yes, let's do that.

Socrates: First we must account for the change from a timocratic to an oligarchic character.

Adeimantus: How does it happen?

Socrates: Suppose a timocratic man has a son. The son begins by emulating his father and walking in his footsteps. But all of a sudden he sees his father crash against the republic, losing everything he has, like a ship that strikes a sunken reef. He may have been a general or some other high officer brought to trial on false charges and either put to death or exiled, deprived of all citizenship, and stripped of his property.

Adeimantus: Such things often happen.

Socrates: The son observes all this and is devastated; through fear he deposes the love of honor and courage from the throne they once occupied in his soul. Humbled by poverty, he turns to making money and by thrift and hard work little by little scrapes together a fortune. Don't you think that such a man would be likely to place greed and the love of money on that vacant throne, treating them like the Great King inside himself, adorning them with tiara, royal collar, and Persian sword?

Adeimantus: I think it is quite likely.

Socrates: Once he makes the rational and high-spirited aspects of his soul sit obediently on either side and teaches them their place, he compels one to calculate the method by which smaller sums may be converted into larger ones and forces the other into admiration of wealth and wealthy people. The only ambition he will tolerate is the desire to get rich and the means that makes it possible.

Adeimantus: No conversion is as quick and certain as when a lover of honor becomes a lover of money.

Socrates: Do you mean that the lover of money is the oligarchic person?

Adeimantus: Yes, and I mean that the individual who evolves resembles the form of government from which oligarchy evolved.

Socrates: Let's see whether they really are alike.

Adeimantus: Yes, let's compare the person and the republic.
[554]

Socrates: First of all they resemble each other by the value they place on wealth.

Adeimantus: That above all.

Socrates: This individual is thrifty and hard working, one who satisfies only the most basic desires and spends money only on necessities, rejecting all other desires as useless and too expensive.

Adeimantus: That's correct.

Socrates: You are describing a stingy person who is only interested in making a profit and hoarding it away—the kind of individual many people envy. Is this the person who resembles oligarchy?

Adeimantus: That's what I think; both the person and the republic place the highest value on money.

Socrates: Then you would not consider such a person to be properly educated.

Adeimantus: No, I don't think so; educated people would not select Plutus, the blind god of wealth, to lead their chorus.[2]

Socrates: That's a good point. Now consider this: Given such poor education, it would seem that the qualities of the drone would emerge, those of both the beggar and the criminal. But such individuals are able to keep those forces in check by a strong will.

Adeimantus: That sounds right.

Socrates: So where should we look to discover these criminal tendencies?

Adeimantus: Perhaps you can tell me.

Socrates: They would probably emerge if such a person were appointed to be the guardian of an orphan and given control of a large estate or provided some similar opportunity for unjustly adding wealth.

Adeimantus: You are probably right.

Socrates: Normally such individuals have a reputation for being honest. They are able to use the better part of their nature to keep their desires under control, not because they are persuaded by reason that such actions are unjust but out of fear of losing the rest of their wealth.

Adeimantus: I agree with your analysis.

Socrates: It is when you put such people in charge of other people's money that the desires of the drone come out.

Adeimantus: They find it hard to resist such temptation.

Socrates: A man like that is at war with himself. He is two men, not one, but generally his better desires prevail over the worse ones.

Adeimantus: I think that's right.

Socrates: For these reasons, this individual will be more decent than many others, but the goodness of a unified and harmonious soul will lie far beyond reach.

Adeimantus: True. **[555]**

Socrates: The oligarchic character will avoid competing for political office or for public recognition out of fear that this would awaken the slumbering desires for honor and fame and require the spending of large amounts of money. Such people, in oligarchic fashion, use only a small part of their resources, losing the battle but saving money.

Adeimantus: Your description is accurate, Socrates.

Socrates: So, there seems to be no doubt that this stingy lover of money corresponds to the oligarchic republic.

Adeimantus: No doubt at all.

Socrates: Then it is time to consider democracy and the democratic individual. We must analyze their origin and nature so that we may compare and evaluate both the individual and the form of government.

Adeimantus: That is the method that we are using.

Socrates: See if you agree with my account of the change from oligarchy to democracy. The rulers in an oligarchy have an unlimited love of money, so they do everything they can to increase their wealth and property—the source of their power. They refuse to pass laws that would curb the excesses of undisciplined young people, because they will profit from their excessive spending. They will lend them money and seize their property when they default on their loans, further increasing their own wealth and prestige.

Adeimantus: That is a probable scenario.

Socrates: It is impossible for the citizens to worship wealth in a republic and simultaneously cultivate the spirit of moderation. They will have to give up one or the other.

Adeimantus: That's clear.

Socrates: We have said that in oligarchic republics people from good families are often careless and extravagant, lose their fortune, and become beggars.

Adeimantus: It frequently happens that way.

Socrates: But they remain in the republic, armed with stingers. Some are in debt, some have lost their citizenship, and some are in both conditions. Pretty soon they begin to hate and plot against the people who took their property and everyone else. Then they call for revolution.

Adeimantus: Such an outcome seems to be unavoidable.

Socrates: The money-lovers in this republic avert their eyes, pretending not to see the people they have already ruined, and continue to insert their own kind of stinger—their money—into unsuspecting victims, collecting interest and expanding their wealth, as parents multiply through their children. In this way they increase the number of beggars and drones.

Adeimantus: Yes, we see them everywhere. **[556]**

Socrates: This corruption spreads like wild fire, and they refuse to quench it either by restricting the way people transfer their property or by another law that compels people to be good.

Adeimantus: What other law?

Socrates: One that requires lenders to enter into contracts at their own risk, placing the burden on them rather than their victims. Do you think that might curb some of the speculation and corruption?

Adeimantus: I think it would.

Socrates: As it is now, the people in power, led by the motives we were just discussing, treat the ordinary people badly, while they live a luxurious life—especially the young people who have never worked a day and become lazy both in body and mind. As a result they are entirely ruled by pleasure and pain.

Adeimantus: That's all they seem to care about.

Socrates: Their only concern is making money, and they are as indifferent to goodness as are the beggars.

Adeimantus: They act as if goodness does not exist.

Socrates: Now let's imagine the rulers and the people they rule thrown together on a trip to a religious ceremony or in military service as soldiers or shipmates or some such activity. When they observe each other during a time of danger, the poor are no longer despised by the rich. The poor person, lean and sunburned, when placed side by side in battle with a rich person who is pale, flabby, panting, and helpless, will probably realize that the rich dominate only because no one has had the courage to challenge them. When they later meet in private, they might agree that these rich people are not worth much in a fight and are easy to defeat.

Adeimantus: Yes, it is easy to imagine such a conversation.

Socrates: If a body is weak, it takes only a small external cause to bring on disease. Sometimes an internal crisis evolves even without outside forces. In the same way, if a republic is weak, it takes little to provoke illness. The democrats line up against the oligarchs, possibly with aid from external allies who are like them; the republic gets sick and wages war on itself. Sometimes this happens even without foreign help. **[557]**

Adeimantus: I can think of several examples of this sort.

Socrates: Democracy comes into being when the poor people have overthrown their rulers, killing some and sending others into exile. Those who remain are given an equal share of freedom and power, often electing the new leaders by lot.

Adeimantus: That is how democracy comes about, whether created by fighting or when the others surrender through fear.

Socrates: What kind of life do they lead? What sort of government is it? Once again we will assume that the individual corresponds to the republic.

Adeimantus: Once again I agree.

Socrates: First of all, they would seem to be free. This kind of republic is free and open, one in which you can say and do whatever you please.

Adeimantus: That's what they say.

Socrates: With this kind of freedom, people can create the life they choose for themselves.

Adeimantus: Clearly.

Socrates: In such a republic, I assume you can find all kinds of different people.

Adeimantus: Probably more than in any other type of republic.

Socrates: Then this would seem to make it the loveliest kind; like an embroidered robe with spangles and flowers, this form of republic would glitter with customs and qualities from all human cultures. Many people will find it to be the most attractive, just as women and children delight in the variety of brightly colored objects.

Adeimantus: Yes, Socrates, they will prefer it over all others.

Socrates: That means it would be a good place to go shopping for a government.

Adeimantus: Why is that?

Socrates: With all that choice, they have a full stock of constitutions. If someone wishes to create a republic, as we are doing now, it would be a good idea to visit a democracy as you might go to a bazaar and pick out one that suits you. Once you have made your choice, then you could use it as the foundation for your republic.

Adeimantus: You would definitely have a lot of samples to choose from.

Socrates: In such a republic you would not have to govern, even if you had the ability, nor would you have to be governed—unless you want to. You would not have to go to war when other people do or be at peace when others are at peace—unless you want to. You have the option to hold office or be a legislator, even if there is a law that forbids you to do so. Is this not a delightful way of life, at least for the moment? **[558]**

Adeimantus: Yes it is—for the moment.

Socrates: Don't you think it is charming how in such a republic convicted criminals remain calm, even if they have been condemned to death or exile, parading through the streets as if nobody saw or cared—like an invisible hero back from the dead?

Adeimantus: Yes, Socrates, we seem to see that more and more often.

Socrates: We should also mention the degree of tolerance found in democracy and the disregard of trifles such as the lofty principles we have been praising as the foundation of the republic. For example, we said that there will never be a good person who has failed to delight in beauty already at an early age and later pursued it as a serious study, except in rare cases. How boldly does democracy discard such ideas, ignoring the activities that cultivate a statesman, being satisfied if a politician merely claims to be a friend of the people.

Adeimantus: An entirely noble form of government!

Socrates: These and similar qualities are proper to democracy, a totally delightful kind of republic, full of variety and diversity, dispensing equality to equals and unequals alike.

Adeimantus: These charms are widely known.

Socrates: Now let's take a look at the individual in a democracy and consider how such a person is created.

Adeimantus: A good idea.

Socrates: It is probable that this kind of individual had a stingy and oligarchic father who tried to rear the child in the same way.

Adeimantus: Exactly right.

Socrates: Like the father, the child represses the pleasures of spending—which are considered unnecessary—and fosters the pleasures of earning money. Perhaps I can make my argument more clear if I distinguish between necessary and unnecessary pleasures.

Adeimantus: I would appreciate that.

Socrates: Necessary pleasures are those we cannot do without and which benefit us. They are properly called necessary, because we are attracted to them by nature.

Adeimantus: That sounds right. **[559]**

Socrates: Then it would be correct to call them necessary?

Adeimantus: Yes.

Socrates: Concerning desires we can get rid of, especially if we begin when we are young—I mean the kind which do us no good and which are often bad—would we be right in saying that they are unnecessary?

Adeimantus: We would.

Socrates: What if we consider an example of each kind so that we may form a general idea of them?

Adeimantus: Yes. Let's do that.

Socrates: Take the desire for eating, I mean basic food to the extent that it is required for health and strength. Would that not fall into the class of what is necessary?

Adeimantus: I think so.

Socrates: The pleasure of eating is necessary in two ways, first as beneficial and also as needed to support life itself.

Adeimantus: Yes.

Socrates: So foods are only necessary when they are good for health.

Adeimantus: That's right.

Socrates: And the desire for the kind of food we can live without, especially if we have good training when we are young, and which might harm the body and undermine moderation and good judgment in the soul—this kind of pleasure we can rightly call unnecessary.

Adeimantus: We can.

Socrates: So we might say that those unnecessary pleasures are a loss, whereas the other ones are a gain—some are productive but others are not.

Adeimantus: You could put it that way.

Socrates: And what should we say about sexual pleasure? Should we apply the same principle?

Adeimantus: Of course.

Socrates: Then should we say that the drone, of whom we were just speaking, overflowing with pleasures and desires of this sort, is governed by what we have called unnecessary desires, in contrast to the thrifty oligarch who is motivated only by the necessary ones?

Adeimantus: I think it is safe to say that.

Socrates: Now let's see how the democratic individual grows out of the oligarchic one. Let's see what you think of my account.

Adeimantus: What is it?

Socrates: When a young person who is reared, as we said, in a crude and stingy way, tastes the drones' honey and spends time with fierce and cunning characters who provide all sorts of fancy pleasures, then the change from oligarchy to democracy takes place.

Adeimantus: That seems to be inevitable.

Socrates: Do you remember that we said revolution comes about in the republic when like-minded forces from the outside help overthrow the existing order, bringing about the change from oligarchy to democracy?

Adeimantus: I do.

Socrates: We have a similar situation in the individual. When a young person encounters desires in others that correspond to similar ones inside, like fosters like, and they ignite passions internal to the soul.

Adeimantus: That makes sense.

Socrates: If the oligarchic side has allies among family or friends, and they scold and oppose this tendency toward unnecessary pleasures, factions and counter-factions arise within the soul and civil war breaks out. **[560]**

Adeimantus: I have often seen it happen.

Socrates: Sometimes the democratic inclinations give way to the oligarchic, leading to the death of some desires and exile for others; a sense of shame enters into the soul, and order is restored.

Adeimantus: Yes, that sometimes happens.

Socrates: But as soon as the old desires are driven out, fresh ones just like them appear. Without skillful nurture by parents, such passions grow strong and plentiful.

Adeimantus: How true.

Socrates: Then these passions lure the young person back into the company of old friends, and together they secretly breed a whole new crowd.

Adeimantus: A familiar pattern.

Socrates: They capture the fortress of the young person's soul once they realize that it is lacking in knowledge, sound practice, and true dialogue, which are the best guards and sentinels of the minds of people loved by the gods.

Adeimantus: That's right.

Socrates: Lying, bragging, and pretending emerge to fill that place in the young person's soul.

Adeimantus: How often it happens that way!

Socrates: So this kind of individual openly returns to live in the land of the lotus-eaters.[3] If any friends of the oligarchic element of this soul try to send help, self-serving words shut the gates of the royal fortress, refusing to let them enter. Such a soul will not even listen to venerable private delegates who come to negotiate. The champions of unrestrained desires win every contest, calling self-control cowardice and shame foolishness, dragging them through the mud and throwing them off the field. They contend that moderation and restraint are unrefined and stingy. Leading a pack of unnecessary passions, they drive the other passions out.

Adeimantus: Those are powerful enemies.

Socrates: Once they have prepared the soul for the great mysteries by purging it of its former qualities, they bring back insolence, anarchy, wastefulness, and impudence in splendid attire, with garlands on their heads and followed by many attendants, they sing their praises and call them by sweet names. Insolence they call good breeding, anarchy becomes liberty, wastefulness is generosity, and impudence is courage. **[561]** Is this not the way the young person acquires a new nature, leaving behind the old one that was educated in the school of necessity and passing into license and lust for useless and unnecessary pleasures?

Adeimantus: Yes, that is obviously the way.

Socrates: After this change takes place, this new individual devotes as much money, effort, and time on unnecessary pleasures as on necessary ones. With good fortune, and if not totally intoxicated by the charms of unrestrained appetites, as time passes it is possible that some of the exiled inclinations will be allowed to return to this soul as it matures. If so, these different sorts of pleasures will be balanced by living in a kind of equilibrium, first enjoying one and, when satisfied, enjoying another, being quite impartial in encouraging all of them as they take turns.

Adeimantus: I know many people who live that way.

Socrates: Then you also know that such people refuse to allow sound words of advice into their fortress. If someone says that one kind of pleasure satisfies good and beautiful desires, and the others satisfy pernicious ones, and suggests that some should be cultivated and encouraged and others ought to be reduced and ignored, such advice will be rejected with the facile answer that all desires and pleasures are of equal value.

Adeimantus: We should not be surprised if this kind of individual responds that way.

Socrates: Yes, they go through the day indulging the appetite of the hour, sometimes getting drunk and listening to sensuous music, and then drinking only water and dieting. Then they take up sports. Next they forget about everything and do nothing. Then they embrace the life of philosophy, which is quickly replaced with politics, where they can say and do anything that comes into their head. If they become interested in the martial arts, they imitate the warrior. If making money strikes their fancy, they start a business. Their lives have neither law nor order; they consider the life of pleasure and freedom to be all there is to happiness.

Adeimantus: Socrates, I think you have done an excellent job of describing the person who thinks that equality is the highest value.

Socrates: Yes, this kind of person is many-sided, uniting pluralistic customs and predispositions, just like the democratic republic. Many other individuals and many republics will admire this person who exemplifies so many different patterns of life.

Adeimantus: Yes, that's how it is.

Socrates: Can we call such an individual the democratic type of person who corresponds to the democratic form of a republic? **[562]**

Adeimantus: That's exactly what we should do.

Socrates: Now comes the most beautiful form of both the individual and the republic—tyranny and the tyrant.

Adeimantus: I'm eager to hear your description.

Socrates: First, my friend, we must explain how tyranny evolves. Would you say that it is likely to arise out of democracy?

Adeimantus: Of course.

Socrates: Can we say that tyranny springs from democracy in much the same way that democracy emerges from oligarchy?

Adeimantus: I'm not quite sure what you have in mind.

Socrates: Did we not say that oligarchy grows from the idea that goodness is the same as great wealth?

Adeimantus: Yes, that is what we said.

Socrates: And did we not also say that the desire for wealth and the neglect of everything else is what leads to the destruction of oligarchy?

Adeimantus: Yes.

Socrates: And democracy is also built on an idea of goodness, but the desire for that good also leads to its downfall.

Adeimantus: What notion of goodness do you mean?

Socrates: Freedom. Have you not heard people claim that freedom is the highest value and that a democracy is the only place to dwell for anyone who is free by nature?

Adeimantus: Yes, Socrates, I have often heard such claims.

Socrates: Well, it seems that the insatiable desire for freedom and the neglect of other values brings about the transformation from democracy to tyranny.

Adeimantus: Why is that?

Socrates: When the thirst for freedom is combined with inept bartenders, people will get drunk from the potent wine of freedom. Unless the rulers are fully amenable and keep pouring, they are accused of being filthy oligarchs and punished.

Adeimantus: Yes, that often happens in democracies.

Socrates: Not only that, but those who obey the rulers are denounced as willing slaves and ciphers; in both public and private affairs they praise and reward followers who act like leaders and leaders who act like followers. In such a republic, could there be any limits to freedom?

Adeimantus: None at all.

Socrates: Eventually anarchy spreads to private homes and even infects the animals.

Adeimantus: Can you explain that to us?

Socrates: You will see parents acting like children and fearing them, and the children begin to behave like their parents, feeling neither shame nor respect in their presence. All of this is justified as freedom. The resident alien is equal to the citizen, the citizen is equal to the resident alien, and they are both equal to the stranger.

Adeimantus: All distinctions disappear in this kind of republic. **[563]**

Socrates: This is true not only of large but of small matters. Teachers begin to fear and flatter their students, and the students ignore their teachers and tutors. On the whole, young and old are alike, all on an equal footing and ready to compete with each other, both in words and actions. Older people descend to the level of the young, constantly imitating them, joking and playing, so that they will not appear to be grim and authoritarian.

Adeimantus: This all sounds quite familiar.

Socrates: The ultimate development of liberty comes when both male and female slaves bought with good money are just as free as the people who purchased them. But I almost forgot to mention the great liberty that is possible for men and women through the equality of the sexes.

Adeimantus: As Aeschylus says, you should speak the words that are on your lips.

Socrates: That is exactly what I am doing. It is hard to believe unless you see how even the animals in a democracy are free from discipline and restraint—more than in any other kind of republic. As the proverb says, the female dog is just like her mistress, and the horses and donkeys march along the road with all the rights and dignity of free people, expecting everybody to get out of the way. Everything is bursting with liberty!

Adeimantus: Socrates, you are describing my own dreams. That's just what happens when I walk in the country.

Socrates: The crux of the matter is that the citizens become so sensitive that they rebel against even the smallest hint of coercion. As you know, they eventually lose all respect for the law, whether written or unwritten, because they will not allow anybody to tell them what to do.

Adeimantus: Yes, I know that quite well.

Socrates: This is the fair and mighty source from which tyranny arises.

Adeimantus: A glorious beginning, to be sure. But what is the next step?

Socrates: We see the same pattern in the destruction of democracy as in the destruction of oligarchy. The same disorder takes over democracy, intensified by the excess of liberty. Excessiveness of anything generally causes a reaction in the opposite direction—a principle that applies to the seasons, to plants and animals, and above all to governments. **[564]**

Adeimantus: That makes sense to me.

Socrates: Too much liberty, whether in individuals or in republics, turns into oppression.

Adeimantus: That is the natural order of things.

Socrates: So tyranny naturally arises out of democracy, and the most aggressive form of tyranny and oppression arise from the most extreme forms of license.

Adeimantus: That is a reasonable account of the matter.

Socrates: But I think you were asking a different question, Adeimantus. You wanted to know what, exactly, is the disorder that arises in both oligarchy and democracy and enslaves both of them.

Adeimantus: Yes, I would like to know that.

Socrates: I was talking about the kind of lazy spenders who are divided in two groups, the more courageous being the leaders and the more timid the followers, the same ones we compared to the drones with and without stingers.

Adeimantus: That's a good comparison.

Socrates: These two groups are a plague in every republic where they appear, being what phlegm and bile are in the body. The good physician and legislator, just like the wise bee-keeper, ought to keep them at a distance and, if possible, prevent their entering. If any have found a way in, then they should be cut out of the hive as quickly as possible—cells and all.

Adeimantus: Yes, that's what should be done!

Socrates: Now, Adeimantus, I have a proposal concerning how we can see this matter more clearly.

Adeimantus: What is your proposal?

Socrates: Let's imagine democracy to be divided into three classes, which, in fact, it is. Because of its liberal nature, the democratic republic creates a class of drones as does oligarchy.

Adeimantus: I agree.

Socrates: But this class is more vigorous in a democracy.

Adeimantus: Why is that?

Socrates: In an oligarchy, they are disqualified from holding power and are therefore untrained and weak. But in a democracy, with few exceptions, they dominate. The shrewdest ones speak and act, and the rest buzz around the podium and will not let the other side present its case. Not much takes place in these republics that is not their doing.

Adeimantus: That's true.

Socrates: There is another class that separates itself from the crowd.

Adeimantus: What class?

Socrates: When everyone is doing business and trying to make money, it is usually the best organized people who form the wealthy class.

Adeimantus: I think we can assume that.

Socrates: Can we also assume that they have the largest amount of honey and that the drones extract the most from them?

Adeimantus: I think it would be hard to extract it from those who have little.

Socrates: So the wealthy class is the pasture of the drones?

Adeimantus: That is a good way to put it. **[565]**

Socrates: There is also a third class consisting of people who work for themselves, stay away from politics, and have few possessions. When they are united they are the largest and most powerful class in a democracy.

Adeimantus: That's true, but they are unwilling to get together unless they get a share of the honey.

Socrates: Do they get a share? This is how it works. Their leaders look for opportunities to plunder the rich, keep most of what they get for themselves, and distribute what is left to the people.

Adeimantus: Well, in that sense I suppose they do share the wealth.

Socrates: And the people whose property is taken away are compelled to defend themselves before the people as best as they can.

Adeimantus: That's right.

Socrates: And when they do, even if they do not intend to bring about political change, they are charged with plotting against the government and favoring oligarchy.

Adeimantus: True.

Socrates: As a result, when they realize that the people seek to injure them—not intentionally but through ignorance and because of slander—they are forced to become oligarchs, goaded by the sting of the drones.

Adeimantus: Exactly.

Socrates: Then both sides initiate impeachment, bring indictments, and conduct trials.

Adeimantus: There is no end to such actions.

Socrates: And the people always seem to find someone to champion their cause and they groom that person for greatness.

Adeimantus: That is their way.

Socrates: This is the root from which the tyrant grows, first appearing as a protector.

Adeimantus: Yes, that is the way it begins.

Socrates: But how does a protector change into a tyrant? Perhaps we can learn from the story about the man at the Arcadian temple of Lycaen Zeus.[4]

Adeimantus: What story?

Socrates: Have you never heard about the man who was turned into a wolf because he ate human intestines mixed in with those of the animals being sacrificed?

Adeimantus: Oh yes, I have heard that story.

Socrates: The protector of the people resembles this man. Armed with the great power of having a submissive mob to command, the former protector does not hesitate to shed the blood of family members. One common method is to bring them into court on false charges and murder them, eliminating human life, and with an unholy tongue and lips tasting the blood of relatives. Those who are not killed are sent into exile, while the supposed champion of the people proclaims that debts will be cancelled and land will be redistributed. After all this, what can happen to such a person other than being killed by enemies or transformed from being human to becoming a wolf—a tyrant? **[566]**

Adeimantus: I see no other alternative.

Socrates: This is the sort of individual who begins by arousing the public against the wealthy class.

Adeimantus: The very same.

Socrates: And if forced into exile and yet managing to return in spite of many enemies, this protector emerges as a full-blown tyrant.

Adeimantus: Now I understand how they originate.

Socrates: Then if they are unable to expel the tyrant or arouse public opinion to issue a death warrant, they make secret plans for elimination.

Adeimantus: That's the usual pattern.

Socrates: Then comes the well-known request for a body-guard, a sure sign of reaching an important stage in a tyrant's career. "Let not the people's friend be lost to them!"

Adeimantus: I can hear it now.

Socrates: The people grant this request, because they only fear for their supposed leader; they have no such worries for themselves.

Adeimantus: No doubt.

Socrates: If a wealthy person witnesses all this and is accused of being an enemy of the people, surely the words spoken by the Delphic oracle to Croesus will come to mind:

> Just then, tender-footed Lydian, by the stone-strewn Hermus
> Flee and do not stay, and do not be ashamed to be a coward.[5]

Adeimantus: Those are wise words, Socrates. Since he was ashamed to escape, he will not be ashamed again.

Socrates: Yes, because anyone who is caught by such a mob will surely be killed.

Adeimantus: It is inevitable.

Socrates: Now our erstwhile protector, rather than lying on the ground "mighty in his mightiness,"[6] is not just victorious over all enemies but stands in the chariot of state holding the reins—having evolved from a protector into a full dictator.

Adeimantus: The transformation is complete.

Socrates: Now we should consider the happiness of the individual and of the republic in which this sort of creature is produced.

Adeimantus: Yes, that comes next in our plan.

Socrates: When first coming to power, the tyrant rejects that label, greets and smiles at everyone, makes public and private promises, cancels debts, and distributes land to the people— pretending to be kind to all.

Adeimantus: That is necessary.

Socrates: Having dealt with the enemies, destroying some and making friends with others, there is nothing to fear from them. The tyrant must then find a reason to wage some war or other so that the people will need a leader to protect them. **[567]**

Adeimantus: We should expect such tactics.

Socrates: This is also a good way to justify raising taxes so that the people will have to work harder simply to provide for their basic needs, leaving no time or energy to plot revolution.

Adeimantus: That is an obvious move.

Socrates: If any of the citizens develop a desire for freedom and are suspected of being disloyal, the tyrant figures out a way to put them in the hands of the enemy. For these reasons, new wars are constantly starting.

Adeimantus: That is inevitable.

Socrates: Eventually the tyrant begins to become unpopular.

Adeimantus: How could it be otherwise?

Socrates: Then some of the influential people who helped the tyrant to power—I mean the most courageous ones—begin to say what is on their mind and to criticize the way things are going.

Adeimantus: That is likely to happen.

Socrates: If the tyrant wishes to stay in power, those people must be eliminated so that eventually not one decent person remains either as a friend or as an enemy.

Adeimantus: That's clear.

Socrates: Constant surveillance is needed to determine who is honorable, wise, wealthy, or brave. This happy leader must be an enemy to all of them and must purge the entire republic by getting rid of everyone who fits that description.

Adeimantus: That would be quite a purge!

Socrates: Yes, it would be just the opposite of how doctors purge the body. They take away the worst and leave the best, but the tyrant does just the opposite.

Adeimantus: There does not seem to be much choice for such an individual.

Socrates: The choice is between living with the worst sort of people and being hated by them, and not living at all.

Adeimantus: Some choice!

Socrates: The more our tyrant arouses hatred among the people, the greater will be the need for loyal bodyguards.

Adeimantus: That's right.

Socrates: Who are these bodyguards, and where can they be found?

Adeimantus: I think they will fly in on their own, if the price is right!

Socrates: Adeimantus, I think you are once again talking about the drones—all kinds of them, this time imported from abroad!

Adeimantus: That's exactly what I had in mind.

Socrates: Don't you think that they can also be found at home?

Adeimantus: What do you mean?

Socrates: How about freeing the slaves of wealthy people and turning them into bodyguards?

Adeimantus: That's a great idea; they can be trusted more than anyone else.

Socrates: What a fortunate person this tyrant is; when the others have all been killed or banished, these bodyguards are the only friends who remain.

Adeimantus: Once again there seems to be no other choice. **[568]**

Socrates: So these are the new citizens the tyrant has created to be companions and admirers, while being hated and avoided by all decent people.

Adeimantus: Of course they would hate and avoid the tyrant.

Socrates: Then it seems that tragedy is a wise thing and Euripides is a great tragedian.

Adeimantus: Why do you say that?

Socrates: Because he is the author of the following wise words: "Tyrants are wise by living with the wise." What could he mean other than that the tyrant lives with wise people?

Adeimantus: That's true. And he also says that tyranny is godlike, a claim made by other poets as well.

Socrates: Therefore, because they are so wise, I trust that the tragic poets will forgive us and anyone else who favors a similar form of government if we exclude them from our republic. We do not welcome those who sing the praises of tyranny.

Adeimantus: Perhaps the more subtle thinkers among them will pardon us.

Socrates: But they will go to other republics, attract crowds with beautiful, strong, and persuasive voices, and lure them into tyranny and democracy.

Adeimantus: They are good at that.

Socrates: And they are paid well and honored for doing it—especially by tyrants, but also in democracies. However, the higher they climb toward the top, where the best governments exist, the less success they have; as if they run out of breath and cannot go on.

Adeimantus: True.

Socrates: But we have strayed from the point. Let's return to the question of how the tyrant will support that fair, large, diverse, and ever-changing army of bodyguards.

Adeimantus: First there is the property of the people the tyrant has eliminated. Then if there is a sacred treasure in the temples of the republic, that would be a good source of income, making it possible to avoid imposing new taxes.

Socrates: What happens when these funds run out?

Adeimantus: Then the tyrant's entire entourage—including both male and female companions—would have to rely on the estate of the father who spawned them.

Socrates: I see what you mean. You are talking about the people, the great mob who produced the tyrant in the first place.

Adeimantus: Yes, that would be a necessary source of support.

Socrates: But what if the people become angry and say that a grown-up child ought not to be supported by the father but that the father should be supported by the child? **[569]** The father did not bring the child into the world simply to serve a crowd of servants and maintain an army of foreign mercenaries. The father was seeking a protector, one who would liberate him from a government run by the rich and noble few. Then they might tell the tyrant to leave and take the bodyguards along, just as a father might expel a drunken party from his house.

Adeimantus: I suspect that the father will discover what a monster he has created; the child will probably be stronger and more aggressive than the father.

Socrates: What do you mean? Are you saying that the tyrant would use violence against the father?

Adeimantus: Yes, by first stripping the father of his weapons.

Socrates: Then this child has become a parricide, cruel and unnatural offspring of a father who ought to be cherished. This is true tyranny. These people tried to avoid the smoke of being slaves of free people and they wound up in the fire of being the slaves of slaves. Freedom, when taken to its extreme, ignoring order and reason, becomes the most bitter form of slavery!

Adeimantus: Yes, Socrates, that is precisely what happens.

Socrates: Then may we conclude that we have said enough about the nature of tyranny and how a republic changes from democracy to tyranny?

Adeimantus: Yes, we have said more than enough.

ENDNOTES

[1] Cf. Homer, *The Iliad*, book xvi.

[2] In Aristophanes' play *Plutus*, the god of wealth is portrayed as being blind. When asked how he lost his sight, he says that Zeus inflicted punishment on him because he threatened that wealth would go only to the just, the wise, and people who live orderly lives. To prevent this kind of distribution, Plutus was struck blind.

[3] "And whosoever of them ate of the honey-sweet fruit of the lotus, [95] had no longer any wish to bring back word or to return, but there they were fain to abide among the Lotus-eaters, feeding on the lotus, and forgetful of their homeward way. These men, therefore, I brought back perforce to the ships, weeping, and dragged them beneath the benches and bound them fast in the hollow ships [100]" (Homer, *The Odyssey*, trans. A. T. Murray, two volumes, books 1–12. [Cambridge, MA: Harvard University Press, 1919], book ix).

[4] "Lycaon brought a human baby to the altar of Lycaean Zeus and sacrificed it, pouring out its blood upon the altar, and according to the legend, immediately after the sacrifice he was changed from a man to a wolf (lycos)" (*Pausania's Description of Greece*, trans. W. H. S. Jones, 4 volumes [Cambridge, MA: Harvard University Press, 1933], 8.2.3).

[5] Herodotus. *Herodotus*, trans. A. D. Godley (Cambridge, MA: Harvard University Press, 1926), 1.55.

[6] Cf. Homer, *The Iliad*, trans. A. T. Murray (Cambridge, MA: Harvard University Press, 1924), xvi. 776.

Book Nine

[571] *Socrates:* Finally we come to the tyrant, who is generated out of democracy. Once again we will ask what kind of people they are, examine the kind of life they lead, and determine whether they are happy or miserable.

Adeimantus: Yes, Socrates, the tyrant is the only one we left out.

Socrates: And did we not omit something else?

Adeimantus: What is that?

Socrates: I don't think we adequately examined the kinds of desires. Adeimantus, until we do, our inquiry will remain obscure.

Adeimantus: Then isn't this the time to do that?

Socrates: That's right, so let's return to our earlier discussion of desire. A while ago we distinguished between necessary and unnecessary pleasures.[1] Even though everyone seems to have desires, in some people they are controlled by law and reason, so that good desires predominate and the bad ones are few and weak or have been eliminated. However, in other people the unnecessary desires are plentiful and strong.

Adeimantus: What desires do you have in mind?

Socrates: I mean the ones that wake up when our reasoning, civilizing, and governing powers go to sleep. Then the wild and savage part of our being, filled with food and drink, rises up and runs around naked, seeking whatever will satisfy its untamed appetites. No crime or vice is too shameful or unnatural for it— including having sex with its mother, or any man, god, or beast, committing the most foul murder, or devouring anything it wants.

Adeimantus: Your description is quite accurate.

Socrates: Now consider a healthy and self-controlled person who goes to sleep after having dined on beautiful words and ideas and gained self-knowledge. The appetites have been satisfied with neither too much nor too little so that they may slumber quietly and not disturb the noblest activity of the soul with their pleasures or their pains. **[572]** The mind is free to think and try to understand what it does not know, whether from the past, the present, or the future. Both the passionate and the willful activities of the soul have been pacified so that a quarrel with someone before going to bed will not disturb thinking, which is the third activity of the soul. In this condition one is most likely to grasp the truth and unlikely to be plagued by wild and lawless dreams.

Adeimantus: I fully agree with you.

Socrates: I have wandered from the main topic of our discussion, but I wanted to make it clear that, even in the best of us, hidden and savage desires exist as part of our nature and reveal themselves in our dreams. Tell me whether you think I am right and you agree with this account.

Adeimantus: Yes, I agree.

Socrates: Remember how we described the character of the democratic person—reared by a miserly father who only encouraged the passion for making money and who disapproved of the childish desire to play or delight in wearing fine clothes and jewelry.

Adeimantus: That is what we said.

Socrates: Then out of hatred for the father's stinginess, the young person was attracted to the ways of a more refined crowd devoted to unnecessary pleasures. Because of a superior nature, this youth was pulled in two directions and settled on a middle way, not one of lawlessness and excess, but a life of measured gratification. This is how we described earlier the way the democrat was generated out of the oligarch.

Adeimantus: Yes, that was and still is our view.

Socrates: Now let's imagine that years have passed and this person has a son who is reared by the new principles. The son is seduced into a lawless life that is called total freedom. His father and other members of his family side with his moderate desires, but his new friends encourage the opposite kind. Eventually these magicians and makers of tyrants fear that they will be unable to hold onto the young man, so they foster in him a great lust that will rule over all his other desires, like a giant drone with wings. [573] Don't you think that is the best way to picture him?

Adeimantus: Yes, Socrates, I think that is an excellent image of such a person.

Socrates: While the other lusts buzz around him, fostered by incense and perfume and garlands and wine and all the other pleasures of a hedonistic life, the sting of desire pierces him and drives his soul into a frenzy. Madness becomes the captain of the guard, and if he finds any ideas or desires that might be considered good and might arouse feelings of shame, it puts an end to them, throwing them out until moderation has been abolished and lunacy reigns.

Adeimantus: I agree. That is how the tyrant comes into being.

Socrates: Isn't this why Eros is often called a tyrant?

Adeimantus: Perhaps.

Socrates: And could we say that a person who is drunk also has the spirit of a tyrant?

Adeimantus: We could.

Socrates: And people who are completely mad will imagine that they are able to rule not only over human beings but even over gods.

Adeimantus: They might say that.

Socrates: So the tyrant comes into existence at the point of becoming drunk, lustful, and mad, whether by nature, habit, or both.

Adeimantus: Exactly.

Socrates: I think we have properly described the origin of the tyrant. But how does such a person live?

Adeimantus: I suspect you could tell us how they might describe their delights.

Socrates: I could. At this stage there will be feasts, parties, orgies, and prostitutes—all the things that the tyrant Eros brings when he sets up house in a person's soul.

Adeimantus: That's a good prediction.

Socrates: Every day and every night their desires will grow in number, becoming stronger and making more and more demands.

Adeimantus: That's inevitable.

Socrates: Yes, and it's also inevitable that people in that condition will soon run out of money.

Adeimantus: True.

Socrates: Next come loans and liens on their property.

Adeimantus: Just as night follows day.

Socrates: When nothing is left, desires will crowd into the nest of the soul like young ravens crying out for food. Goaded by them, and especially by Eros whom they worship, tyrants will look for someone they can cheat and property they can acquire, whether by fraud or violence. **[574]**

Adeimantus: Sad but true.

Socrates: No matter how it is gained, money is needed to avoid horrible pangs and pains.

Adeimantus: That's right, Socrates.

Socrates: Just as new pleasures defeated and replaced the old ones in their soul, such young tyrants, after depleting their own share of property, will claim the right to more than their father and mother and take a slice out of theirs.

Adeimantus: No doubt.

Socrates: And if their parents will not agree, they will try to cheat and deceive them.

Adeimantus: They will try anything.

Socrates: And if that doesn't work, they will use force.

Adeimantus: They probably will.

Socrates: And if their parents still resist, would they hesitate to tyrannize them?

Adeimantus: No, I would have little hope for such parents.

Socrates: In the name of Zeus, Adeimantus, don't you think that a tyrannical son would even attack his dear old mother, the one who brought him into existence, on account of an affair with some new mistress who is not at all necessary? Would he bring them under the same roof and give her authority over his mother? Or would he treat his aging father, who has long been an indispensable friend, in the same way for the sake of a youthful and disposable lover?

Adeimantus: Yes, Socrates, I'm afraid he would.

Socrates: Then a tyrannical son turns out to be a true blessing for his father and his mother!

Adeimantus: Yes, a real prize.

Socrates: After he has taken their property and consumed it, and pleasures are swarming in the hive of his soul, might he not break into a house or steal from people traveling at night or clean out a temple? While all of this is going on, the opinions about what is good and what is bad that he learned as a boy are thrown away and replaced by the ones that had been repressed. These new opinions come with lust and serve as its bodyguard. Fantasies that once appeared only in his dreams while he followed the laws established by his father and the democratic constitution of his soul are now free to appear in daylight. Under the tyranny of lust, he constantly does while awake what he previously did only sometimes in his dreams. He is willing to commit murder, eat anything he pleases, and perform any other horrible act. [575] Freed from all control, Eros has become a dictator in the republic of his soul. He promotes anarchy and encourages whatever it takes to maintain himself and his wild mob, which has either come in from the outside through reckless intercourse or has been released from within by bad habits. Is this an accurate picture of the life of the tyrant?

Adeimantus: Yes, you have described it well.

Socrates: If there are only a few such people in the republic and the rest are moderate, they go someplace else to guard some other tyrant or become mercenaries fighting in a war. If there is no war, they will probably stay home and cause trouble in the republic.

Adeimantus: What sort of trouble do you mean?

Socrates: They become thieves, burglars, pickpockets, muggers, temple robbers, and kidnappers. If they are clever speakers, they become informers, take bribes, and give false testimony in court.

Adeimantus: Yes. But these seem to be relatively minor offenses when the perpetrators are few.

Socrates: True, small and large are comparative terms. These acts affecting a republic don't even come close to the evils caused by a tyrant. But once this mob grows in size, becomes aware of its power, and is supported by the unsuspecting citizens, it selects the person with the most tyrannical soul to become the leader.

Adeimantus: That makes sense, because such a person will be the most effective dictator.

Socrates: If the people yield, that's fine, but if they resist, tyrants will treat them the way they did their own father and mother. Now that they have the power, they will attack the dear old fatherland and motherland, as the Cretans say, and they will bring in their lackeys to serve as rulers. That is clearly the goal of the tyrant's desires and passions.

Adeimantus: Exactly.

Socrates: Should we assume that such people already reveal their character in their private lives before they rule in the republic? First they only associate with people who flatter them, and if they desire something from somebody else, they grovel before them, willing to do anything. But as soon as they get what they want, they treat them like strangers. **[576]**

Adeimantus: That's a familiar pattern.

Socrates: They are either masters or slaves, never friends of anyone. A tyrant never tastes true freedom or true friendship.

Adeimantus: Never.

Socrates: Should we call them deceitful?

Adeimantus: That's a good word for them.

Socrates: Adeimantus, if our previous view of justice is correct, we could also call them unjust.

Adeimantus: Yes, I'm sure we were right about that.

Socrates: Then we can sum up the worst people by saying that they behave as badly while awake as they do in their dreams.

Adeimantus: That's true.

Socrates: Such a person is the product of a tyrannical nature that acquires total authority. The longer they live, the worse they get.

Glaucon: Socrates, I think that you and Adeimantus have accurately described the tyrant.

Socrates: Then, Glaucon, can we also conclude that the most wicked person is also the most miserable? Even if this is not the opinion of the majority, can we agree that the person who has tyrannized the longest and most completely will truly have the most unhappy life?

Glaucon: That is inevitable.

Socrates: And do we also agree that the tyrannical person resembles the tyrannical republic, the democratic person resembles the democratic republic, and so on?

Glaucon: How could it be otherwise?

Socrates: Can we also say that goodness and happiness in the republic can be compared to those same qualities in the person?

Glaucon: We can say that.

Socrates: Then if we compare a republic ruled by the true sovereign that we described a while ago with a republic under the rule of a tyrant, how do they compare from the standpoint of goodness?

Glaucon: They are at opposite extremes; one is the best and the other is the worst.

Socrates: Then it is obvious which is which, and I can ask whether you would come to the same conclusion about their relative happiness and misery? We should not allow ourselves to be blinded by the impression tyrants and the few people around them make; but we should consider that kind of republic and examine every part of it and only then make a judgment.

Glaucon: That's a good proposal, and I think it will become clear to everyone that tyranny is the most miserable form of government, and the happiest republic is ruled by a true sovereign.

Socrates: [577] Do you also think it is a good procedure to rely on the judgement of someone who has the power to understand a person's character—someone who would not be dazzled by the external splendor of tyranny, as a child might, but would have clear insight? I assume that we would pay attention to someone who has lived under the same roof with a tyrant and has observed both the daily life of the family, where the tyrant does not wear a costume, and times of public danger. I would propose that kind of person as a judge of the happiness and misery of the tyrant as compared with other people.

Glaucon: That is the right procedure.

Socrates: Then let's imagine ourselves to be that judge and that we had such experience with a tyrant. That way we will have someone to answer our questions.

Glaucon: Yes, let's proceed that way.

Socrates: We will continue with the parallel between the individual and the republic. With that in mind, and glancing from one to the other, please describe their qualities.

Glaucon: Which qualities do you mean?

Socrates: Let's begin with the republic. Would you say that a republic ruled by a tyrant is free or enslaved?

Glaucon: No republic could be more enslaved.

Socrates: But don't we find both free people and slaves in such a republic?

Glaucon: I see what you mean. There are a few free people, but the people as a whole, especially the best of them, are miserably and disgracefully enslaved.

Socrates: Then if the individual is like the republic, would not the same hold true of the individual whose soul is servile because the noblest elements of the soul are meager and enslaved, ruled by a part that is worthless and depraved?

Glaucon: That is inevitable.

Socrates: Glaucon, would you say that this is the soul of a slave or a free person?

Glaucon: No doubt it is the soul of a slave.

Socrates: And a republic that is enslaved under a tyrant is far from having achieved autonomy.

Glaucon: Yes, Socrates, a long way.

Socrates: And the soul of the tyrant—I mean the soul taken as a whole—also lacks self-determination. Driven by insane desire, it lives in constant terror and disorder.

Glaucon: A pitiful condition.

Socrates: Does a tyrant rule a rich or poor republic?

Glaucon: Poor.

Socrates: Like the tyrannical soul, it will be poor because it is always insatiable.

Glaucon: That's right. **[578]**

Socrates: It would seem that such a republic and such an individual would always be filled with fear.

Glaucon: No doubt.

Socrates: Is there any republic in which you will find more tears, sadness, groaning, and pain?

Glaucon: Certainly not.

Socrates: And is there any individual in whom you will find more of that kind of misery than in the tyrannical individual, who is always driven mad by desire and lust?

Glaucon: No, this is by far the worst.

Socrates: Then it was in light of all these evils and others like them, that you said the tyrannical republic is the most miserable of all.

Glaucon: That's what I said, Socrates, and I was right in saying so.

Socrates: Yes, and when you see the same evils in the tyrannical person, what do you say?

Glaucon: I say that person is the most miserable of all people.

Socrates: I think you are wrong.

Glaucon: Why do you say that?

Socrates: I don't think that individual has reached the extreme limit of misery.

Glaucon: Then who is more miserable?

Socrates: The one I'm about to mention.

Glaucon: Who is that?

Socrates: A tyrannical person who does not live a private life but has the misfortune of becoming a public tyrant.

Glaucon: Based on what we said before, I suppose you are right.

Socrates: Glaucon, when we are considering such important matters, dealing with which life is good and which is bad, it is not enough to suppose. We need rational justification.

Glaucon: That's quite true.

Socrates: Then let me try to prove this claim.

Glaucon: I'm eager to hear what you have to say.

Socrates: Consider the case of rich people who live in a republic and have many slaves. They resemble the tyrant in that both have slaves; the only difference is that the tyrant has more of them.

Glaucon: Yes, that's the difference.

Socrates: These people are secure and do not fear their slaves.

Glaucon: What should they fear?

Socrates: Nothing. But do you know why?

Glaucon: Yes. The reason is that all of the citizens protect each other.

Socrates: Fine. But now let's imagine that one of these slave owners is carried off by a god and placed in the wilderness where there are no other citizens to help. Let's say it is a man with a whole household, including fifty or more slaves. Would he not be afraid that his slaves might revolt and kill him along with his wife and children?

Glaucon: He would have good reason to be terrified. **[579]**

Socrates: He would be compelled to flatter several of his slaves, promising them favors and even freedom. Against his will, he would become a slave to his slaves.

Glaucon: He would if he valued his life.

Socrates: Now imagine that the same god who carried him off put him down among neighbors who oppose slavery itself, threatening the most severe punishment for anyone caught holding slaves.

Glaucon: His plight would be even worse; enemies would surround him on all sides.

Socrates: Isn't this the kind of prison in which every tyrant is confined? The soul of a tyrant is filled with greed, lust, and fear. Unlike free people, tyrants dare not travel abroad to enjoy the sights. They are like a woman who is confined to the house, envying those who can go where they wish and see what they want.

Glaucon: Yes, they are in a kind of prison.

Socrates: With such a plentiful harvest of evils, am I correct in saying that the tyrant, lacking self-control—the one you just described as the most miserable of all people—would be even more miserable living a public life? Would it not be a worse fate to have to rule over a republic rather than a private life? Having to rule over others while being unable to rule over oneself is like becoming paralyzed and then being expected to go out to fight with other people.

Glaucon: Socrates, I think what you say is true; that is a good comparison.

Socrates: Do you now agree that this is the most miserable condition and that the public tyrant leads a worse life than the private one, as we said before?

Glaucon: Yes, I agree.

Socrates: Then it is true, in spite of popular opinion, that to be a tyrant is really to be a slave, forced to praise and flatter the most vile people. If you know how to view their soul as a whole, you will see that because tyrants are unable to satisfy their many desires, they are really the poorest people of all. Throughout their lives they live in terror and are plagued by convulsions and pains, similar to the agony of the republic they resemble.

Glaucon: Once again that resemblance is quite clear. **[580]**

Socrates: As the power of the tyrant increases, so do jealousy, deception, injustice, unholiness, and loneliness. By encouraging and fostering every shameful desire, the tyrant becomes supremely miserable and makes everybody else equally miserable.

Glaucon: No sensible person could deny that.

Socrates: Come, then, and take the role of the final judge in a contest, deciding once and for all which of the five kinds of life is most happy, which is second, and so on. How do you rank the royal, timocratic, oligarchic, democratic, and tyrannical forms of life?

Glaucon: That's easy, Socrates. From the standpoint of goodness and badness, happiness and unhappiness, I would rank them in their order of appearance, as if they were choruses entering the theater.

Socrates: Shall we hire a messenger, or shall I announce the result: The son of Ariston judges that the best and most just people are also the happiest, because they reign over themselves. He also claims that the worst and most unjust are also the most miserable, tyrannizing themselves and their republic.

Glaucon: Socrates, you made the announcement.

Socrates: May I also add that this is true whether they are visible or invisible to gods and to people?

Glaucon: Yes, I would like you to add that!²

Socrates: Well then, this ends the first proof, but there is another one that I think has some merit. Let's see what you think.

Glaucon: What is it?

Socrates: The second proof is based on the nature of the soul. Just as we have distinguished three activities of the republic, we can distinguish three activities of the soul; those distinctions lead to a new demonstration.

Glaucon: What is this proof?

Socrates: The proof is as follows: three kinds of pleasure correspond to the three kinds of activity of the soul. We can also identify three kinds of desire and three kinds of rule.

Glaucon: I don't quite understand. Can you explain what you mean?

Socrates: People learn through one kind of activity and become angry or willful through another kind. The third kind has many forms, so we could not give it a single name, but its primary activity involves the great strength and power of desire for the pleasures of food, drink, sex, and the other sensual appetites. This third activity is also related to the love of money, because these desires are most easily gratified by spending money. [581]

Glaucon: Yes, we were right about that.

Socrates: Perhaps we can say that the various desires and pleasures related to this third kind of activity are all concerned with profit. That would allow us to give it a single head and call it by a single name. Shall we call it the desire for money and profit?

Glaucon: That sounds good to me.

Socrates: Can we also say that the willful activity of the soul is determined to rule, conquer, and become famous?

Glaucon: Certainly.

Socrates: So we can call it competitive and ambitious.

Glaucon: Yes, Socrates, that is quite appropriate.

Socrates: On the other hand, the activity through which we learn only seeks to know the truth and has little concern for profit and fame.

Glaucon: Especially when we compare it with the other two activities of the soul.

Socrates: We might call that kind of activity the love of learning or the love of wisdom.

Glaucon: Either term would be appropriate.

Socrates: So it would seem that this principle rules some souls and one of the other two dominates others.

Glaucon: Yes.

Socrates: Then may we assume that there are three kinds of people: lovers of wisdom, lovers of combat, and lovers of profit?

Glaucon: Exactly.

Socrates: Each kind of person prefers a different kind of pleasure.

Glaucon: True.

Socrates: If you were to interview each one and ask what they think is most pleasant, they will praise their own form of life and condemn that of the others. Lovers of profit will condemn combat as foolish and learning as useless—unless they contribute to making money.

Glaucon: You hear such talk all the time.

Socrates: What about the lovers of combat? Will they not consider delight in wealth to be vulgar and the pleasure of learning, if it brings no honor or fame, to be mere smoke and nonsense?

Glaucon: I think they might use stronger language than that.

Socrates: But lovers of wisdom would probably say that the other pleasures are nothing when compared with the constant delight of pursuing truth and reality. They would probably call the other pleasures necessary, meaning that they would ignore them in favor of true pleasure, if there were no need for them.

Glaucon: We should be aware of that.

Socrates: So when there is disagreement about which kind of life is the most pleasurable and the least painful—I don't mean which life is better or worse or noble or base—how can we determine which one tells the truth? **[582]**

Glaucon: Socrates, I really don't know.

Socrates: Consider the criteria we should use. Is there any better basis for judgment than experience, thinking, and reason?

Glaucon: No, those would be the best criteria.

Socrates: Then let's think it through. Of the three individuals, which has the most experience with all of the pleasures we listed? Does the lover of profit have more experience of the pleasures of learning and seeking the truth than the lover of wisdom has of the pleasure of making a profit?

Glaucon: No, the lover of wisdom has the advantage. Ever since they were children, philosophers have tasted all three kinds of pleasure, but the lover of profit has little interest in the process of learning about the nature of things and would have a difficult time tasting the sweetness of it.

Socrates: So the lover of wisdom surpasses the lover of profit by having both kinds of experience.

Glaucon: By far.

Socrates: How should we compare the lover of wisdom with the lover of combat? Do philosophers have greater experience with the pleasures of honor or do the lovers of combat have greater acquaintance with the pleasures of learning?

Glaucon: All three kinds of life bring honors to the degree that they achieve their goals. The wealthy, the brave, and the wise all have their admirers, and when they are honored they experience its pleasure. But only the lover of wisdom knows the delight that comes from considering all of existence.

Socrates: Then using the criterion of experience, the philosopher will be the best judge.

Glaucon: The best by far.

Socrates: Only that kind of judge will use reasoning to understand experience.

Glaucon: Precisely.

Socrates: And the method by which such judgments are made is not the tool of either the lover of profit or the lover of combat but only of the lover of wisdom?

Glaucon: What method?

Socrates: The one we earlier called dialectic.[3]

Glaucon: Of course.

Socrates: And that kind of reasoning is proper to the lover of wisdom?

Glaucon: Yes.

Socrates: If wealth were the criterion, then what the lover of profit praised and criticized would serve as the standard.

Glaucon: That's right.

Socrates: Or if honor or victory or courage were the standard, then the lover of combat would be the best judge.

Glaucon: Clearly.

Socrates: But since experience, thinking, and rational explanation are the criteria—

Glaucon: —then it necessarily follows that what the lover of wisdom and of explanation judges to be best, reveals what is true.

Socrates: Among the three pleasures of the soul, the pleasure from the activity of learning turns out to be the greatest; and the person in whom this is the guiding principle has the most pleasant life. **[583]**

Glaucon: There is no doubt about it. Lovers of wisdom are in the best position to judge the value of their own life.

Socrates: And what does the judge say is the next best life?

Glaucon: It would be the lover of combat and honor, whose way of life is closer to the judge than that of the lover of profit.

Socrates: So you would place the lover of profit last?

Glaucon: I would.

Socrates: Glaucon, so far the just person has twice conquered the unjust person. Now, in the tradition of the Olympic games, comes the third contest—the one that is sacred to Olympic Zeus, the savior. I have heard it said by a wise person that only the pleasure from wisdom is true and pure; all others are mere shadows. As in wrestling, the third fall is decisive.

Glaucon: That's right, Socrates, but what is your strategy?

Socrates: If you will answer my questions, we can discover it together.

Glaucon: Ask your questions.

Socrates: Tell me, then, is pain the opposite of pleasure?

Glaucon: Of course.

Socrates: And is there an intermediate state of mind, which is neither pleasure nor pain?

Glaucon: Yes.

Socrates: In that condition the mind rests from both.

Glaucon: You could say that.

Socrates: Do you remember what people say when they are sick?

Glaucon: Remind me.

Socrates: They say that nothing is more pleasant than health, but they didn't realize that until they got sick.

Glaucon: Yes, I remember hearing that.

Socrates: And when people are suffering from extreme pain, you have probably heard them say that nothing is more pleasant than getting rid of their pain.

Glaucon: I have.

Socrates: In fact, there are many cases in which people praise ending the pain, not the experience of some positive enjoyment, as the greatest pleasure.

Glaucon: Yes, the absence of pain is experienced as pleasant.

Socrates: And when the experience of pleasure ends, that kind of rest will be painful.

Glaucon: I guess so.

Socrates: Then what we called the intermediate state of mind will be both pleasurable and painful.

Glaucon: That seems to follow.

Socrates: But how can what is neither pleasurable nor painful be both?

Glaucon: It seems impossible.

Socrates: Both pleasure and pain arise in the soul and are activities of the mind?

Glaucon: Yes.

Socrates: But we just saw that the intermediate state is at rest, not in motion. **[584]**

Glaucon: We did.

Socrates: Then does it make sense to say that the absence of pain is pleasurable or that the absence of pleasure is painful?

Glaucon: It would seem to be nonsense.

Socrates: Then our experience of this intermediate state is an illusion, not reality. In other words, when we are resting from both pain and pleasure, when compared to pain that condition seems to be pleasure and when compared to pleasure it seems to be pain. But all of these appearances, when compared to true pleasure, are simply a kind of magic trick.

Glaucon: Based on what we said before, that's a sound inference.

Socrates: Then let us seek the kind of pleasures that do not follow pain and dispel the illusion that pleasure is only relative to pain or that pain is only relative to pleasure.

Glaucon: What pleasures do you mean? Where shall I look for them?

Socrates: There are lots of them. Consider the delightful experiences of smell, which can be quite profound but are not preceded by pain. They are generated without warning and disappear without leaving any pain.

Glaucon: I can think of many examples of such pleasure.

Socrates: Then let's not believe that pure pleasure is the stopping of pain or pain simply the ending of pleasure.

Glaucon: Yes, we should dismiss any such notion.

Socrates: But we must admit that a large number of intense pleasures we experience through the body are a relief from pain.

Glaucon: That's true.

Socrates: And don't you think that the same is true of pleasures and pains we experience through anticipation?

Glaucon: I do.

Socrates: Would you like to hear an analogy of such experience?

Glaucon: I would.

Socrates: In nature we can distinguish among upper, middle, and lower regions.

Glaucon: Yes.

Socrates: If someone were to go from the lower to the middle region, wouldn't that person have the impression of going up? And someone standing in the middle, looking back would have the idea of being in the upper region?

Glaucon: Without seeing the highest point, how could such a person think otherwise?

Socrates: But when taken back to the lower region, that same person would have the experience of descending.

Glaucon: No doubt.

Socrates: These experiences would be shaped by ignorance of what is really upper, middle, and lower.

Glaucon: I agree.

Socrates: Then we should not be surprised if people who do not know the truth have wrong ideas about many other things, including pleasure, pain, and the intermediate state between them. When they experience pain they really are pained, but when they move from pain to the neutral state, they have the illusion of satisfaction or even pleasure. **[585]** Because they do not know true pleasure, they make a mistake in comparing pain with the absence of pain—like comparing black with gray instead of white.

Glaucon: No, Socrates, that would not surprise me. In fact, I would be surprised if such a person could make true distinctions.

Socrates: Now think about it another way. Can we say that hunger and thirst are a kind of deficiency in the body?

Glaucon: Yes.

Socrates: Can we also say that ignorance and thoughtlessness are a deficiency of the mind?

Glaucon: We can say that.

Socrates: So food and wisdom fill those voids and satisfy the respective needs of body and mind.

Glaucon: They do.

Socrates: Which is more likely to provide genuine satisfaction, something that is more real or something that is less real?

Glaucon: Clearly it would be what is more real.

Socrates: Then what kind of things do you think are more real, the ones satisfied by bread, drink, seasoning, and other kinds of bodily food, or the ones nourished by true opinion, knowledge, and goodness as a whole? Think about it this way: some activities are concerned with what is unchanging, immortal, and true; others are occupied with the changing, and the mortal. Which activities and objects are closer to being itself?

Glaucon: Activities concerned with objects that are unchanging are far more excellent.

Socrates: And does the essence of the unchanging also participate in both knowing and being?

Glaucon: Yes. Knowledge and being are directly related.

Socrates: And is it less concerned with truth?

Glaucon: No, not at all.

Socrates: So what is less true is also less real?

Glaucon: Correct.

Socrates: Then, in general, the kind of activity that serves the body is less true and substantial than the kind that serves the soul?

Glaucon: Far less.

Socrates: And that means the body is less true and less real than the soul?

Glaucon: Naturally.

Socrates: May we conclude that whatever is more real and filled with what is more real has more existence than what is less real and is filled with what is less real?

Glaucon: That sounds right to me.

Socrates: And if pleasure comes from what harmonizes with nature, whoever is filled with being will experience genuine joy and pleasure, but whoever is filled with something less real will be less satisfied and will only experience lesser and passing pleasure.

Glaucon: That necessarily follows.

Socrates: Glaucon, this means that those who do not experience wisdom and goodness, but devote themselves to feasting and partying, live their lives in the lower and middle regions. **[586]** They move aimlessly through life, never entering the true upper region. They neither look for it nor find their way there, never filled with being nor tasting genuine and lasting pleasure. They look down at their banquet table, like cattle in a feed lot. With their eyes cast toward the earth, they feed and fatten and breed. In their excessive need for such things, they kick and butt each other with horns and hooves of iron, killing each other out of insatiable hunger. They are not able to fill their being with anything of substance nor are they able to retain what they receive.

Glaucon: Socrates, you speak like an oracle as you describe the life of the masses.

Socrates: Their pleasures are mixed with pains. But isn't that inevitable? Their pleasures are shadows of true pleasures, like the pictures an artist might draw using light and shade. This intensifies their mighty appeal, fosters mad passions and leads to fights, as Stesichorus says the ignorant Greeks fought over the shadow of Helen at Troy.[4]

Glaucon: I don't see how it could be any other way.

Socrates: Isn't it the same with the willful activity of the soul? The person dominated by the love of honor and success will act through envy and ambition, be violent and competitive, and angry without reason and good sense.

Glaucon: Yes, that's what happens.

Socrates: But may we say that even the love of wealth and the love of honor can contribute to true pleasure whenever they are guided by reason and knowledge in the quest for truth? In this way they would be following what is natural to them, assuming that what is best is what is most natural.

Glaucon: Yes, Socrates, we can say that. I agree that what is best is what is most natural to us.

Socrates: When the whole soul is guided by the love of wisdom, each activity following its own nature in harmony with the others, then each will enjoy the best and truest pleasures proper to it. **[587]**

Glaucon: Exactly.

Socrates: But if either of the other activities dominates, it fails not only to acquire its own genuine pleasure, but also compels the others to pursue shadows of pleasures foreign to them.

Glaucon: No doubt.

Socrates: And the greater the separation between them and the love of reason and wisdom, the more strange those pleasures become?

Glaucon: How true.

Socrates: And as the distance from reason increases, the more they separate from law and order?

Glaucon: That's clear.

Socrates: The lustful and tyrannical desires are at the greatest distance?

Glaucon: Yes.

Socrates: But the royal and orderly desires are the closest?

Glaucon: Yes.

Socrates: Then the tyrant will live the least pleasant and the true sovereign the most pleasant life.

Glaucon: Yes again.

Socrates: Glaucon, do you know how to measure the distance between them?

Glaucon: No, Socrates, you will have to tell me.

Socrates: There seem to be three kinds of pleasure, one is genuine and two are counterfeit. The tyrant flees from the domain of law and reason and dwells beyond the border of the counterfeit, with satellite pleasures as slaves. We can express the degree of the tyrant's inferiority with a number.

Glaucon: Socrates, I really don't know how you would do that.

Socrates: The way we count in Greece, you would agree that the tyrant is in the third place from the oligarch, with the democrat in the middle.

Glaucon: Yes, I would agree about that.

Socrates: That means the tyrant is coupled with an image of pleasure that is three times removed from the pleasure of the oligarch.

Glaucon: I suppose so.

Socrates: Now the oligarch is three times removed from the sovereign, assuming the royal sovereign is the same as the aristocrat.

Glaucon: Yes, three times would be right.

Socrates: Therefore, a number that is three times three separates the tyrant from true pleasure.

Glaucon: That's clear.

Socrates: Then the shadow of tyrannical pleasure lies at a distance determined by geometrical progression.

Glaucon: I'm beginning to understand.

Socrates: Now, if we consider the line that represents the interval between tyrannical pleasure and true pleasure as it relates both to the square and the cube, it is easy to see how great the distance becomes.

Glaucon: It would be easy for a mathematician.

Socrates: Likewise, instead of going from the tyrant to the sovereign, if you invert the order and consider true pleasure from the point of view of the sovereign, you will find that when the multiplication is finished, the sovereign lives 729 times more pleasantly than the tyrant (who lives 729 times more miserably than the sovereign), the interval being the same between the two. **[588]**

Glaucon: What a wonderful calculation, Socrates! I am overwhelmed by the enormous distance between the just and the unjust person, as measured by relative pleasure and pain.

Socrates: And it is an accurate and true calculation, Glaucon, because it is a number central to human life, its days and nights, months and years.

Glaucon: Yes, how true.

Socrates: Then if the good and just people exceed bad and unjust people to this degree, imagine the superiority of their lives in grace, beauty, and goodness!

Glaucon: By Zeus! Immeasurably greater!

Socrates: At this point of our discussion, Glaucon, it would be appropriate to go back to the beginning of the argument. As I recall, it started when someone said that injustice benefits a completely unjust person who gives the impression of being just. Didn't someone say that?

Glaucon: Yes, someone said that.

Socrates: All right, now that we have determined the power and quality of justice and injustice, let's have a word with him.

Glaucon: What shall we say to him?

Socrates: Let's create an image of the soul so he can see what he said.

Glaucon: What kind of image?

Socrates: An image like the ones encountered in ancient mythology, such as Chimera, with parts from a goat, a lion, and a snake; Scylla, a woman, dog, and serpent; and Cerberus, a three-headed dog and snakes, and many others whose bodies contain several images in one.

Glaucon: Yes. I've heard that many such creatures have existed.

Socrates: Now try to imagine one single many-colored beast with several heads arranged in a circle, each head from a different animal—some wild and some tame. Imagine also that it can generate them and change at will.

Glaucon: Socrates, you are asking for a work of great skill, but since language is more malleable than beeswax, I have formed such a creature.

Socrates: Now make another one, this time a lion, and a third in the form of a human being, the first larger than the second one, and the second larger than the third.

Glaucon: That is much easier. I have done it already.

Socrates: Then fuse all three so that they grow into a single being.

Glaucon: Done.

Socrates: Now shape it into the image of a person who, from the outside, appears to be a human being to those who cannot see inside.

Glaucon: I have accomplished it.

Socrates: Now let's say to that person who insists that injustice is more profitable than justice that he is really claiming that a person benefits by feeding and strengthening the many-headed beast and the lion, with all their qualities, and by starving, and weakening the human being. [589] This means that the human will be at the mercy of the other two and dragged along in whatever directions they want to go and will not encourage them to adjust to each other and become friends. Rather, one should let them fight and devour each other.

Glaucon: Yes, that is what it means to encourage injustice.

Socrates: But the advocate of justice replies that it is better to devote everything we say and do to strengthen the ability of the human being to govern the entire person—like a good farmer watching over and tending young plants—controlling the desires of the many-headed beast, using the strength of the lion to tame and cultivate them in harmony with each other and with ourselves.

Glaucon: I agree that this is what the advocate of justice would say.

Socrates: Then from every point of view, the advocate of justice is right, but the person who praises injustice is deceived. Whether we consider pleasure, honor, or profit: those who advocate justice speak the truth, but those who condemn it speak from ignorance.

Glaucon: They don't know what they are saying.

Socrates: Unjust people do not intend to make such a mistake. So, we should try to persuade them gently—something like this: "My friend, what is your opinion about the customary distinction between what is good and beautiful and what is harmful and disgusting? Don't you think that the good and beautiful tames what is wild in us and makes it human, or even divine? Otherwise the wild will overpower the tame and become harmful. How could they deny this, Glaucon?

Glaucon: They could not deny it if they take my advice.

Socrates: But if they do admit it, we could follow up with another question: How can people benefit when they receive gold and silver on the condition that they enslave the best part of themselves by the worst? Can you imagine selling your son or daughter into slavery, especially if you were to sell them to brutal and evil people? Would any amount of money justify such a transaction? And would we not be equally miserable if we were to sell what is divine in us to desires that are godless and brutal? **[590]** Think of Eriphyle, who was bribed with a necklace to betray her husband.[5] Wouldn't this bargain be even worse?

Glaucon: Answering for the advocate of injustice, I would say that this would be a lot worse.

Socrates: And don't you think that the reason we object to immoderate desire is that it unleashes the many-headed beast in us?

Glaucon: I think we can say that.

Socrates: And we condemn willfulness and hostility because they unduly nurture the lion and the serpent in us?

Glaucon: Yes.

Socrates: But at the other extreme, we denounce softness and luxury because they weaken this same activity of our soul and make us cowards.

Glaucon: True.

Socrates: And we censure greedy people for using flattery and dirty tricks to subordinate the high-spirited animal to the unruly beast for the sake of money of which there is never enough? Already at a young age, such people develop the habit of abusing and subduing the lion and turning it into a monkey.

Glaucon: They certainly do.

Socrates: Why do manual work and laborers have such a bad reputation? Isn't it because people say that what is best in them is naturally weak so that they lack the power to control the wild beasts, claiming that all they know is how to serve and flatter them.

Glaucon: That's a good explanation.

Socrates: Therefore, in order to be ruled by what is best in them, they ought to be the servant of the best. Rather than being a slave to others to their detriment, as Thrasymachus claimed, they should all be ruled by the divine wisdom within them. If that is not possible, they should be governed by a common external order, established by all alike so that we may dwell as friends.

Glaucon: Those are wise words, Socrates.

Socrates: Clearly this is the purpose of the law, which is allied with everyone in the entire republic. It is also the responsibility and control we have over children, not allowing them to be free until the best in us has helped them set up a republic in themselves, guided and guarded by the best in them. Then we can let them go. **[591]**

Glaucon: That is clear, both about the true purpose of law and the education of children.

Socrates: Then, Glaucon, how could it possibly be shown that a person profits by doing what is unjust, immoderate, or shameful, even if it brings great wealth?

Glaucon: There is no way that could be demonstrated.

Socrates: What if the injustice goes undetected and the person is never punished? Would that person not get worse? But if caught and corrected, the savage part might be pacified and tamed. Once the gentle part of a person is freed, the entire soul can achieve its proper nature and acquire justice, moderation, and wisdom. Would this state of mind not surpass the beauty, strength, and health of the body to the extent that the value of a person's soul surpasses that of the body?

Glaucon: This is true, in every respect.

Socrates: Then would people, in their right mind, not wish to devote their whole life to this purpose? Would they not begin by valuing those studies that nurture these qualities of mind and pay less attention to the others?

Glaucon: They would.

Socrates: They would avoid cultivating savage and irrational pleasures of the body and would regard even health as secondary. Being beautiful or strong or healthy would not be important concerns unless they foster moderation and promote the harmony of the body in symphony with the soul.

Glaucon: They must do that if they intend to be like true musicians.

Socrates: They will also observe the principle of order and harmony in acquiring wealth and possessions, refusing to be dazzled by the opinion of the majority which would encourage them to heap up riches that would actually bring countless evils.

Glaucon: That is a temptation they should avoid.

Socrates: Instead they will look at the republic within themselves and guard against disturbing their internal order either by too much or too little wealth, regulating both income and expenses as carefully as possible.

Glaucon: True.

Socrates: For the same reason, they will enjoy and accept any public or private honors they think will make them better, but will avoid those that could undermine their internal order. **[592]**

Glaucon: Socrates, if that is their primary concern, they will have nothing to do with politics!

Socrates: By the dog of Egypt, Glaucon, they certainly will! In their own republic they will, but perhaps not in their native land—unless by some divine intervention!

Glaucon: I understand. You are referring to the republic of words we have established in our dialogue. I don't think it actually exists.

Socrates: Perhaps a model of such a republic exists in the heavens for anyone to see who wishes to live accordingly. And whether it actually exists or not, they will want to live according to the order of that republic and no other.

Glaucon: That is certain.

ENDNOTES

[1] See *Plato's Republic*, 558.
[2] See *Plato's Republic*, 366.
[3] See *Plato's Republic*, 533.
[4] Cf. *Plato's Phaedrus*, 243. According to the story told by the poet Stesichorus, Helen was not responsible for the war, because it was not she but her ghost that was present at Troy. Thus, the foolish men who fought for ten years were only fighting over a shadow.
[5] See Homer, *The Odyssey*, xi. 326.

Book Ten

Socrates: **[595]** Glaucon, as I reflect on the many aspects of ordering our republic, I think what we said about poetry is one of the best.

Glaucon: What do you have in mind, Socrates?

Socrates: Our rejection of imitation. Now that we have distinguished the specific activities of the soul, it is clear why imitation should not be admitted.

Glaucon: Why is that?

Socrates: Let's keep this between us because I would not like to have it repeated to the tragedians and the other imitators. To you I will say that imitation is detrimental to the intelligence of the audience because many people are not aware that the only remedy is knowledge of its true nature.

Glaucon: I don't understand the point you are making.

Socrates: Well, I will explain it to you, though even now I hesitate because of the love and respect I have had for Homer since I was a child. He is the ancestor and teacher of the great tragic writers. But a person should not be placed above the truth, so I must speak my mind.

Glaucon: I fully agree.

Socrates: Then listen. No, even better, please answer my questions.

Glaucon: Go ahead.

Socrates: Can you tell me the general nature of imitation? I really don't know what it is.

Glaucon: If you don't know, what are the chances that I do?

Socrates: Doesn't a person with weaker eyes often see some things sooner than one with keen vision? **[596]**

Glaucon: True, but in your presence I'm not eager to lead the discussion, even when I might have something to say. Perhaps you should begin.

Socrates: Then would you like to proceed with our usual method, thinking of many particular things and considering them as a single idea? Do you understand what I mean?

Glaucon: I do.

Socrates: Then think of any particulars you please, such as beds or tables. Are there not many of each in the world?

Glaucon: Yes.

Socrates: But there are only two ideas of these objects: one of "bed" and one of "table."

Glaucon: True.

Socrates: And we usually say that a person who makes a bed or a table, or any other thing we use, does so by considering the idea, but does not make the idea itself.

Glaucon: Of course.

Socrates: But now I would like to know what you would call another kind of maker.

Glaucon: What kind?

Socrates: One who makes all the works of all the other workers.

Glaucon: That would be an extraordinary person.

Socrates: Just wait, it gets even better. The maker I have in mind makes not only every kind of instrument but also plants and animals on earth, including the maker, as well as the earth itself, the heavens, all things in the heavens and under the earth, and even the gods.

Glaucon: You are describing a marvelous magician!

Socrates: Don't you believe me, Glaucon? Would you completely deny the existence of such a maker? Or could there be at least one who could do all of these things to some degree? Don't you see that there is a way in which you could do this yourself?

Glaucon: Me? How could I do that?

Socrates: It would be easy. There are many ways, but the quickest would be to carry around a mirror and catch the sun, the heavens, the earth, plants, yourself and the other animals, and the rest of the natural and artificial world.

Glaucon: But Socrates, you would only capture the appearance of things, not their reality.

Socrates: Bravo! That's exactly my point. Now consider representational painters. Wouldn't we say they are that kind of maker?

Glaucon: I suppose you are right.

Socrates: But is what they paint unreal? Isn't the painter also making a bed, in a certain way?

Glaucon: Such a painter only makes the appearance of a bed.

Socrates: **[597]** Then what about a carpenter? Didn't you just say that such a person does not make the idea of the bed itself, but only a particular bed?

Glaucon: Yes, I did say that.

Socrates: Then if the carpenter does not make what it truly is, but only a likeness, it would be wrong to say that the work of a carpenter or any other craftsperson is the real thing.

Glaucon: At least that would be the opinion of people who devote themselves to this kind of reasoning.

Socrates: So we should not be surprised that the work of the carpenter falls short of what is true.

Glaucon: Not at all.

Socrates: Would you like to use these examples to try to understand what an imitator is?

Glaucon: That's a good plan.

Socrates: Then it seems that we have three beds. The first one exists by nature. Who could have made it but the god?

Glaucon: No one else could have made it.

Socrates: A carpenter makes the second one?

Glaucon: Yes.

Socrates: And a painter makes the other one?

Glaucon: Yes.

Socrates: Therefore, there are three kinds of bed and three kinds of maker: the god, the carpenter, and the representational painter.

Glaucon: I agree that there are three kinds of maker.

Socrates: But the god, whether by choice or by necessity, made only one bed. Two or more such beds could not exist in nature.

Glaucon: I don't understand. Why not?

Socrates: Because even if the god had made only two, a third one would necessarily exist as the idea by which the other two participate in the true idea of the bed.

Glaucon: I understand.

Socrates: Now that we know this, we can say that the god, not wishing to be a particular carpenter making a particular bed, created the unique one that exists by nature.

Glaucon: That makes sense.

Socrates: Shall we call this the true act of creation?

Glaucon: I think that would be right, because the divine is the natural creator of this and everything else that truly is.

Socrates: But doesn't the carpenter also make a bed?

Glaucon: Yes.

Socrates: And would you call the painter a maker and creator?

Glaucon: No, I would not.

Socrates: Then what is the painter's relation to the real bed?

Glaucon: I think it would be best to say that a representational painter imitates what has already been created.

Socrates: Good. Then if we count nature as first, would it be fair to call the person whose work is three steps away an imitator?

Glaucon: Yes it would.

Socrates: And the maker of tragedies is also an imitator and, therefore, third in line of succession from the king—from truth? Can we make this claim about all imitators?

Glaucon: It seems to follow from what we have said.

Socrates: Then we agree about the imitator. **[598]** Now I have a further question about such painters. Do they imitate that one which originally exists in nature or only what the others make?

Glaucon: They imitate only what the others make.

Socrates: As those things are or as they appear? You should make that distinction.

Glaucon: What do you mean?

Socrates: I mean that you can look at a bed from one side, from the opposite side, or from many other angles. It appears to be different from each perspective, but the bed continues to be itself. Would it not be the same with all other objects?

Glaucon: Yes, they continue to be what they are; they only appear to be different.

Socrates: Now let me ask my question another way. Does representational painting imitate things as they are or as they appear? Speaking generally, does it imitate appearance or reality?

Glaucon: Appearance.

Socrates: Then the power of imitating is a long way from reality. It seems to be able to make everything because it only grasps a little of it—its appearance. So we will not deny that such a painter can represent a shoemaker, a carpenter, or any other craftsperson, even without knowing anything about their craft. A skillful representational painter will show a picture of a carpenter from a distance to make children and simple-minded people believe that they are looking at a real carpenter.

Glaucon: Of course.

Socrates: So, my friend, whenever anyone claims to have found a person who knows all the crafts and everything else others know, and knows it better than anyone else, I think we can assume that such a person is naïve and has met some magician or imitator who supposedly knew everything. It is easy to be deceived when you are unable to distinguish among knowledge, ignorance, and imitation.

Glaucon: That is true.

Socrates: And we hear such people say that the writers of tragedy, with Homer leading the way, know all of the crafts, and everything about human affairs, including what is good and bad, and even about divine things. When they say that good poets, in order to create something beautiful, must be experts of their subjects, or not be able to create at all, we should consider whether they are not being similarly misled. **[599]** Seeing their works, people might not have suspected that they were looking at imitations three times removed from reality, which can be made without knowledge because they are mere appearances, not real substances. Or is it possible that good poets really do know the things about which many people believe they speak so well?

Glaucon: Socrates, I think this subject needs much more reflection.

Socrates: If a person were able both to create the original as well as make an image of it, would you say that making the image would be the best one could do? Would you allow this to direct your life when you could do much better?

Glaucon: I would not prefer a life of imitation.

Socrates: People who really know what they are imitating would devote themselves to reality, not to imitations. They would leave for posterity many beautiful works, being praised rather than praising others.

Glaucon: Yes, that kind of life would bring greater honor and profit.

Socrates: Then I think we should demand an explanation from Homer or any other poet, but not about medicine or any of the crafts of which they know only incidentally. We will not ask whether they have cured patients or left behind medical students, as Asclepius did, or whether they talk about medicine without genuine knowledge. But it would be appropriate to ask about war, military tactics, politics, education, and the other great and inspiring subjects of his poems. We might proceed like this: "Friend Homer, if you are not three steps away from truth and goodness; if you know what activities make people better or worse in private or public life; if you are not a mere imitator, please tell us what republic was ever made better through your effort? Lycurgus contributed to the civic order of Sparta, and other people have served many large and small republics in the same way. But who says that you have been a good legislator or otherwise improved any republic? Italy and Sicily would mention Charondas, and we Athenians would designate Solon. But what republic has anything to say about you?" Glaucon, is there any republic Homer might name?

Glaucon: I don't think so. Not even the Homer Society[1] would say that he was a legislator.

Socrates: And when Homer was alive, did he wage a successful war against anyone or advise anyone who did? **[600]**

Glaucon: No.

Socrates: Did he invent something useful for the crafts or for business, as did Thales from Miletus, Anacharsis the Scythian, and many other ingenious people?

Glaucon: He did nothing of that kind.

Socrates: If he was not engaged in public service, did he contribute privately to the education of individual people? During his lifetime, did he have devoted friends and followers to whom he passed on a Homeric way of life, similar to the one Pythagoras invented and which continues to distinguish his followers?

Glaucon: No, Socrates, there is nothing like that recorded about him. Think of Homer's companion Creophylus, whose name "meat tribe" always makes us laugh; we might justly ridicule him for his lack of culture because of the way he neglected his friend, Homer?

Socrates: That is what tradition says. But can you imagine, Glaucon, that if Homer really had been able to educate and improve humanity, if he was really knowledgeable rather than being an imitator, that he would have lacked followers who honored and loved him? Or consider Protagoras of Abdera, Prodicus of Ceos, and a host of others who lead their private students to believe that they could never manage their own house or their republic unless they put them in charge of their education. These educators are so much loved for their wisdom that their companions all but carry them around on their shoulders. Would contemporaries of Homer or Hesiod have allowed either of them to beg their way as rhapsodists if they had been able to improve humanity in this way? Surely they would rather have parted with gold than with these teachers, demanding that they stay with them in their homes. If the masters would not stay with them, the disciples would have followed them wherever they went until they had learned enough.

Glaucon: Yes, Socrates, I think that is true.

Socrates: Then we can conclude that all mimetic poets, beginning with Homer, are only imitators. They copy images of goodness and the other subjects they treat, but they never reach the truth. **[601]** They are like those painters who, as we said, make the likeness of a shoemaker even if they know nothing about making shoes. This is good enough for people who know no more than they do and who judge only by colors and shapes.

Glaucon: That's right.

Socrates: By analogy, we can say that mimetic poets, who know only how to imitate, paint each of the crafts with nouns and verbs but lack understanding of their true nature. Other people, who are as ignorant as they are, judge only from their words, supposing that if they speak of making shoes, military strategy, or anything else in meter, harmony, and rhythm, they are speaking beautifully. Such is the mighty spell naturally cast by melody and rhythm. I think you know that, because you have often observed the quality of poetic compositions when they are merely recited and stripped of the colors that music adds to them.

Glaucon: Yes, I have.

Socrates: They are like young people whose faces were never beautiful but blooming, and now their bloom has passed away.

Glaucon: Exactly.

Socrates: Now reconsider this: The maker of images, the imitator, knows nothing of true existence but only of appearances. Is that not so?

Glaucon: Yes.

Socrates: Then let's not leave this explanation in the middle but treat it fully.

Glaucon: Proceed.

Socrates: Think of a representative painter who paints reins and a bridle.

Glaucon: All right.

Socrates: But leatherworkers and metalworkers actually make those things.

Glaucon: Yes.

Socrates: But does the painter know the correct form of the bridle and the reins? Not even the maker would know that; only the equestrian who knows how to use them knows their true nature.

Glaucon: Right.

Socrates: And does this hold true in general?

Glaucon: What do you mean?

Socrates: I mean that there are three kinds of art: one that uses, one that creates, and one that imitates.

Glaucon: I understand.

Socrates: So the goodness, beauty, and rightness of every tool, every living being, and every action relate to their natural or practical use.

Glaucon: True.

Socrates: So, the person who uses something has the greatest experience of it and tells the maker of that thing about the good or bad qualities that manifest themselves in using it. For example, a musician who plays the flute will tell the maker which flutes perform well and will suggest improvements; a good flute maker will respond accordingly.

Glaucon: Of course.

Socrates: The user knows what is a good or bad flute; the maker trusts and follows the user's instructions.

Glaucon: Yes.

Socrates: The tool is the same for both, but the maker believes what is good or bad by listening to the user who knows.

Glaucon: Precisely. **[602]**

Socrates: Now what should we say about the imitator? Does the person who draws a flute know from using the flute whether the drawing is good and beautiful? Or will the instructions from others determine whether the drawing is correct?

Glaucon: Neither.

Socrates: Then the imitator has neither knowledge nor correct opinion about what is good or bad about it.

Glaucon: I suppose not.

Socrates: Are mimetic artists wise and educated about their creations?

Glaucon: No, Socrates, just the opposite.

Socrates: Yet, Glaucon, they continue to go about their work without knowledge and only imitate what appears to be good and bad and what looks beautiful to ignorant people.

Glaucon: That's all.

Socrates: So, we agree that the imitator has no knowledge worth mentioning and that imitation is a kind of game without substance, especially when written in iambic or heroic verse and in tragic or epic form.

Glaucon: That's true.

Socrates: Then can we conclude with certainty that imitation really is three times removed from reality?

Glaucon: It is.

Socrates: And to which human power does imitation correspond?

Glaucon: I don't understand your question.

Socrates: Let me put it this way. If you look at an object up close, it looks large, but when seen from a distance, it seems to be small.

Glaucon: True.

Socrates: Again, an object that looks straight when out of the water appears crooked when immersed in water. Also, an object that appears convex becomes concave because of the different ways we see colors. Our mind is constantly plagued by such confusion. Illusory painting, juggling, and various kinds of magic tricks and clever devices impose that kind of deception and exploit this weakness in our nature.

Glaucon: I agree.

Socrates: But measuring, counting, and weighing graciously come to our aid, and what appears to be larger or smaller or full or heavy no longer deceives us but submits to calculation, number, and weight.

Glaucon: They provide a powerful antidote.

Socrates: This must be the work of the reasoning and computing power of the soul.

Glaucon: No doubt.

Socrates: And this is what measures and determines that some things are equal or that some are more or less than others. But doesn't this often contradict what appears to be?

Glaucon: Yes. **[603]**

Socrates: Didn't we already say that it is impossible to think contradictory ideas about the same thing at the same time?[2]

Glaucon: We did, and we were right when we said that.

Socrates: Then the power of the soul that thinks according to measurement must be different from the power that thinks contrary to measurement.

Glaucon: It must.

Socrates: And what measures and calculates is the best?

Glaucon: Certainly.

Socrates: And what opposes them is inferior to it?

Glaucon: That necessarily follows.

Socrates: That's what I had in mind when I said that imitation in all its forms, including painting and drawing, is far from truth; it associates with and is the companion and friend of what is remote from reason. It is neither sound nor true.

Glaucon: Now I understand, and I agree.

Socrates: Then imitation is an inferior breed that mates with an inferior breed and produces inferior offspring.

Glaucon: That's an appropriate metaphor.

Socrates: Does this apply only to sight, or is it also true of hearing, so that it includes what we are calling mimetic poetry?

Glaucon: It probably applies to mimetic poetry as well.

Socrates: But let's not rely only on the analogy with painting. Instead let us consider the aspect of thinking associated with mimetic poetry and examine whether it is superior or inferior. Mimetic poetry imitates human action that is either voluntary or involuntary, and people expect good or bad results such as pleasure or pain. Is there anything else we should say about it?

Glaucon: No, Socrates, I think that is enough.

Socrates: When people act in these ways, are they in harmony with themselves? Or is it, as we found with sight, full of confusion and contradiction? Do we find additional strife and inconsistency? But now that I think about it, we don't need to raise this question again, because we already proved that the soul is always full of contradictions of this kind.[3]

Glaucon: Yes, and we were correct.

Socrates: True, but we did leave something out that should now be added.

Glaucon: What was that?

Socrates: Didn't we say that a good and reasonable person who has the bad luck to lose a son or anything else that is dear, will bear the loss better than someone who has not?

Glaucon: Yes.

Socrates: We should now consider whether such a person will suffer no grief or, if that is impossible, will be moderate in grieving.

Glaucon: I think that such people will be moderate.

Socrates: Would they be more likely to fight and control their sorrow when they are alone or when others see them? **[604]**

Glaucon: They are more likely to struggle against grief when observed by others.

Socrates: But when left alone, they will probably say or do things that they would be ashamed to have someone else see or hear.

Glaucon: I agree.

Socrates: Isn't it reason and custom that encourage them to resist, while suffering itself urges them to indulge their grief?

Glaucon: I think that's right.

Socrates: But when a person is drawn in two opposite directions, to and from the same object, that seems to indicate that two different forces are at work.

Glaucon: Of course.

Socrates: And isn't one of them easily persuaded to follow custom?

Glaucon: What do you mean?

Socrates: I mean that law and custom indicate that it is best to retain our composure in the face of suffering, because there is no way to know whether such things are really good or bad, and nothing is gained by taking it so hard. Anyway, human affairs should not be valued beyond their importance. Excessive grief interferes with what is most required at such times.

Glaucon: What's that?

Socrates: Deliberating. If you throw dice, you have to follow what reason prescribes and accept the numbers that come up. That is better than acting like children who take a fall and then waste time crying and rubbing the place that hurts. We should accustom ourselves to finding a cure for sickness and injury, replacing cries of grief with effective treatment.

Glaucon: Yes, Socrates, that is the best way to deal with fate.

Socrates: And what is best in us is ready to act according to reason?

Glaucon: That's clear.

Socrates: But what inclines us to dwell on our troubles and wallow in sorrow, of which it never gets its fill, we shall call irrational and self-indulgent, and brand it as an ally of cowardice.

Glaucon: Yes, those are fitting terms to use.

Socrates: Doesn't this temperamental aspect of our nature provide a multitude of subjects for imitation? On the other hand, a wise and even-tempered disposition is difficult to imitate and, when someone tries, hard to appreciate, especially by the people who flock to such shows—they are strangers to that way of being.

Glaucon: Yes, Socrates, I agree. **[605]**

Socrates: That means mimetic poets do not naturally satisfy the aspect of the soul that desires wisdom. Wishing to be popular, they devote their attention to the passionate and multicolored temperament that is more suited to imitation.

Glaucon: That is where they focus their attention.

Socrates: Then, Glaucon, we can capture and place the mimetic poet side by side with the representational painter. They resemble each other in two ways. First, the things they produce are a long way from truth, and second, they both deal with what is inferior in the soul. So, we shall exclude imitation from our ideal republic, because of what it awakens and feeds and encourages in the soul by undermining reason. Just as we cannot allow the bad elements in a republic to take power and the good ones to be eliminated, we should also refuse to let mimetic poets create a bad form of government in our soul. We cannot allow it to foster irrational activity that cannot distinguish between more and less, one that thinks exactly the same thing is both great and small, and one that produces images that are far removed from what is true.

Glaucon: I agree.

Socrates: But we still have to present the strongest part of our indictment—the power of mimetic poetry to corrupt those who are good, which is a terrible thing.

Glaucon: If that is the result, it is terrible.

Socrates: Well, listen and see what you think. Consider the response of even the best people when they hear a passage by Homer or one of the writers of tragedy in which the heroes are represented as laying out their sorrows in a long speech, or possibly singing, and beating their breast. Don't people delight in being overcome by sympathy, captivated by the excellence of that poet who most arouses their feelings?

Glaucon: Yes, I confess I have experienced that myself.

Socrates: But when some tragedy occurs in our own life, we prefer the opposite kind of response, enduring such grief quietly and calmly; what enraptures people in the theater is not considered worthy of a man but acceptable of women.

Glaucon: That's true.

Socrates: Do you think it is right to praise such performances and take delight in watching such behavior in others when we detest it and are ashamed of it in ourselves?

Glaucon: No, it would be unreasonable.

Socrates: But it does make sense from another point of view. **[606]**

Glaucon: What point of view?

Socrates: Think about that aspect in our soul that is hungry for sorrow and the satisfaction that comes from crying—the one we try to keep under control when we encounter personal misfortune. This is the same desire that is satisfied and delighted by mimetic poets. The best part of our nature, if reason or habit has not adequately educated it, lets down its guard over that desire, thinking that there is no disgrace in praising and pitying someone who claims to be a good person but indulges in excessive grief. What would be the point of rejecting the poem or play as a whole and losing the pleasure it gives? Few people realize that by enjoying emotions that belong to someone else we necessarily bring them into ourselves. They do not know that if we foster a feeling such as pity through viewing the misfortunes of others, we cannot easily control that same feeling when it arises from our own suffering.

Glaucon: That is an important realization.

Socrates: Doesn't the same principle apply to humor? Jokes you find disgusting and would be ashamed to tell in public are amusing when you hear them from a comedian or from someone in private conversation. As in the case of excessive grief, the desire for ribald amusement you normally suppress is unleashed and you applaud it on stage. In spite of your own repulsion at being a fool, you are lured into becoming a clown in your daily life.

Glaucon: I'm embarrassed to think of it.

Socrates: And the same goes for lust and wild anger and all the offensive desires and pleasures of the soul that pervade our lives. Mimetic poetry feeds and waters such passions that ought to be dried up. They are allowed to rule us, whereas we ought to rule over them in order to make our lives better and happier, rather than worse and more miserable.

Glaucon: I cannot disagree with you.

Socrates: Glaucon, when you meet people who praise Homer for being the educator of Greece, who laud him for his contribution to the management and administration of human affairs, and say that we should read him and follow him to regulate our whole life, then you should respect the good intentions of people who are doing their best to be helpful. **[607]** Be ready to grant that Homer is the poet's poet and first among tragedians, but remember that so far we have only admitted hymns to the gods and eulogies for good people into our republic. If we admit the honeyed Muse, whether lyric or epic, pleasure and pain will rule our republic rather than what is best—law and reason common to all people.

Glaucon: That's quite true, Socrates.

Socrates: So we have simply recollected the course of our reasoning for expelling mimetic poetry from our republic. But to avoid the charge of being too harsh or provincial, we should say that the quarrel between poetry and philosophy is an ancient one. This is clear from poetic expressions such as "the yelping hound howling at her master," or "mighty in the vain talk of fools," and "the mob of sages circumventing Zeus," and "the subtle thinkers who are beggars after all," and countless other signs of the age-old tension. But let us announce that if poetry of any kind can justify her existence in a well-ordered republic, we would be delighted to admit her. We have always been conscious of her pleasure and charm, but we have a sacred obligation to the truth. Glaucon, my friend, are you not as enchanted as I am, especially when we consider the work of Homer himself?

Glaucon: Yes, I am greatly charmed.

Socrates: Then shall we propose that she be allowed to return from exile on the condition that she defend herself in lyric or any other poetic form?

Glaucon: Certainly.

Socrates: And I think we should also allow her defenders, who are lovers of poetry but not poets, to speak on her behalf in language without meter. Let them show that she is not only pleasant but also useful to republics and to all human life. We will be happy to listen, because if it can be proved that poetry is beneficial as well as delightful, we will surely benefit ourselves.

Glaucon: We certainly would!

Socrates: Otherwise we must give her up, just as lovers stay away from each other when they think their love is not good for them. We are lovers of the kind of poetry by which we have been educated in our beautiful republic, so we would delight in having her appear at her best and truest. **[608]** But if her defense fails, then even if our ears hear her, our soul will be protected from her charms by the magic power of the arguments we have just given. That way we can avoid the childish love the masses have for her. We will take care not to be seduced by such poetry because it should not be pursued or taken seriously as a way to truth. Those who listen to her must fear for the safety of the republic within them, so they should pay careful attention to our words of warning.

Glaucon: I agree with you for all the reasons you have given.

Socrates: Glaucon my friend, this is a mighty struggle, much greater than it seems. At stake is whether a person is to be good or bad; so we should not be diverted from the pursuit of justice and goodness by honor or money or power or even by the enchantment of poetry.

Glaucon: Given everything we have said, I agree with you, and I think anyone who has heard the argument would also agree.

Socrates: But we have not yet mentioned the greatest prizes and rewards for goodness.

Glaucon: If they are even greater than the ones we just discussed, I cannot imagine what they could be.

Socrates: Can anything great be accomplished in a short time? Consider how brief is the period from youth to old age when compared to all of time.

Glaucon: As much as nothing.

Socrates: Should an immortal being invest so much into a short period rather than the whole?

Glaucon: Probably not, but I'm not sure what you mean.

Socrates: Glaucon, don't you know that the soul is immortal and imperishable?

Glaucon: No, Socrates, I can't say I know that. Do you mean to say that you can prove it?

Socrates: Yes, I believe I can—and so can you, because it's not difficult.

Glaucon: It's difficult from my perspective; so I'd like to hear from you why it's not difficult.

Socrates: Then listen.

Glaucon: I'm all ears.

Socrates: Do you call some things good and others bad?

Glaucon: Certainly.

Socrates: Do you understand them the same way I do?

Glaucon: How do you understand them?

Socrates: Would you agree that what corrupts and destroys is bad and what saves and improves is good?

Glaucon: I would. **[609]**

Socrates: Would you also say that everything has a specific goodness and badness? For example, ophthalmia is harmful to the eyes, disease to the body as a whole, blight is bad for grain, rot for timber, and rust for iron and bronze. For almost everything there is at least one inherent evil or a disease peculiar to it.

Glaucon: That seems to be true.

Socrates: Whatever is afflicted in this way is made bad by it and eventually dissolves and dies?

Glaucon: Yes.

Socrates: What is inherently bad in each thing is what destroys it; but if that does not demolish it, then nothing will; because what is good for it cannot destroy it, nor can what is neither good nor bad for it.

Glaucon: That would be impossible.

Socrates: Then if we find any existing thing in which some badness exists but does not dissolve or destroy it, then can we say that the thing itself will not be destroyed?

Glaucon: That sounds reasonable.

Socrates: Does the soul have something that makes it bad?

Glaucon: Yes, all the things we just talked about—injustice, excess, cowardice, ignorance.

Socrates: But does any of these conditions destroy it? We must take care not to make the mistake of assuming that unjust and foolish people are destroyed when injustice is discovered in their soul. Consider an analogy with the body. What is bad for the body is disease, which depletes, decays, and eventually annihilates it. And so it is with the other things we were discussing; they are destroyed through their own inherent evil. Is this not true?

Glaucon: Yes.

Socrates: Let's think about the soul in the same way. Do injustice and other bad qualities in the soul waste and destroy it? Do they attach themselves to the soul and consume it until it dies and separates from the body?

Glaucon: No, that's not what happens.

Socrates: Then it would be irrational to suppose that something could be destroyed through the badness of something else when it could not be destroyed by its own evil.

Glaucon: Yes, that would be unreasonable.

Socrates: Then what is bad in the food, Glaucon—being stale, rotten, or whatever else destroys the food—will not itself destroy the body. But when what is bad in the food harms the body, then we would say that the body suffers from disease, and that it dies from a condition internal to itself. So we will say that the body cannot be destroyed by a different badness that is external to it, but only by what becomes bad within itself. **[610]**

Glaucon: That is clear.

Socrates: For that same reason, if what is bad in the body cannot produce what is bad in the soul, we should never think that the soul, which is one kind of thing, can be destroyed by badness that is external to it and belongs to another kind of thing.

Glaucon: That's a well-reasoned explanation.

Socrates: Then either we would have to refute that argument or, if it is a sound inference, never say that fever, or any disease, or a slit throat, or even cutting the entire body into tiny pieces will destroy the soul. Such things cannot harm the soul unless the soul itself becomes unjust or unholy. But we should not suppose that the soul, or anything else, that is not destroyed by an internal evil, could be destroyed by an external one.

Glaucon: True. It would be impossible to prove that it was death that caused a person's soul to become unjust.

Socrates: But if someone, who does not believe that the soul is immortal, denies this and says that people really do become unjust and bad by dying, then I suppose we would have to admit that injustice, like a disease, is fatal to the unjust. That would mean evil has a power that destroys from the inside, sometimes killing a person sooner and sometimes later, and quite different from what currently takes place where unjust people are executed for their injustice.

Glaucon: It seems to me that if injustice were fatal to unjust people, that would not be so bad, because it would bring an end to all troubles. But I suspect that this is not true and that injustice is more likely to kill other people while keeping the killers alive and even wide awake! Death and injustice, as we can now see, dwell far apart.

Socrates: Well observed, Glaucon. So, if in that case even the inherent natural evil of the soul is unable to kill it, then surely no external evil could ever destroy the soul or anything else.

Glaucon: Exactly.

Socrates: Then if no evil, neither internal nor external, destroys the soul, it is clear that it exists forever; and if it necessarily exists forever, then it is immortal. **[611]**

Glaucon: It must be so.

Socrates: That is our argument, and if it holds up, then we can also conclude that the number of souls in existence remains constant. If no soul is destroyed, then the number could not decrease. Nor could anything immortal increase, because it would have to come from something mortal. Eventually everything would be immortal.

Glaucon: That's true.

Socrates: But we should not believe that; it would be unreasonable. We must also reject the view that the soul is by nature many, diverse, and filled with variation and self-contradiction.

Glaucon: I don't understand what you mean.

Socrates: I mean that if soul is immortal, it is difficult to understand how it could be composed of many elements, and not necessarily the best of them, as we have seen.

Glaucon: It seems unlikely.

Socrates: The immortality of soul is proved by the arguments we have just examined and by other ones. But to know its true existence, you must look upon soul not as we see it now, distorted by communion with the body and other impediments, but with the eye of reason through which we see it purified and as it truly is. Then its beauty will be evident and you will find that it recognizes justice and injustice much more clearly, as well as all the other things we have described. Even though what we said about the soul was correct as it presently appears to us, we have seen it only like those who contemplate the image of the sea-god

Glaucus. His original form cannot be seen; some parts of his body have been broken off and crushed and otherwise damaged by the waves; incrustations of seaweed and shells and stones have grown over them, so he is more like a sea-monster than what he was before. We see the soul in a similar condition, disfigured by ten thousand injuries. But Glaucon, that is where we'll find it.

Glaucon: Where?

Socrates: In its love of wisdom. We will notice what it yearns for and what it seeks, given its kinship with the immortal, eternal, and divine, and what the soul would be like if it could pursue fully and totally what it desires and be lifted out of the water and debris in which it is now immersed. What if it were freed from the stones and shells and earth and rock that cover it in wild variety, and from what is often considered to be the good life? **[612]** Then you might see its true nature, knowing for sure whether it is a single form or many. Its present shape and its conditions in human life we have amply explained.

Glaucon: We certainly have.

Socrates: Glaucon, now we have completed the argument you and Adeimantus requested, ignoring the rewards and public acclaim that Homer and Hesiod invoke.[4] Have we showed the intrinsic nature of justice and demonstrated that it is best for the soul? Are you convinced that a person should do what is just even with [the power to become invisible by possessing] the ring of Gyges and the helmet of Hades?

Glaucon: Yes, Socrates, I am well satisfied with the argument.

Socrates: Then I assume it would not hurt to explore the rewards for justice and goodness the gods and human beings give to the soul both in this life and after death.

Glaucon: Not at all.

Socrates: Will you return what you borrowed during the argument?

Glaucon: What was that?

Socrates: I granted that the just person should appear to be unjust and that the unjust person should appear to be just. I did that because you said that even if it is impossible to conceal the reality from gods and human beings, it should be assumed for the sake of the argument so that we could compare justice itself with injustice itself. Do you remember?

Glaucon: It would be unjust for me to forget.

Socrates: Now that we have rendered our judgment, I demand on behalf of justice that you acknowledge the glory she receives from gods and human beings. She has been shown to be real and not to deceive those who possess her, so we should also restore the appearance of justice to her, so that she may wear the other crown of victory that rightly belongs to her and she shares with the just.

Glaucon: That is a fair demand.

Socrates: Will you grant, as the first debt you will repay, that the gods know the nature of both the just and the unjust?

Glaucon: I grant that.

Socrates: Then if they know both of them, would you also admit that one of them is a friend of the gods and the other is their enemy, as we said in the beginning of our discussion?

Glaucon: I would. **[613]**

Socrates: Can we assume that the friends of the gods receive from them only what is good, except whatever bad consequences derive from a prior offense?

Glaucon: Certainly.

Socrates: Isn't this how we should think about the just person, even if troubled by poverty or illness or anything else that seems to be a misfortune? In the end everything will work for the good, both in life and in death, because the gods will take care of those who desire to become just and divine, as far as human beings can, by pursuing goodness.

Glaucon: Yes, if they are like the divine they will never be neglected.

Socrates: And may we assume the opposite for the unjust person?

Glaucon: For sure.

Socrates: Is this the victory prize we said the gods confer on the just person?

Glaucon: Yes, I believe it is.

Socrates: And what do just people receive from human beings? In reality, we see that clever but unjust people are like runners who start well but fade in the final stretch. They sprint at the beginning, but in the end they look foolish, slinking away with their ears on their shoulders. But the true runner comes first to the finish and receives the crown. Then is this the way of just people, that the ones who persevere in every action and occasion throughout life are honored and carry off the prizes bestowed by human beings?

Glaucon: In my opinion that's true.

Socrates: Now you must allow me to repeat the blessings you formerly attributed to the unjust. I say of the just that as they grow older, they can become rulers, marrying whom they wish and giving in marriage whomever they wish. Everything you said of the others I now say of them. On the other hand, of the unjust I say that most of them, even if they escape in their youth, are eventually discovered and look foolish. When they are old and miserable they are insulted both by citizens and foreigners. As you said, they are beaten and racked and burned and suffer in ways unfit to be told in polite company. Confirm now that you have heard me say that too, and that it is so.

Glaucon: I will, because I believe what you say is true. **[614]**

Socrates: Then are these the prizes and rewards and gifts that gods and human beings bestow on the just in the present life— above and beyond the blessings that come from justice itself?

Glaucon: Yes, Socrates, and I would say that these rewards are beautiful and lasting.

Socrates: But these things are nothing, either in number or size, when compared with what awaits both the just and the unjust after death, which will be far more and greater. All of this should be heard so that both the just and the unjust receive the words they are due.

Glaucon: Speak on, Socrates. There are few things I would rather hear!

Socrates: Then I will tell you a story—not one of the long tales Odysseus tells to Alcinous—but one about a brave man named Er, the son of Armenius, a Pamphylian by birth. He was killed in battle, and ten days later, when the bodies of the dead were recovered and brought home to be buried, all of them had rotted— except his. On the twelfth day, as he was lying on the funeral pyre, he returned to life and told about what he had seen in the other world. He said that when his soul departed he went on a journey with a great company. They came to a mysterious place where there were two chasms in the earth located near each other; above them were two similar openings in the sky. Judges were seated in the space between. They told the just, after they were judged, to ascend by the heavenly path situated on the right side. They had the signs of judgment marked on their foreheads. In a similar way, the unjust were commanded by the judges to descend by the lower way on the left side. They had signs of their evil deeds placed on their backs. As Er drew near, they told him that he was to be the courier from that other world to human beings, and they told him to hear and see everything that could be heard and seen in that place.

On one side he saw souls departing for either heaven or earth, once their sentences were announced. At the other two openings, different souls were arriving, ascending or descending—some coming up out of the earth, dusty and worn with travel, and some coming down from heaven clean and bright. Always when they arrived they seem to have been on a long journey, joyfully going out into a nearby meadow and camping there as if they were at a festival. When they found someone they knew, they embraced and conversed, the souls coming from earth eagerly inquiring about the things above and the souls that descended from the sky asking about the things of earth. And they told one another about what had happened on the way, some weeping and grieving at the remembrance of what they had seen and suffered during their journey beneath the earth, a trip that lasted a thousand years. |615| Others were describing heavenly blessings and visions of inconceivable beauty.

Glaucon, I don't have enough time to tell everything, but here is a summary. Er said that for every wrong anyone had done, they suffered tenfold—lasting a thousand years, ten times the hundred-year span of a human life. For example, if there were any who committed murder, betrayed or enslaved republics and armies, or been guilty of any other evil act, for each and all of them they received punishment ten times over. The rewards for benevolence, justice, and holiness were in the same proportion. Er recounted even greater retributions for impiety to the gods, disrespect to parents, and suicide. I will omit as not worth recording what he had to say about young children who died shortly after they were born. He said that he was present when one of them asked another: "Where is Ardiaeus the Great?" (Now this Ardiaeus was the tyrant of a city in Pamphylia, who had murdered his aging father and his elder brother and committed many other abominable crimes a thousand years before the time of Er). The answer was: "He comes not hither, and will never come." Er said: "This was one of the terrible sights I witnessed. Ardiaeus and several others, most of them tyrants, but some of them private individuals who had committed great crimes, approached the mouth of the chasm, expecting to return to the upper world. Instead of allowing them to pass, the opening gave a great roar, as it did when any incurable or unpunished criminal tried to ascend. Then wild men of fiery appearance, who knew the meaning of that sound, seized and carried off several of them, including Ardiaeus. |616| They bound them head, foot, and hand, threw them down, flayed them with scourges, and dragged them along the side of the road, carding them on thorns like wool, proclaiming their crimes to the pilgrims as they passed and announcing that they were being taken away to be cast into Tartarus. Of all the terrors of that place, there was none like that of hearing this sound. When there was silence, they ascended with joy." Glaucon, these were the penalties and retributions, and there were blessings just as great.

They were allowed to remain in the meadow for seven days, and on the eighth day they were required to proceed on their journey. On the fourth day from that time they came to a place where they looked down from above on a shaft of light, like a column extending through the heavens and the earth. Its color was similar to that of a rainbow, only brighter and more pure. Another day's journey brought them to the center of the shaft of light where they saw the ends of the chains holding it that reach all the way from heaven. This light is the belt of heaven, which holds together the circle of the universe, like the main girders of a trireme [or similar warship]. From the ends of the chains is fastened the spindle of Necessity, on which all the revolutions turn. The shaft and hook of the spindle are made of adamant, and the whorl, [the flyweight that regulates the speed of the spindle], is partly made of adamant and partly of other materials. The form of the whorl resembles that of the whorls used by our spinners, but somewhat different. Er described an arrangement in which one large hollow whorl has been scooped out to house a smaller one placed inside it. In that one is placed a smaller one, and another, and another, and four others, making eight in all—like a nest of boxes. Their edges are turned up, and taken together they form one continuous whorl. The spindle pierces the entire system, going directly through the center of the eight. The first whorl, located on the outside, has the broadest rim. The seven inner whorls have the following proportions: the sixth is the second largest, the fourth next in size to the sixth, then comes the eighth; the seventh is fifth, the fifth is sixth, the third is seventh, and last and eighth comes the second. **[617]**

The largest is spangled, the seventh is brightest, the eighth is colored by the reflected light from the seventh, the second and fifth resemble each other, having a more yellow color than the preceding one. The third has the whitest light, the fourth is reddish, and the sixth is second in whiteness. The spindle has a uniform motion, but as it revolves in one direction, the seven inner circles move slowly in the opposite direction. Of these the eighth is the fastest, next are the seventh, sixth, and fifth, which move at the same speed. Third comes the fourth, and the third is fourth, with the second fifth.

The spindle itself turns on the knees of Necessity. On the upper surface of each circle stands a siren, rotating with them and singing a single note, making a single sound each different from the others. The eight together form a harmony. Three more figures, each sitting on a throne, are placed at equal intervals. These are the Fates, daughters of Necessity, who are clothed in white and have garlands on their heads. Their names are Lachesis, Clotho, and Atropos. Their voices join the harmony of the sirens—Lachesis sings of the past, Clotho of the present, and Atropos of the future. Clotho periodically uses her right hand to push the outer whorl of the spindle, Atropos touches and guides the inner ones with her left hand, and Lachesis alternates between the whorls, first with one hand and then with another.

As soon as they arrived, the souls were required to approach Lachesis. A messenger from the gods arranged them in order and then took lots and samples of lives from the knees of Lachesis. Climbing to a high place, the messenger spoke: "Hear the word of Lachesis, the daughter of Necessity. You ephemeral souls, behold a new cycle of mortal life. Your guiding spirit will not choose you, but you will choose your guiding spirit. The one who draws the first lot will have the first choice of a life; that will be your destiny. Goodness has no master, so she will favor you or not, depending on whether you honor or dishonor her. You make your own choice and are responsible; the god is blameless." Having said this, the messenger threw the lots into the crowd, and everyone—except Er who was forbidden—picked up the closest one and looked at the number inscribed on it. **[618]** Then the messenger placed samples of the various kinds of life on the ground in front of them. There were many more than the number of souls in the crowd, and there were all kinds of them, including every animal and every sort of human life. For example, they included the lives of tyrants that last a whole lifetime, others that end early in poverty, exile, and begging. There were lives of famous men, some who were known for their form and beauty and strength, for their success in games, or for their high birth and the qualities of their ancestors. There were others that were infamous for the opposite qualities. There was a similar display of lives for women. The specific character of the soul was not determined, because that depends on the kind of life chosen and how it is lived. But there were many elements mixed in, such as wealth and poverty, disease and health, and various intermediate states and conditions.

This, my dear Glaucon, is a time of great danger for a person. To prepare for it, we must be extremely careful, putting aside every other pursuit and focusing on how to distinguish among good and bad lives and finding teachers who can foster that ability, always being sure to choose the better life to the extent that is possible. All of the specific and general issues we have been discussing should be taken into account. We should learn the role of beauty when it is combined either with poverty or wealth in a particular soul. We should assess the true value of a noble or a humble birth, of living a private or a public life, of strength and weakness, of cleverness and dullness—of all the natural and acquired gifts of the soul, individually and in combination. By considering all of these things, we will be able to determine which is the better and which is the worse life. When the time comes to choose, we will be able to call bad the kind of life that will make our soul unjust and good the kind that makes it more just. We should disregard everything else. As we have seen, this is the best choice both for this life and after it is over. **[619]** We must take with us into the underworld an adamantine regard for what is true and right, so that there too we may not be dazzled by the desire for wealth and the various other temptations that await us. We must learn to resist tyranny and similar evils, lest we do irreparable damage to others and suffer even worse ourselves. We must learn how to choose the moderate life and avoid the extremes both in this life and in whatever might come; this is the way to genuine happiness for a human being.

According to the report from Er, this is what the messenger of the gods said: "Even for the person who chooses last, it is possible to choose wisely and live diligently and select a happy and desirable existence. The one who chooses first should not be careless, and the one who comes last should not be discouraged." Just as the messenger spoke those words, a thoughtless and greedy man who had first choice rushed forward and grabbed the life of greatest tyranny, not realizing that among other evils this included eating his own children. When he realized this and understood what was included in that choice, he began to beat his breast and cry about his selection. He had ignored the warning from the messenger; instead of blaming himself for making a bad choice, he accused chance and the gods for causing his bad fortune. He was one of those who had come down from heaven. In a former life he had dwelled in a well-ordered republic, but his former goodness was only a matter of habit. It did not come from the love of wisdom. This often happened with people who came down from heaven, because they had no experience of life, whereas those who came up from below usually had seen plenty of trouble and were in no hurry to choose. Both because of inexperience and due to the element of chance involved in the lottery, many of the souls exchanged a good life for a bad one, and many others exchanged a bad life for a good one. However, if a person is dedicated to the love of wisdom and is reasonably fortunate in getting a decent number in the lottery, it is possible to be happy in this life, in passing to another life, and in returning to this one—as the messenger reported. Instead of being rough and made underground, the trip might be smooth and heavenly.

Er said that the choosing of the lives was a sight to behold—sad and funny and bizarre. Generally the souls chose according to the condition of their previous life. **[620]** For example, he saw the soul that was once Orpheus choosing the life of a swan because of his hatred for women, refusing to be born of a woman because women had murdered him. He also saw the soul of Thamyris choosing the life of a nightingale. On the other hand, birds, such as swans and other musicians, chose to be human. The soul that received the twentieth lot chose the life of a lion. This was the soul of Ajax, the son of Telamon, who refused to be a man because he remembered the injustice he received in the judgment concerning the arms of Achilles. Next he saw Agamemnon, who selected the life of an eagle, because—like Ajax—he hated human nature due to his sufferings. Around the middle of the drawing was the lot of Atalanta. Seeing the great fame of being an athlete, she was unable to resist the temptation. After her came the soul of Eoeus, the son of Panopeus, who passed into the nature of a woman adept in the arts and crafts. One of the last to choose was the jester Thersites, who chose the form of a monkey.

The soul of Odysseus made the last choice of all. He recalled his former labors and was deterred from a life of ambition. He looked around for a long time seeking the life of a private person free from meddling in other people's affairs. He had difficulty finding such a life but eventually discovered it lying in a corner neglected by everyone else. He was delighted to choose it and said that he would have selected it if he had been first instead of last. Not only did people pass into animals, but also there were both wild and tame animals that changed into each other and into corresponding human natures, the good into the gentle and the bad into the savage in all sorts of combinations.

All of the souls had now chosen their lives, and they went in the order of their choice to Lachesis. She sent with them the guiding spirits they had chosen to guard their lives and fulfill their choice. The guiding spirit first led the soul to Clotho and placed them into the revolution of the spindle impelled by her hand, in this way confirming its destiny. Next it carried them to Atropos, who spun the threads and made them irreversible. **[621]** From there they passed beneath the throne of Necessity without turning around and finally marched through scorching heat to the Plain of Oblivion, a barren waste without trees or greenery. Toward evening they camped by the River of Forgetfulness, whose water no vessel can hold. They were all required to drink a certain amount, but those who were not saved by wisdom drank more than was necessary. Those who drank forgot everything about this place. When they had gone to sleep, in the middle of the night there was a thunderstorm and an earthquake, and like shooting stars they were instantly sent in all directions to their birth. Er was prevented from drinking the water, but he could not recall how he was returned to his body. In the morning he awoke to find himself lying on the funeral pyre.

In this way, Glaucon, the tale has been saved and has not perished. It may be our salvation if we obey the words that have been spoken so that we can pass safely over the River of

Forgetfulness and our soul will not be corrupted. I advise that we hold fast to the heavenly way and always seek justice and goodness, remembering that the soul is immortal and able to survive every sort of good and every sort of evil. In this way we will be dear to each other and to the gods, both while remaining here and, when like victors in the games, we go round to gather our prizes and receive our reward. All will be well with us in this life and in our future pilgrimage of a thousand years.

ENDNOTES

[1] The Homeridae ("sons of Homer") was a clan of rhapsodes centered in Chios who claimed Homeric descent and thereby a prerogative of reciting Homer's poetry. The clan eventually became a guild, admitting non-descendants of Homer.

[2] Cf. *Plato's Republic*, 436.

[3] Cf. *Plato's Republic*, 439.

[4] See *Plato's Republic*, 357–367.